A Wonderful Wife

A Wonderful Wife

Virender Kapoor

B L O O M S B U R Y

NEW DELHI • LONDON • OXFORD • NEW YORK • SYDNEY

ISBN 978 93 854 3662 8
2 4 6 8 10 9 7 5 3 1

Bloomsbury Publishing India Pvt. Ltd
DDA Complex, LSC Building No.4
Second Floor, Pocket C – 6 & 7, Vasant Kunj
New Delhi 110070
www.bloomsbury.com

Typeset by Manmohan Kumar
Printed and bound in India by Replika Press Pvt. Ltd.

To find out more about our authors and books visit www.bloomsbury.com. Here you will find extracts, author interviews, details of forthcoming events and the option to sign up for our newsletters.

Dedicated to my wife Laxmi who means so much
to me and my family

CONTENTS

PRELUDE

A wonderful wife is a unique creation. It has been crafted by a dozen husbands plus one. A common trait in all these gentlemen is that they all love and value their wives.

Love is the most often used word and most men and women use it without even understanding its real meaning. Without being poetic, romantic, philosophical or judgmental I would use the dictionary meaning of the word love. Love is fondness, attachment, yearning, adulation, warmth, caring and even devotion. Oh! It is pretty serious. In such a context, the pseudo-modern expression of 'I love you' generating an instant response of 'I love you too' appears to be weird if not crass or frivolous.

Poets, priests, Sufis and saints have written about this human emotion more than any other, for centuries. They did this because it was the *raison d'être*: reason for our very existence.

A husband and wife value each other because they need each other. They value each other because both are a part of an intrinsic system. The comfort is due to a feeling of permanence, which was ineffaceable and innate. In their minds it is an unbreakable bond which makes them one. That comfort alone lets them take each other for granted – yes for granted. In a crisis each expects the other to say 'Main hoon na'. Which translates into 'I am there for you'. Since humans don't trust humans, they brought God into it. God and religion make it more solemn, ceremonial and even imposing. Therefore for centuries on, marriages have the blessings of God. But things have changed and are continuing to change fast.

In the last two decades either we have dumped God or our values or maybe both. People in the West were the first ones to be hit because they became rich first. The decades of the sixties and the seventies belonged to America. The Second World War was over a couple of decades ago and the ugly scars had by now healed. The world was good and safe. Money, affluence and material comforts were suddenly available in abundance.

This was also the era of opportunity in the United States. Women wanted to participate and thus started the race for gender equality. A very strong women's movement dubbed as women's lib started in the 1960s and 70s, which was a struggle for equality and sought to free women from male supremacy. Some called it radical feminism which was more militant in its approach. At the Miss America Pageant in September, 1968, hundreds of women activists tossed women's feminine products into a trash can. Though they did not burn bras, it was popularly called a bra-burning event. The movement gathered momentum almost simultaneously in Europe and Australia.

It caught the fancy of the media and of course the world. It did give women equality and better prospects but it had a devastating effect on the family front. The number of divorces shot up to four times between 1970 and 1996. Gradually, better sense prevailed and the American divorce rate is nearly twice that of 1960 but has declined since the early eighties when it touched the highest point. In 1992, John Gray published his book 'Men are from Mars and women are from Venus'. He demonstrated, through this seminal work that men and women are indeed born different – they are two different species. Such a simple and obvious fact required a 286-page book to reveal. It also proves another point that it is very difficult for humans to convince humans. I do not think this book was written in the wake of or in response to the women's movement, but the timing could be a coincidence. India hit its watershed year in 1991, which was thirty years after America and the rest of the western world had tasted the 'blood of affluence'.

We got out LPG –Liberalisation, Privatisation and Globalisation mantra, which took Indians to cloud nine. Booming economy and opportunities galore, hit us like a sledge hammer. It took ten years to sink in and India was rocking.

As an aftermath, simple Indian families started feeling the heat. From Hyderabad to Himachal Pradesh, or Mumbai to Meghalaya, it started taking its toll on our family life. The young generation got too much too soon and took every comfort for granted if not as a right. Divorces in Delhi alone shot up from 100 in 1980 to almost 10,000 cases per year in the first decade of the new millennium. Young couples probably got so engrossed in themselves individually, that they forgot the meaning of co-existence. It was, I, me, myself and everybody was as if on his or her own.

Our basic cultural foundation got shaken. The elders still believed in family values and remained firmly committed to the Institution of marriage but could do little to help their children hold on to their marriages. We are now in the middle of that turmoil. However modern we may become, our emotional needs will not change; in fact should not change. Yet the formal association of a man and woman as a married couple, is on a shaky wicket today.

Fortunately, majority of couples of yesteryears lived happily and created homes and families for themselves. Perhaps they did not get swayed by these 'free for all' freedom storms and lived their lives well. Most marriages of this millennium have also been blessed by God and Sanity. Such married couples who are truly blessed are living a perfectly happy life, in fact making the most of it.

A wonderful wife is a tribute not only to women but to togetherness, co-existence and a symbiotic relation between the men from Mars and the women from Venus.

It is a narrative that spans three generations. A dozen people talk about their marriage, about a woman in their life and how they cherished this as they moved on together to experience life.

Married for forty years, my own experience would not have been good enough to prove the point that marriage is one of the essential rituals of life which provides a woman and a man a home. It may have its ups and downs but gives a couple the security and sense of well being that nothing else can.

People who are just out of their honeymoon to those married for more than four decades have shared their experiences. I am thankful to each one of them for coming forward to write about their family life, their wives and their children. Their experiences are very personal and that is all the more reason for me to feel humbled by their contribution.

Men and women can be equal but can never be identical. They together make a home for themselves, clearly understanding that they are different but need each other to spend their lives meaningfully. It may not be pink throughout, but it does have numerous shades of pink.

This book is about staying together through thick and thin and making the best of it.

Virender Kapoor.

A GOOD WIFE AND
NOT-SO-GOOD WIFE

*Marriage is a book of which the first chapter is written in
poetry and the remaining chapters in prose.*
— Beverley Nichols

A myth called a perfect wife

No individual is perfect. And when you look at someone in a particular role or a specific context, perfection could be far from true.

Human beings are individually so complex and unique that when they interact with each other the outcome is highly unpredictable. A husband and wife relation is such that they are connected to each other twenty by seven. Whether they are in the same room or in different cities or even in different continents they are, mentally and emotionally, always connected to each other. They are concerned about each other even if they are far away. That is the beauty of this relation. There is some sort of permanency and interdependability which keeps this relation going. This works perfectly well, despite the fact that both husband and wife are individually imperfect individuals. The outcome of this interplay is always unpredictable but at the end of it, it is manageable. How good is very good and how good is not so good, depends on an individual's perception and is very subjective. Therefore one thing is certain that a wife can never be perfect whichever way you look at it. Yet, without being a perfect wife she can be good.

As two people spend time with each other they not only begin to understand each other's nuances, and idiosyncrasies, but they also mature individually. Therefore, as time passes, their perceptions about each other also undergo a change. You start seeing positivity in each other which you couldn't notice earlier. You start understanding your wife, her logic, her suggestions better and better, as you both grow.

> *When I was a boy of fourteen, my father was so ignorant; I could hardly stand to have the old man around. But when I got to be twenty one, I was astonished as how much the old man had learnt in seven years.*
>
> – Mark Twain

In marriage, husband and wife both mature with time. If both are well-meaning and sensible, they can make a beautiful home and a wonderful life for themselves.

Beauty baffles brains

Men are probably hardwired to go head over heels for beautiful women. That hour-glass figure is something men can't ignore because they are programmed that way. Such a perfect figure signals a healthy mate. Men seek beautiful, healthy women for evolutionary reasons. This was ingrained in the human species for both men and women, over the 80,000 generations that our ancestors lived. 'Mate and vacate' was a fair deal millions of years ago. But today in an organised society, these signals can often be misleading for both the genders.

Choosing a life partner is more than just a beautiful face.

Albert Einstein said, 'God does not play dice'.

In selecting a life partner God does play dice. An ancient saying that *Zar, Zamin* aur *Joroo* all three are gods gifts. *Zar* are the children or off spring, *zamin* is landed property and *Joroo* is your wife.

That is why it is said that marriages are made in heaven. While one cannot totally discount the looks of a man or a woman you have to spend your life with, there are certainly other much more important factors which need to be considered which ultimately bring happiness in life.

A sensible wife is on top of the stack. This could be one of the most important factors in selecting a girl for yourself. Rest everything will fall in place. Looks could be a bonus.

Sensible means mature, having a sense of responsibility and above all sense of ownership. The ownership factor translates into 'my home is our home'.

Some men become victims of 'designer spouse syndrome', where bullshit baffles brains. From day one, they know what they are getting into: 'bankruptcy'. This species is a by-product of the modern 'eruptive affluence' in urbane society. They are gasoline guzzlers and would not stop spending on themselves even if they are broke and dead. Courtship to captaining the ship in such a case can literally take the wind out of you. So beware.

I have seen men of substance being left without any substance, if they don't take care of these factors. One wrong decision, a wrong partner and your life can become very unpleasant.

The greatest day in your life and mine is when we take total responsibility for our attitudes. That's the day we truly grow up.
– John C. Maxwell

Nature's Kaleidoscope

It is very difficult to predict the behaviour of an individual, especially in the long run. Courtships could be the 'best foot forward' phase for both men and women.

As far as physicals are concerned, they are there for you to see. Looks are easiest to judge and hence they say looks can be deceptive. In marriages 'first impressions' need not be deal-clinching impressions. Even looks are a part of the pedigree.

My uncle, who a long time ago, went to see a girl said 'see the mother of the girl first. You will know how she would look when she turns fifty!' Bang on. Same goes for a boy. That's maximum bang for the buck.

Behaviour or what we also call the 'nature of a person' is the most deceptive bundle of traits of a human being. Imagine a scenario where a couple has four sons out of wedlock. One becomes a doctor, another actor, yet another pilot and the fourth one, a goon. They went to the same school, had the same neighborhood and to top it all, had the same DNA! Many people argue that it depends on how you bring up your children, what *sanskar* you give to your children and how you yourself behave in front of them. But in that case all four sons were brought up in the same environment. As far as 'sanskars' are concerned, it is a twister. OK. Parents want to give *sanskars* but are the children ready to accept these. This is the most important aspect as far as upbringing is concerned. All parents try to give the right *sanskars* and values to their children but some children just refuse to accept these. Mendel's law of heredity and modern genetics indicate that we may inherit traits and diseases not only from our parents but probably from any of our ancestors going back, seven generations. Therefore, while looks are literally on face value, human nature and behaviour maybe very complex to discern. With this kind of a situation one has to be lucky to get a sensible spouse.

In my case I was very lucky to get a sensible wife. About three to four decades ago, men got married by the time they were around twenty five. I was just twenty three. I lost my father when I was in my teens. My brothers and sisters were married by then and I was still a teenager. Being the youngest of the four siblings I was a little lost because of these circumstances. I found my first family when I joined the National Defence Academy, on my way to become an officer in the Armed forces. It is one hell of a place to be – the Indian Army. It's not a life style – it is a way of life. It is one big family whose bonds can't be described in words. It provides you an emotional comfort, camaraderie, sense of belonging, brotherhood, mentors, and fatherly figures, all in one single organisation. You feel that you belong to every cantonment and every cantonment belongs to you. You feel like a prince, with a meagre salary.

'There is no personal charm so great as the charm of a cheerful temperament.'

– Henry Van Dyke

When I got married, my salary slip reflected a figure of Rs 600 per month and after standard deductions I got just over Rs 500 in hand. This was in 1974. My bank balance was less than Rs 3,000 but I had a huge family – the Indian armed forces.

My wife knew my financials very well before we decided to get married. My precondition was that we will not take anything from her family. I was against any dowry; I was trying to follow my father's footsteps, who, I was told, took nothing in dowry, when he married my mother in Lahore, before the partition.

Our total assets were four odd trunks, two hold-alls and four wrought iron chairs. I was posted in a field area where families were permitted. Our first home was a tent, with an attached toilet, which was also a tent, but a smaller one. In a couple of months a 'Basha' was built for us, and we now had the luxury of four walls and a roof. A Basha is a hutment made of mud walls and a thatched roof. The bathroom was still a small tent. Trunks were used as settees and a few wooden packing cases, used for packing rum joined together, made our dining table. The kitchen was also a makeshift tin roof shack with very limited utensils, one cooker and a kerosene stove. But it was fun to start life like that. We started with almost nothing. Again, the Army teaches you and grooms you to live well in any situation. You could live in a bunker, a tent, a Basha or in a huge bungalow, you learn to live well and, above all, be happy. You can eat with a pauper or dine with a king, you are equally comfortable and can pull it off pretty well.

This is the only organisation, where you could be having your lunch in a mess tin sitting in a dusty bunker and later in the evening having an elaborate five-course dinner being served in a spectacular dining hall with bagpipers playing music in the background.

'Nobody can make you feel inferior without your consent,' said Eleanor Roosevelt and she was dead right.

We never felt inferior to anyone! When we interacted with our civilian friends or some rich relatives, we never felt that they were so much richer, had big cars or maybe a huge bank balance.

I feel it's all in your mind. It is more important for a wife to feel that way. And a sensible wife feels that way. I fail to understand as to how this pseudo modern expression called 'peer pressure' can actually make people feel inferior. Self-esteem comes from within and not by way of what kind of money you have. You may have less but you can still live in style. You define your own style statement. I have met some women who wear only cotton saris and look extremely graceful, often giving many-a-woman in chiffons a run for their money.

I remember that old song picturised on Raj Kapoor, 'Mana apni jaib se garib hain, phir bhi yaaron dil ke ham amir hain', which translates into 'I agree I don't have too much money in my pocket, but I am a rich hearted guy'.

Need a bit of that Jazz

You need two to tango and that's what you are when you get married. But you need some Jazz. It depends entirely on you, what instruments you use. It will be great music with any instrument as long as you want to dance and you love music. You may not have an expensive Jazz Piano, a drum set and a saxophone to start with, but you can dance to the tune of a trumpet or a trombone and a Goema if you want to dance.

'Don't keep counting the score, enjoy the match', and that's the essence of lifetime of happiness. Your happiness doesn't depend so much on outside factors but depends on how happy you want to be with what you have. It is unfortunate that some young couples keep searching for that happiness chasing big cars, designer homes and five star comforts. Yet they are unhappy. Today, I see men who are forty years old, behaving like five-year olds. They get so fascinated with new gizmos like smart phones, thin laptops and shoes that they get desperate to acquire these. And they get bored with these as quickly as a child would. It is something like when a child says,

'I need a ball, I need a ball'. Once he gets his ball the next day he starts crying, 'Oh now I need that doll, that doll.'

My wife was very happy and enjoyed every moment of our stay in that remote area. She never complained. Coming from a background where there was no one in the armed forces in her entire family, she took this as an adventure of sorts, making every day a picnic.

From a field area, I got posted to Lucknow, which was a paradise as compared to the conditions we were living in. here one actually feels the theory of relativity discovered, theorised and explained by Albert Einstein. Lucknow is no Paris but coming from a place where we lived in tents had our fair share of dust storms and sweltering heat, Lucknow was more exciting and comfortable than Paris for us. We had fantastic company and made the best of it.

'Most folks are as happy as they make up their minds to be.'
– Abraham Lincoln

Awadhi cuisine, Biryani, Kebabs and Kulfis are things we sank our teeth into very often. Mohammed Bagh club, which reminds you of the British aristocracy, was the place for Saturday Tambolas and poolside lunches. We built our itinerary at Lucknow, known for best chinhat crockery and chicken embroidery. We gradually bought our kitchen ware and built our simple yet satisfying wardrobes. We did this all with a two-wheeler and less than thousand rupees a month.

We could do this because my wife is frugally extravagant or sometimes extravagantly frugal. I feel slight deprivation keeps us together. We managed to buy a carpet for our drawing room, crafted some Ikebana flower arrangements from the bamboo that grew in the backyard of our sprawling bungalow, in the cantonment.

We realised that life can be beautiful if you want it to be beautiful. We were chasing no money, no great stuff but we enjoyed every bit of it.

We are both mad about dogs and love all animals. We met a couple through a common friend who were dog lovers and wanted to give away the pups their mother had delivered. They didn't want to sell the pups but wanted to give them for free only to those homes where those pups would be loved. We were interviewed. And we both passed with flying colours. Eventually they agreed but were not prepared to give a single pup and the logic was that two would be able to give company to each other! This was like take one get one free! We agreed and were blessed with two lovely, piknese pups. We named them Sherry and Whisky.

Count your blessings, don't mount your blessings!

We were building a home together, we were not rich but were very happy. Our son Samir was born at Lucknow, and soon we moved to Pune on posting. I had to undergo a three-year degree in Engineering and that is a great place to be. All your course mates are there with you. When we reached the College of Military Engineering, CME for short, very few of us were married at the beginning of the course. We were all young captains. By the end of the course there were hardly a couple of bachelors left out of a total of sixty. Almost fifty marriages took place in a matter of eighteen months.

It was something like a 'marriage a fortnight' affair. Every newly-married couple was greeted with a traditional 'scootercade'. As none of us had a car, all couples were on their motorbikes or scooters and took the newly-married couple for a drive around the campus, honking and hooting away to glory. At night there was usually a potluck dinner where each couple pooled in a dish and we also pooled in liquor, which was always overflowing.

Such a place is pretty fertile. Pregnancy was in the air. All sixty of us were successful in contributing to the demographic dividend of India's population.

What can be called 'audacity of enjoyment', the CME open-air theatre where two movies were screened every week, was jam-packed regardless of what movie was being screened! Some of the serious, studious guys would give an occasional miss, if there was an exam next day. Ladies! No way! All of them with prams in tow and some with bumpy stomachs would watch every movie.

On occasions watching a movie was no less than an adventure camp. In Pune when it rains, it actually pours. In an open-air theatre, while it was pouring cats and dogs, everybody was sitting pretty with rain capes on and umbrellas out. Incorrigible as we were, men had a drink in hand and hot samosas and snacks from the tuck shop moved around in paper bags. It was always more of a picnic, the movie was just incidental.

We enjoyed every moment, and not to give credit to our brave heart wives would be very unfair.

I really feel, enjoyment is a state of mind. We all built homes from scratch. Most had the blessings of their parents, some had to depend on God but we enjoyed with meagre resources and went on to build our dream homes successfully. In building a home together there is a sense of achievement. When we bought our first refrigerator, a white coloured, 165 litres Kenvinator, it was party time. We could chill our beer and make our own ice! We actually always needed an excuse to have a party.

Today people are not satisfied with a double door or even a French door machine with a capacity upwards of 900 litres. I ask them, 'Do you need to sleep in it?'

> *'Contentment consists not in adding more fuel, but in taking away some fire.'*
>
> – Thomas Fuller

Taken for Granted

If husband and wife don't take each other for granted then who else will they take for granted?

The dictionary meaning of the expression 'Taken for granted' is 'To expect someone or something to be always available to serve in some way without thanks or recognition'. Marriage is a relation where artificial 'thank you's' are not necessary. It is an extremely formal relation in one sense of it but this relationship has no formalities and niceties. Courtesies and caring are different from mere words.

You are actually together during good as well as bad times. If a husband falls sick then does he have to even think whether his wife will care for him during sickness? Similarly, if the lady of the house falls sick, who will provide for her? Who will look after her? Obviously, her husband. We both had a share of our good and bad times individually but it was given that one had to be available for the other. I think this is the biggest plus point of a happy married life. You always have that psychological comfort of mutual support. It is the greatest and most trustworthy relation, provided you build that trust.

There is one quality, which women have, and the men folk don't – sense of sacrifice. For instance if a husband needs to change eating habits because of health reasons, his wife will change the regular menu to a 'special health food menu' which she would also happily eat every day. This is what love and caring is all about. Men in most cases will not do this for their wives.

> 'Strong women need not declare they can carry all the burdens
> in life. They just quietly do it and survive with a smile.'
> – Princess Maleiha Bajunaid Candao

Was my mother an unhappy woman?

The partition of India in 1947 was one of the worst human tragedies. It was also one of the largest mass migration of some ten million people. Families on both sides lost almost everything including many close relatives, who were killed in the riots which killed millions.

My parents, who were a rich and mighty family in Lahore, became refugees overnight. They lost their home which was not short of a palace I am told. They left behind their factories, jewellery and bank accounts and were asked to take refuge in their own country, which was now divided in two.

I was born after the partition and saw my parents struggling to build their home once again. It happened to the entire family, my uncles and aunts were all in the same boat.

Imagine if the wives had not stood by their husbands or failed to give their husbands the badly-needed moral support, what would have happened?

Probably our generation learnt a bit of our tenacity from our parents. How did they manage to travel by public transport, having left behind a dozen cars, horse buggies and tongas? It was resilience and mutual support that saw them through. They still lived with honour and a smile on their face. India as a nation state, at that point in time, was struggling to find its feet. There were very little opportunities available for anyone to make money.

I cannot remember an occasion where there were any arguments between my parents leave aside fights for lack of resources, shortage of money or general discomfort they were going through. Can this credit be given only to the men folk? What about women, their wives who were a part of this story and this terrible twist of fate? Most of my uncles and aunts had three or four children to feed and bring up. They did it pretty well despite this calamity.

If I look back, one thing I distinctly remember is that none of the women ever looked unhappy. Though they had gone through hell and were still struggling to keep the boat afloat.

Truly these were the women of substance, who believed in 'Sanjha Choolah', a common hearth. They were not silent sufferers as many modernistic thinkers would like to portray. Today, they portray a woman of substance as someone who will fight only for herself, for her rights, equality, money, position and being on the top. But yes, only for herself.

Such women of yesteryears probably never required to go to any ashram, because each one of them was herself an ashram. They did not preach honesty but lived by it. They never preached team work, sharing and caring as we do. But they demonstrated all of that gracefully and without any pomp and show and without taking any credit for it.

The amount of trust between husband and wife was total. Trust is like integrity. It is either there or it's not there. You can't be somewhat trustworthy.

A woman is like a tea bag, you can't tell how strong she is
until you put her in hot water.

– Eleanor Roosevelt

A woman can do anything to save or make her home. It is an old saying that a man will not be able to bring down a home even with an axe but a woman can make a home with just a needle. This is the spirit of being together and the strength of a woman which men can never have.

Woman is stronger than man in many ways. Physically, she may be frail, short and slim but she has tremendous capacity to bear pressure and pain. She can be a man's most trusted, dependable 'rough weather' friend. During my most difficult days, my wife has stood by me as a strong pillar of support. In whichever way I may look at it, she has been stronger than me on every count.

That sixth sense

Whether we call it gut-feeling, intuition or hunch, women generally have a better ability than men in this area of excellence. it is referred to as the 'sixth sense' because we are all familiar with the five senses that we all posses-touch, taste, vision, hearing and smell.

One reason for this could be God's gift to understand their children's demand or requirements better. This goes from womb to tomb. When a newborn baby cries, it is the mother who can understand what he/she wants, milk or water or just a hug. Even as children grow into adults, the mother's instinct is still active. Possibly, this develops further as extra-sensory-perception over a period of time.

Some argue that men fall for women mostly for their looks and their Judgment is based on the requirement of mating in the true sense of 'expansionism by reproduction'. But women choose men on the basis of their sincerity, stability and ability to be a long-term partner. This obviously requires some internal radar or computation mechanism which men don't have. Intuition and sixth sense are closely related to Emotional Intelligence which is closer to the heart than head.

As Blaire Pascal said, 'The heart has its reasons which reason knows not'. In this sense, the sixth sense falls in this grey area of human understanding.

Mother's Instinct

Closely related to the sixth sense is the mother's instinct and 'protective' nature. You take any species of animals or birds, this is a very visible trait.

'Kids always stay with the mother', she keeps an eye on the kids till they are ready to fend for themselves and are able to protect themselves from other animals or natural dangers. A polar bear, a grizzly bear, a zebra, a lion, or a dog, they all have this instinct which is hardwired into them. Mother is the biggest teacher, she teaches them not only to walk and run but also how to hunt and stay away from trouble.

Similarly for us humans, our mothers are the best teachers. We may think that we have become smarter or wiser but mothers are ahead of us, especially in instilling morals and putting us on the right track.

If any mother doesn't teach her children morals and sense of right and wrong, then it is an aberration, and that too, a pretty skewed one.

> 'God could not be everywhere and therefore he made mothers'.
> – Jewish Proverb

In this area, motherhood has taken a big hit. In the last couple of decades, especially in India, women have started competing with men in every possible way. It may be good for them but it has a big negative impact on their children.

It is starkly visible. It beats basic logic and the laws of nature. Today a modern mother is prepared to leave her three-month-old child in a day care facility or a crèche from 8.30 am to 8.30pm every day for a full working week! Just for a few dollars more or to pursue her career because she wants to beat someone at her work place. In several cases, a mother is also ready to leave that three-month-old in the day care facility even on a Sunday because that is the day for her to chill! This sends a chill up your spine! Fathers are equally to blame for this. This is what will happen if we go against the very nature which is the basis of our existence.

Our greed, that comparison with others, our freedom and personal comfort, has beaten nature and God put together. We are getting into a 'tit for tat' situation. The same kids are going to send us to old age homes. And this is already happening.

If mothers of mothers or mothers-in-law of mothers are welcome in their homes, in most cases it is because they are safe, free and reliable nannies and not grandmothers. It is sad but true, that some take them as grand servants and not grand parents

Women are stronger than men in many ways and do have that intuitive ability. God has given them all this for a reason. They must not spend all that in competing with the environment, with other men and women and ultimately lose something much bigger in life.

They can be modern yet be traditional.

Maternal Blindness

Closely linked to mother's instinct is a type of mother's irrational love and skewed judgment. There are different types of blindness related to our vision. Snow blindness, night blindness and colour blindness are the most well-known ones. Then there is also blindness of the mind and of the heart. Maternal blindness is that shortcoming of a mother, which clouds her rational judgment because of her warped emotional attachment to one of her children. This manifests in different ways.

When mothers start favoritism at home between siblings the results can be catastrophic and the scars can be deep and painful.

Sometimes the youngest son becomes the blue-eyed boy and in some cases the most handsome one. A beautiful daughter is given preferential treatment over a daughter who is not so charming.

For the 'chosen one' everything is forgiven and forgotten. Unfortunately, this behaviour is disturbing for others in the family.

In several cases, parents treat their children according to their own childhood experiences. For instance, if a woman was given a damper treatment by her parents as compared to her brothers, she may end up giving preferential treatment to her daughters. In this case a son feels that he is being given step-motherly treatment. This kind of parental prejudice can really complicate relationships in a family.

So much so, a mother may go against her husband because of this distorted perception. Here a daughter or a son becomes more important than her husband. Emotions can play havoc with lives if people are not careful with their interpretations and maintaining a balance within relationships.

Wife is a rough weather friend

In our modern lexicon we try to use this word 'friend' very extensively. Most don't understand the real and true value of this. A husband and wife are not only friends but partners for life. They are there to stand by each other in good as well as bad times. Many great and successful men give credit for their success to their wives. Actors, film directors, entrepreneurs and senior corporate professionals, when they look over their shoulders, they will find a supportive wife. And many of them have put this fact on record.

From the time I started writing, I had full support of my wife. I could concentrate on my work only because she took a lot of load on herself to allow me that freedom.

Narayan Murthy, the founder of Infosys, truly acknowledges his wife, Sudha Murthy's contribution to his success. He says, 'she sacrificed so much for me and the children, giving up her job as a manager in Mumbai in 1981 and moving to Pune. Without her I am not sure if I would have been able to found Infosys with six of my colleagues"

In the nascent stage, Infosys had very little money even to sustain their business. His wife let him mortgage her jewellery for raising Rs 10,000 which was required by Infosys those days. If husband

and wife have a good understanding and trust each other's abilities, then a lot can happen. Today many husbands and wives don't trust each other and I doubt if something as personal as jewellery for a woman would be put at stake for a husband's progress.

Producer director David Dhawan also gives credit to his wife for supporting him during his struggling period. He was trained as an editor at FTII (Film and Television Institute of India) Pune. He became a very successful and sought-after editor of Hindi cinema. His wife asked him to go in for direction as he had a dream and also had the ability to direct films. She looked after the home and children, as he went on to become a very successful film director.

In an interview, Javed Akhtar talking about his wife Shabana Azmi on their thirtieth wedding anniversary said, 'Our friendship is so strong that even marriage could not break it'.

That is why it's said, 'Behind every successful man there is a woman'.

It is a three-legged race

In a marriage, husband and wife not only walk together, they are in a way tied together. That may be the significance of tying the knot.

Putting it differently, it is something like a three-legged race that one plays at school. Right leg of one is tied to the left leg of the other partner and you are supposed to run together. Understanding, synchronization and above all supporting each other all throughout is important in case you want to run without running down your partner.

But once you are in sync, it is a pleasure to glide along. Eventually you finish the race not only without pain, but come out with flying colours.

Significance of a wedding ceremony and rituals

In a Hindu wedding, the bride and the bridegroom make a lifetime's commitment to each other. They do this in public and in front of the sacred fire. They go around this sacred fire seven times, each round being a specific commitment. These are known as 'saat-pheras' or seven rounds. Significance of each round is as follows.

Round 1. Here the man asks the woman to walk with him, step-by-step and he promises to take care of her. The bride reciprocates by saying that she submits to him and asks him to give her the responsibility of their home, food and finance, which he agrees.

Round 2. Man asks the woman to fill his heart with courage and strength so that together they can build a secure future for their children. She agrees and commits to rejoice in his happiness and be grieved in his bad times.

Round 3. He agrees to consider all other women his sisters. She commits to lead her life as a chaste wife.

Round 4. He thanks her for filling his life with auspiciousness and sacredness. She accepts and agrees to keep him happy in every way possible.

Round 5. They both ask for longevity of their loved ones so that they may share in the prosperity that this union is about to bring.

Round 6. Man asks the woman to fill his heart with joy and peace at all times. She agrees.

Round 7. This last round unites the two souls with God. Now they are completely one body and soul and they agree to keep their marriage intact for ever.

This is the seriousness with which a marriage is taken by every society and religion.

At the end of the marriage ceremony, as per Hindu customs, a woman leaves her home to join her new family. This is called 'vidai'.

Very simply, the essence of it is commitment and mutual happiness forever. A woman leaves her home, not to join her new family but to create her new family. And that is the big difference.

You start a new life and new people come in your life, new relations are made. Relations do have names. Hindus depended purely on religion, rituals and God. But westerners brought law into these relations. For instance the husband's younger brother is called 'Devar 'but westerners call him brother-in-law. The husband's mother is called a 'Saas' and the wife is called a 'Bahu'. Westerners call them mother-in-law and daughter in law respectively. It is a matter of perception.

It's not just the two of us

Bill Withers' classic song, 'Just the two of us, we can make it if we can try. I see the crystal raindrops fall and the beauty of it all – Just the two of us'.

In love and good times it is just the two of us. But marriage is not just the two of us. It's a family stupid!

A man and a woman must understand that the innermost core of their family is just the two of them, always and every time. But they should not forget that together they create a family, which is a much larger sphere of influence and existence. They have to carry the entire flock together as they move forward in life.

> *A family is a risky venture, because the greater the love, the greater the loss... That's the trade-off. But I'll take it all.*
>
> – Brad Pitt

I was lucky that my wife understood this pretty well. Even if there were some problems between the two of us, they never got conveyed to either my folks or hers. Every married couple has arguments, tiffs and fights. But they are like little sparks which are handled easily. The moment you involve the jungle it becomes a bushfire and it is time for the fire brigade!

Privacy is something that everyone needs. At the same time get-togethers are important. In the good old days, people were not so much privacy conscious as we are today. A summer holiday meant that our parents would take our cousins and friends along for almost a month-long holiday to a hill station. We would all bunk together in the same room not looking for any particular comfort for ourselves. Mothers behaved like mothers. And they were mothers to all.

Gods couldn't have been crazy

John Gray in his well researched book, 'Men are from mars and women are from Venus', goes into great detail to demonstrate how men and women are different. Very simply, they are two different species. That is why they are known as the opposite sex, feminine and masculine. His argument is that if men and women start understanding each other it can bring a lot of peace and happiness.

We expect the opposite sex to be more like ourselves. We desire them to 'want what we want' and 'feel the way we feel', he says. As the magic and 'high' of love recedes and its 'business as usual', the feeling of 'lived happily ever after' could disappear.

With the best intentions from both husband and wife, the feeling of love continues to decline. Problems creep in. Communications are no more smooth. Misunderstandings, mistrust, and resentment become a routine.

'When men and women are able to understand and respect the differences then love has a chance to blossom' he emphasises.

Some very specific traits of men and women which may seem trivial are very important.

Women behave very differently compared to men and they expect men to understand this.

For instance, a woman wants a man to only listen to her. She doesn't expect him to get down to solving every problem she talks about! As men are, they feel that if she is complaining, then he must get to the bottom of it and make all efforts to solve that problem. Women actually want empathy whereas he thinks she wants a solution. Men therefore must give a patient hearing to what a woman says, without too much of a reaction or even action. In most cases, hearing her out would be better than attempting to solve the problem. But by nature men feel that she wants a solution.

God probably put a mother in every woman. Therefore, by their very nature, they like to nurture those who are close to them. When she nurtures her husband, he feels she is trying to control him. In the worst case it appears that she is nagging him.

Men usually want to control things. They value power efficiency and competence. They value achievement and drive. For them success is primarily through accomplishment. That is why he thinks he is the solution provider and wants people to accept his solutions.

On the other hand, women value love and communication in a relationship. They feel that in a relationship, they experience fulfilment through sharing and giving.

Lines of intellect govern men-women: by curves of emotion.
                                                              – James Joyce

Women are compulsive counsellors. That is why they are the best teachers for their children. They always advise you for your own good. They are well-meaning and advise you on spirituality, morals, healing, human values and everything that can cultivate in you. This, many grown up men don't like. Especially from their wives. They may still accept it from their mothers but not their wives. For women offering help is a way of life but for men taking help may be offensive. Women don't like to prove their competence. Offering constructive criticism is an act of love and nurturing. They advise because they care for you. Complaining is also a way of life for them. They just want someone to listen to them.

Women therefore make great teachers. My wife has taught school children for over thirty years. She was always praised and admired by her peers, supervisors and the children. Using the same ability she now runs eight playschools very efficiently. Her involvement is total and within a short time, her schools got wonderful rankings..

Men are motivated and empowered when they feel needed and if they can be of some use to others. Women, in contrast, get motivated when they feel cherished, adored and admired. This is closely linked to the mother's instinct. Mothers have to look after their children; they are ready to sacrifice for their family, sometimes in the most unexpected ways. Women are givers and men are providers. But a woman, when upset, needs someone to be at her side, a companion who is prepared to listen to her.

Do women like chivalry? Yes, they do. Qualities such as bravery and gallantry are appreciated by women. They want a man to protect their honour and dignity. Maybe amongst the young men today this trait is on the wane.

My wife has always demonstrated this strong trait of doing for others, especially at home. She would meet all the demands of her two sons. As far as food is concerned, instead of ordering meals from outside she would cook them at home. Giving medicine, checking fever or looking after their homework was a part of her duties. We lived in some of the most difficult areas, wherever my job in the armed forces took us. Some locations had hardly any markets. With very limited resources also, she could come up with exotic food.

As John Gray says women need caring, validation, appreciation, respect and, to some extent, devotion. Many of them want visually demonstrative dialogue. I, for one, may not be very vocal about my appreciation. If, for instance, I like the food on the table, I may not say, 'Oh, it is a fantastic meal'. I will rather demonstrate by eating more!

Men on the other hand need trust, encouragement and appreciation. Trust is something which both men and women expect from each other. That blind trust is the basis of any lasting relationship. I feel that trust between the two of us has been the biggest strength and gave us that comfort from which we both benefitted.

Men and women can be equal but can never be identical

God has created us differently. Very differently. Then how can we be identical.

In this mad race for equality, women have forgotten this fundamental fact. Why should they compete to be identical when they are so different? They have tonnes of strengths and plus points, In fact more than men in whichever way you look at it. Then why this fight for frivolous equality.

Why does society, media and law try to make them identical? Neither should men try to become what women are nor should women try to become what men are. Because they are so different.

> 'On the left side of a strong woman, stands a strong man; he is strengthened by her character.'
> – Ellen J. Barrier

Small things of God

Small things in life need to be enjoyed and probably they can give us maximum joy. We have unfortunately forgotten how to enjoy what we have and are always looking for what we don't have. Today we are running after that mirage. The mirage is becoming bigger and bigger everyday which is entirely the creation of our materialistic society.

The song Aashiyana says it all,

'Itni si hansi
Itni si khushi
Itna sa tukda chand ka.
Khwabon ke tinkon se
Chal banayein aashiyaan'

It basically reflects two feelings: one, that a little laughter and happiness is all that you require. A man and woman can make a home together, gradually, starting from scratch.

Most of us must have heard this saying so many times, but very few would have understood the true meaning of this. Hardly anyone would have taken this seriously to be applied in life.

It is like reading a religious scripture hundred times over and not understanding a word of it.

If we can be a little contented with what we have and a little patient with what we don't have, life can be worth living. If couples can learn to live within their means, they don't have to search for happiness.

'Who is rich? He who rejoices in his portion'.
– Talmud

Trust is the key

Trust and faith are two issues that are of paramount importance in every relationship.

Boss and subordinates must have, colleagues amongst them must have business partners must have, friends must have, brothers must have. If you can't trust your boss, you will not be able to work and if you can't trust colleagues and friends you won't survive.

It is one of the key parameters on which a marriage is founded. Trust is something that is the most comforting feeling in a marriage. If husband and wife have to cover their tracks at home all the time, what kind of life will that be? This will happen only if you don't trust each other.

When you talk of a common hearth or 'Sanjha Choola' it is acknowledging the common wealth principle. Then how can you and why should you have separate bank accounts, lockers and property.

I have had a joint bank account with my wife from day one. We have everything in our joint names. I let my wife run the house and take care of finances. If I am not hiding anything from her then I may as well have things absolutely transparent. And the same applies to her. She knows the inwards and therefore should be able to manage the outwards also. This can happen only if your wife is 'sensible'.

Today unfortunately your whole relation is based on mistrust, as you look at it as a contract. In the modern world, after trust and faithfulness, comes the division of household work. Who will wash the utensils, who will do the laundry and who will drop the kids to school and it just goes on.

Even in an employment agreement one would not expect such rigidity. Most employment contracts would read, 'I agree to do whatever work is assigned to me by my company through my supervisors. If required I will take an extra load in addition to what is given in my Job description'. You are flexible and willing to accommodate at your workplace then why not at home. This is applicable to husband and wife both. A marriage will never be smooth sailing if it is stricken by STDO – 'spousal trust deficit disorder'.

Ego: the killer

Nature has given ego to every man and woman in equal measure. Our ego seeks gratification, fulfilment, indulgence and even satisfaction. Ego actually destroys us because if our ego is not satisfied we feel restless, we feel small, we feel hurt. Most of the times these are personal fixations. Ego is seductive. It leads to emotionally-charged and tense situations like 'who will blink first'. That is why it is quite common to hear, 'Oh, he has made it an ego issue', which can be interpreted as 'If his ego is not satisfied he will not budge'. In politics, offices and workplace this is common.

We normally use others as punching bags to satisfy our ego and fill that personal void. To look big we try to make the other person feel small.

We take these ego trips often at the cost of hurting others. Our ego is satisfied if we feel empowered, we feel in control of things and we can even manipulate people and circumstances to satisfy our ego.

While spiritual ego focuses on 'we and collective good', human ego is focused on 'I'.

All saints, gurus and scriptures tell us to shed our ego. At home, if you are looking for collective good and happiness, it is better to keep egos in check.

How can two helmsmen rowing together have egos? Because the purpose is to collectively take the boat forward. We handle ego issues at home through little arguments and discussions. This is one area where 'work is in progress'. As long as your ego doesn't give you sleepless nights and skirmishes and do not take the shape of a war, it is fine. We have been able to manage quite well for the last forty years now.

Rubber Band theory

I feel, sometimes a bit of separation keeps the relationship alive. In the armed forces it is a matter of routine to be posted to remote areas which are usually non-family stations. Even while being at family stations one has to go for training exercises for a considerable period of time, each year.

These separations, though unpleasant, help in keeping the warmth alive in a family. About two decades ago, husbands and wives used to communicate mostly through letters because telecommunication was not that reliable in remote areas. There were no e-mails, sat phones or cell phones those days. There was, therefore, a sense of inquisitiveness. One waited for a letter very eagerly, and then these were also preserved for some time.

During courtship, I was posted to a field area, and my would-be-wife was at Ajmer. Our primary means of communication was letter-writing but I would get an occasional kick by managing to put a call through on her landline number at home. Imagine in 1973, with very little telecom infrastructure available, you are trying to put a long distance call through, from a remote area.

It was an exercise by itself. Those days the only telecom company was Department of P&T (Post and Telegraph) and even DOT had not come into existence. For long haul communications we had to take their help. I belong to the Army Corps of Signals, who are responsible for providing communications to the entire Army. I always had one of my linemen present at their communication node as a routine. His job was to ensure that all our communication circuits, routed through civil infrastructure, were always up and functioning.

But with my courtship having started, he had one more task on hand, 'to patch me on a reasonably good circuit up to my bunker on one side and connect me to Ajmer ensuring I could speak to my would-be-wife at least twice a week'. This was usually done late at night so that the subscriber at Ajmer was available at home and the call did not miss the target. In addition, it was easy to get speech circuits late at night, when one could speak for hours without interruptions.

These calls were real moral boosters, when you are sitting in a bunker, out in the wilderness. This is where that song '*Itni si Khushi*' would sum up the situation.

I feel for us humans a bit of depravity keeps us alive and kicking.

For a fairly long time during our marriage, we would manage to speak to each other infrequently during some of the separation periods. But it was something which one would look forward to.

'Distance is the strongest bridge for love'. Sounds weird, but it is a fact.

John Gray in his book, 'Men are from Mars and women are from Venus', nicely portrays the need for men to sometimes pull away from women. He says, 'A man automatically alternates between needing intimacy and autonomy'.

He compares men to rubber bands, after sometime of being close to a woman, they need to move away for a while. After a while they come back, pulling back exactly like a stretched rubber band.

In many professions, separation becomes inevitable. People who are into sales and marketing need to travel for a considerable period of time in a month. Many high-flying jobs involve frequent travel. In the armed forces also separation is an unavoidable professional hazard. Many who served the armed forces would have stayed with their families for only fifty percent of their length of service. In such a case, wives play a very important role. They are the ones who need to run the show alone. Bringing up children, managing home, money matters and even little emergencies have to be handled by the lady of the house.

I feel most women do this astonishingly well. It also brings that extra zing in life and a bonding within the family. You all look forward to being together and rejoice. When one comes back home after several months of separation, it is party time and one makes the best of it. It breaks the monotony of 'always being together', which may at some point become boring.

Without a family, man, alone in the world, trembles with the cold.

— Andre Maurois

Home, sweet Home

There is nothing like sleeping on your own bed. You may go out for a family outing for a week to the most exotic locations, but coming back home is something which we all cherish. Your home is the most comfortable and the most familiar place on earth.

In the armed forces, like many central government jobs, we get transferred every two to three years to new locations. During the 1980's and 1990's, there were no packers and movers; we had to pack our stuff ourselves. Wives played a very big role in packing which was a week-long affair. In fact, in our case the responsibility of packing was taken entirely by my wife. Clothes, crockery, cutlery, kitchenware, furniture, all was to be packed into trunks and taken along. Shortage of accommodation has always been a perennial problem with the army and invariably one would first move into a temporary makeshift accommodation for a few months before getting a proper house. This added to the problem of packing. It was done in such a way so as to facilitate unpacking in two phases. Our wives did this marvelously. We have stayed in tents, bashas, two room apartments and sprawling bungalows. It surprises me as to how we managed all that. Each type of accommodation had its own challenges and each one offered something very unique. With the support of our wives, we enjoyed every bit of it.

I remember moving into a Basha which was our second house (the first being a tent), in a semi-field area. It had mud walls, a rustic door, picked up from a village. The roof was made of bamboos and raven grass (locally known as 'sarkanda'). During summers it used to get very hot and staying indoors under that was very difficult because of the heat. Our administrative officer (a local guy) suggested that we give it a coat of mud and cow dung, a neat coat on top of the roof would keep away the heat. He told us that it was a time-tested method. I agreed and he got it done for us very quickly. Yes, it was something that worked; especially in the afternoons when the sun was at its brightest and temperature was close to 48 degrees celcius in the desert.

Having settled down, we called a few friends over for dinner. It was hot, so most of the men opted for beer, which I gladly poured into glasses and we all settled down under the cow dung-covered, thatched roof. Soon it started raining, but we were pretty safe and dry inside our basha. I realised that it had started raining heavily. The second-in-command of the regiment was also amongst the guests. He preferred his whisky with soda and I promptly served him that.

To my horror I found his whisky changing to the colour of rum. I quickly picked up his glass to check. I found I had poured him the right drink but the drippings from the roof, along with cow dung, had done the damage. I quickly replaced his glass and managed to avert the disaster. Post-dinner when I narrated this to the rest of the friends, they all had a hearty laugh. At night, it became a storm and the entire basha was leaking. Our bedroom was like a swimming pool and we spent the night with our hurricane lantern as there was no electricity.

Early morning, we woke up with a thud. Our rear wall had collapsed and we were both looking into my commanding officer's bedroom that was the next Basha. He was equally drenched. We were all in the same boat.

It just depends on how you take these things. One could have cribbed and complained but we enjoyed every bit of it. Life is like that; one must make the best of it. Army teaches us adaptability and I feel this is the biggest learning for our wives. They can make a home anywhere and under any circumstances.

Getting along with people is an art which wonderful wives have

In the armed forces, we have colleagues from all over the country. Yet we have a spirit of camaraderie amongst officers which no other organisation has. This equation can quickly change if their wives don't get along with each other.

Two men may get along with each other very well and could be the best of friends. In case their wives don't get along, this friendship won't last for long.

We did have our differences of opinion regarding some friends, but they were not escalated to levels which would break down friendships. Again, sensible wives get along with most others.

Great expectations

In the last two decades, India has witnessed a huge social turmoil. It is a society in transition. Sudden affluence, availability of things, loan facilities, plastic money, overdose of media and over activism about individual freedom and rights have considerably changed the social fabric and value system.

For the older generation it was more to do with survival and making a better life. For husband and wife it was more symbiotic, and interdependence was at the core of family values. Today it is more individualistic, which has to an extent made life chaotic.

Money was essential for happiness even earlier and no family or a relationship could survive only on love and fresh air. But that happiness was mostly based on contentment. People were happy with limited resources.

Today money is required to splurge and meet one's greed. When so much surplus money or disposable income suddenly becomes available, it is most likely that young couples will go bananas. That is why they are going crazy.

> *'To be content with little is difficult; to be content with much, impossible.'*
> – Marie von Ebner-Eschenbach,

The most intriguing part of this upheaval is that despite this sudden affluence, husbands and wives are in debt. They swipe a credit card as if they will never have to return that money. It is bad financial planning. I have been saying this earlier, that women are more sensible than men in this regard. But within a cluster of women some are very sensible, some sensible and some, could be very senseless or even downright doltish.

Middle-class values may seem outdated, but they are the most effective values. These are the values that can also be called 'Indian values.'

Before the 1990s, we believed in celebrating sacrifice and duty over success and materialistic achievements. Such people joined the police and the armed forces. It was education and power over wealth and that's why people joined civil services. We believed in co-existence over competition. That's why families survived. It was respecting the hierarchy rather than equality.

"Middle class sounds so middle class" some may argue. But these values are fundamentally very sound. Many 'nouveau-riche' people have not been able to handle that success appropriately. They gained something in terms of real estate, big cars and fat bank balances but lost out on these very basics, which actually account for all good men and also all good women.

At the same time, many who earned good money remained grounded and stuck to these values. I feel they benefitted the most. Even if middle-class values were values of compulsion, rather than choice, these were good to keep our sanity and our feet on the ground. We have started aping westerners especially the Americans. Remember when you ape, you look like an ape. We learnt all the wrong things from them (which could be right in their context) but we never learnt the right stuff from them.

We aped them for rights, liberty and individual freedom, but never wanted to learn responsibility and responsiveness from them. Because it is easy to have rights but difficult to be responsible. We learnt to dress up like them, speak like them, eat like them but never tried to learn to be punctual or law-abiding like them. Again easy versus difficult.

Unfortunately, we made a hash out of it and many of the upward mobile and pseudo-moderns have collectively created nothing more than a pseudo-modern society.

This has impacted our homes. It will be great if we learn good things from the west and keep our Indianness intact. We can be modern and yet remain traditional. If husbands and wives can do this much, life can be very pleasant.

'Throw away' culture

All of us have an emotional attachment with things given to us by our parents, some special gifts or even letters written by our loved ones. We foolishly preserved them and some of them we still possess. But can these acts of being possessive about some weird, old things be called foolish? I think not. Relationships, family and home are all about strong feelings, emotions and attachment. How can you love someone or care for someone if you don't have any feeling of attachment towards him or her? Without attachment it becomes a synthetic relationship. And that is what we have come to, what I commonly refer to as 'Plug and play relationship', is a by-product of this synthetic emotional aloofness.

When we lose a cat or a dog, why do we feel sad? We feel sad and even break down because we are attached to them. Humans are so sensitive that those who love plants feel very sad even when a plant in their garden decays or dies.

The materialistic culture has ushered in the throw-away culture. Ever-changing models of cars, cell phones and new TV systems push us to discard the old and buy new ones.

Indirectly it also creates that emotional aloofness in us. A popular advertisement on TV by olx.com is pretty illustrative. A father is playing a piano and his two young sons crack a good price for his old desktop computer and suggest selling it. The old man reacts and says, 'I wrote the first letter to your mother on this very desktop, how can I sell it?' The boys say, 'Oh, it is so old now, what's the use?' Dad responds, OK. Tomorrow when I become old, will you sell me too?'

It is definitely impacting our emotional sensitivity. A time may come, when we become like robots: intelligent, smart, efficient but not emotional.

Robots don't feel nostalgic about anything, but we humans do. Going back to your old school, visiting your college or your native place means a lot to most of us. Because we are humans, we feel that way.

Families, societies and even nations exist because of emotions and attachments. Emotions are for our collective good. But when we start loving ourselves so much, we are automatically detaching ourselves from others and are heading for the Emotional Deficiency Syndrome. This is one of the major reasons for men not preferring to opt for armed forces as a profession across the world, today.

We have mistakenly shifted the goal posts

There is no such thing as public opinion. There is only published opinion.

– Joseph Goebbels

We are rapidly trying to change the rules of the game; the game called 'family life'. We have not learnt anything from the west, their failings, their problems and what they have gone through in the recent past. We have mistakenly shifted the goal posts, individuals have done this by being over-assertive, exercising freedom of choice and looking for that personal space.

Just as climate change is going to affect the coming generations, societal changes are destroying our homes and will impact our children. Both are man-made disasters and the world is paying the price. Women's very nature is being tampered with by women themselves. They are being goaded by the media and some opinion makers to do this. When so much is happening around you and people around you are thumping the table all the time for freedom, liberty and rights, it is bound to incite an individual. It is like a non-smoker in a room where everyone is smoking heavily. A non-smoker will surely inhale some of the smoke even if he doesn't want to. Some men and women therefore become victims of passive smoking'.

'We should celebrate rising divorce rates', read a headline on the editorial page of a New Delhi-based tabloid. Another mainstream paper puts it on the front page, 'Seventy-year-old woman wants divorce after fifty three years of marriage!' This is a favourite past-time of some of our socialite ladies and gentlemen. It gets you in the limelight and the media gets its highest TRPs. Who would not like to read about a seventy-year-old woman wanting a divorce?

The former CM of Delhi, Ms Sheila Dikshit, who herself is seventy years old, blames the 'Intolerance' between couples for rising divorces. She also says that financial independence could be one of the factors, though that does not mean that you lose your family life in the process.

The unfortunate part of this situation is that some of these modern thinkers many times become victims of this liberation storm, which they themselves have crafted to a large extent. Sometimes, taking a closer look into their personal lives may be pretty revealing.

Public opinion and Goebbels trap

Public opinion is not necessary made by public at large. Therefore *public opinion may not be created by the public but it is created for the public for sure.*

All Germans did not want to mercilessly kill Jews during the Second World War. But it was being portrayed thus throughout

Germany. Later the entire world felt that all Germans were barbaric and heartless.

> *It would not be impossible to prove with sufficient repetition and psychological understanding of the people concerned that a square is in fact a circle. They are mere words, and words can be moulded until they clothe ideas in disguise.*
> – Joseph Goebbels

Joseph Goebbels, who was the propaganda minister in the Nazi government of Adolf Hitler, was one of the major contributors to building public opinion amongst Germans to wage a war against the rest of Europe after the First World War.

In a similar way, public opinion regarding social issues is also created by some opinion makers and the media. Today traditional media coupled with social media (which is also dominated by opinion makers) is a very potent weapon, which can sway public opinion very quickly and very strongly. The media cleverly uses the celebrity brigade to endorse such opinions. Celebrities themselves are looking for publicity and this vicious circle goes on.

Once a public opinion is created, then anyone speaking against it is made to shut up. In a way it becomes a fashion statement and no one dares to say anything different else he or she becomes a laughing stock. These are like 'untouchable truths'. Social desirability is another key component to the formation of public opinion. Social desirability is the idea that people in general will form their opinions based on what they believe is the prevalent opinion of the social group they identify with.

> *Public opinion is no more than this: what people think that other people think.*
> – Alfred Austin

Fight for your rights, fight for your individual comfort and fight for your individual freedom are the constructs on which the new social order is being built. Unfortunately, very few talk about responsibility, morals, commitment, sacrifice, tolerance or harmony. These are difficult and therefore conveniently labeled as outdated and old-fashioned.

Vanity of profanity

People keep testing the environment to gauge 'how much is too much'. It is reflected in our cinema, our writings, in the media and in our general conversation and behaviour.

The language of cinema and songs has changed over the last two decades. Directors, lyricists and actors keep pushing the envelope of profanity. 'If something crass has been accepted by the censor board, let me try something even crasser next time', is the philosophy. If this much of nudity has been accepted, let me try to experiment with something hotter next time. In a way you keep pushing the society under the garb of freedom of expression, freedom of art, freedom of choice, choice of clothes and this list goes on. Society becomes a mute spectator and watches the drama helplessly.

Values, morals and dignity are again just words, which can be interpreted and misinterpreted at the same time.

Artists, writers and film-makers are told by the courts to apply self-censorship on their craft. But cheap popularity and money is all that matters, who cares for morals and values.

If anyone tries to point out an error, the same groups of liberals huddle up in front of the cameras to ask him, 'who are you to ask us this?' And the matter is summarily disposed off. The person questioning the wrong is made to look like an idiot.

Such is the fear of punishment by these self-appointed modernistic gurus that, even parents can't speak their mind.

Expressions in fashion

Instead of going for semantics, today we are getting bogged down with syntax. Let me explain the difference. Semantics is about the meaning and substance and syntax deals with phraseology.

We are now bogged down with mere rhetoric and expressions of freedom, love and celebration. These give us a false sense of freedom and self-respect.

Men and women have suddenly realised the need for personal space, personal identity, personal freedom and equality all like never before. Women start a new family and a new blood line. You need not bury your past but you are starting something new for sure.

Women across the world, including the western world, would assume her new husband's family name or surname after marriage. All over from England, Australia, New Zealand, Pakistan, India, Philippines, Canada and the US, this tradition is followed. Therefore, children of these marriages are given their father's surname.

To keep the notion of independence and identity intact, now some women in India are not prepared to shed their original surname while taking the surname of the husband after marriage. For instance, if a girl named Miss Sakshi Sharma marries Mr. Rohit Ganguly, she would call herself Sakshi Sharma Ganguly after she gets married. This is mere syntax and doesn't really change anything as far as substance is concerned.

Unfortunately, these are nugatory protests against existing norms, which add to the repelling forces between individuals.

In front of the holy fire, the vows are taken in public to unite; but if retaining a surname can give the comfort of individual identity, then so be it.

Some of the recent words and expressions of the modern lexicon are quite amusing. They are used without much thought or even intent. Its melodramatic use of expressions like trauma, break-up, relationship, empowerment, compatibility, unable to handle it and so on, which is quite intriguing.

Compatibility

The dictionary meaning of compatibility is 'a state in which two things are able to exist or occur together without problems or conflict'.

This is probably the most often used or misused word today in the context of marital discord. You don't have to give any reasons for the conflict because this word itself is good enough a reason or shall we say excuse to fall apart.

Men and women are anyway two different species, with different emotional, physical as well as mental make-up. They were created differently by nature and were not built as compatible beings. Yet their roles, strengths and abilities are such that they complement each other in union.

Since both men and women today have become so individualistic and are not prepared to give an inch of their space, they automatically become strong candidates for incompatibility.

Remember 'only plugs and sockets are compatible; human beings have to co-exist'.

> *Marriage is an alliance entered into by a man who can't sleep*
> *with the window shut, and a woman who can't sleep with*
> *the window open.*
> — George Bernard Shaw

Compromise

In today's world of liberated conscience, the word compromise makes people jump out of their seats. I don't know why, but men and women take it almost like an abuse.

I remember having conducted a seminar on work life balance almost ten years ago, where I had invited senior executives from the industry to be a part of the panel discussion.

While we were discussing the issue of women at workplace and how they need to deal with pregnancy at work, some interesting reactions came our way.

One lady, who represented a leading global consulting company as a panelist, said that when she was expecting her child during her career, she took a clean break of three years to devote time to her child. She lost out on her promotion and it did impact her career progression. 'Was it worth it?' I asked. 'Of course it was worth it!' she responded.

'Oh, so a little compromise was worth it', I said.

'No way! It was not a compromise!' she shouted.

I was surprised at this reaction. What is a compromise?

It is a trade-off, you give some and you take some, you lose something to gain something. It is a happy medium. Again this was a reaction to syntax and not focusing on semantics.

Our whole life is one big bloody compromise! You don't get the right team to finish your project. Your boss is not what you want him to be. Your neighbour is an ass and you have to put up with a lousy government. The tax structure doesn't suit you. There is too much pollution in the city. Power cuts are killing your business; you need to live in a flat as you can't afford a bungalow. The courier services are lousy. Your son performs poorly at school. You can't afford a holiday in the Bahamas and you end up going to Bandipur National Park instead. And you are still living and putting up with all this bullshit! Is this anything other than compromise?

Then what's the big deal if you need to compromise a little to live a happy married life?

We need to follow some rules and regulations

Rules and regulations are made to regulate the way we live. Without rules, there will be a total breakdown of our society. Rules and regulations demarcate certain boundaries for us. For instance, there are traffic regulations that we need to follow. You can't overtake from the right at certain places, this is a rule that everyone has to follow. You either drive on the right side or the left side of the road, but you can't be driving in the middle of it! It cannot be free for all. You can't say 'It's my choice and I will decide whether I drive on the right side or the left side of the road since I pay the road tax'.

Social behaviour too is rule-bound and society itself lays down certain rules. There may not be formal or legal rules for establishing or maintaining friendship but for marriage, parents and children, there are rules that need to be followed.

Therefore, a slight pressure of society or the fear of God is good for any civilization. You may not have archaic rules but you need *some* rules which everyone must follow.

> *Do not free a camel of the burden of his hump; you may be*
> *freeing him from being a camel.*
> – G.K. Chesterton

Impact of broken homes on children

When a marriage breaks down and ends in a divorce, it is not only something that affects just husband and wife. Earlier people were of the opinion that if parents were unhappy in a marriage, so were the children. And a natural assumption was that a divorce will make parents as well as the children happy. This is an absolutely wrong notion. In fact, children suffer the most when their parents split up and get divorced.

Children look up to their parents as people with supernatural abilities. They expect them to sort out their differences amicably. They hold them in high esteem and that is why even if a small child gets to learn about an act of infidelity committed by any of the parents, he gets very upset and shaken. He is unable to forgive and digest this act of betrayal. For children, divorce shatters the basic psychological comfort and safety which he expects his parents to provide him throughout his life. Children strongly believe that there is only one correct relationship and that is their father and mother being together. When this relationship is disturbed or broken, they feel betrayed and for them it is in conflict of their basic understanding of family life. When a divorce takes place children nurse a grudge against both the parents.

A divorce leaves some scars for life and for all of them a divorce negatively taints their view of relationships.

Judith Wallenstein, a psychologist, followed a group of children of divorced parents for twenty years. She interviewed them after eighteen months and then five, ten, fifteen and twenty five years after the divorce. She was expecting that by then they would have forgotten the event and would have bounced back. What she discovered was disturbing. Even twenty years after the divorce, they experienced fear of loss and fear of conflict. Twenty years is a long time.

During childhood, such children were at a risk of suffering academically, indulging in crimes, drug and alcohol abuse. But as they become adults, they are averse to love affairs and suffer unstable marriages. Judith observes through her research that these children demonstrated a sense of being abandoned by both parents. Parents take a divorce for their own needs and to find happiness again with someone new. As it stands today, many second marriages also end up in divorce and the mirage of happiness still remains a mirage even after the first divorce.

> *Having children makes you no more a parent than having a*
> *piano makes you a pianist.*
> – Michael Levine

'After divorce, both the parents get involved in rebuilding their own families, economically, socially and sexually, often forgetting that they have not only abandoned their partners but their children as well', she observes.

Unfortunately parents and children's needs are out of sync for many years after the divorce. Obviously, children see their parents running for their own happiness, chasing their own dreams, leaving them in a lurch. What a pity.

A divorced husband and wife may lead their new lives with more vigour, but the children think of their loss every day. There have been cases where both mother and father refuse to take the custody of the child, where can such a child go?

Kerby Anderson in an article says, The breakdown of the American family is at the root of nearly every other social problem and pathology'. Karl Zinsmeister, of the American Enterprise Institute, says, 'There is a mountain of scientific evidence showing that when families disintegrate, children suffer emotional scars that last for life. Drug crisis, education crisis, and juvenile crime, all trace back to one source: broken families'.

I have drawn many examples from the west, because they were hit before us, in the 1970s and 1980s – and we were hit almost thirty years later. But the damage is the same for us as well.

One thing which we must take note of is that western society is self-centric and society-centric. An individual looks after his own freedom and also takes care of his obligations towards society. The society and the system is also capable of helping individuals during their crisis.

In India, we are individual-centric and family-centric. A person doesn't care so much for society but is very close and caring towards his family. Our society and the system is also not geared up to support people in personal crisis. If we lose our family bonding it is unimaginable as to what will happen to us.

At this rate, it may take us just four to five generations in the future to become social tribes where children belong to a tribe and not a family. Individuals will mate and vacate and one would neither be able to establish blood lines nor even family trees. Everyone will be an individual, just 200 to 300 years from now. This will be the greatest future shock!

The fifth stage of life – A new paradigm

As per Hinduism, human life is to be broadly lived in four stages. These are known as Ashrams.

The first Ashram is 'Brahmacharya' where a man lives as a student and learns practical and spiritual knowledge from his guru. He remains single till he is twenty five.

The second Ashram is 'Grihastha' when he gets married and looks after his family.

The third Ashram is 'Vanprastha', when his responsibility as a householder comes to an end. His children are grown-up and he, by now, has grandchildren. He goes away from his home and spends time in relaxing and praying.

The fourth Ashram is 'Sanyas' when he devotes his time to spirituality to attain ultimate happiness. If we club the third and fourth stage together, it broadly identifies with a sense of happiness, satisfaction, achievement and fulfillment. The new age has added to the troubles of couples, who spent their lives, more or less peacefully with their spouses, lived for each other, lived by each other and followed and fulfilled their commitment to their marriage. By and large, they sailed through these Ashrams or stages of life quite well. For them there is something beyond the third and fourth stage of life, created by their children. While they planned to bask in the sun, and spend the rest of their days peacefully, they were hit by a new stage in life where they witness the divorce of their children. They helplessly watch their children breaking all the promises to their spouses often being caught between the 'who is right and who is wrong' predicament.

They are unable to understand the hard battle lines being drawn between the husbands and wives of today, whom they find totally unrelenting and incorrigible. Oh, they are from the old school of thought, a little old-fashioned, pliant, understanding, sometimes meek, adjusting, relenting and sometimes prepared to sacrifice for others. This is what their children perceive them to be!

No parents like it when the homes of their children are destroyed. It may be a son or a daughter, he or she is after all their own flesh and blood. If they have grandchildren, the pain becomes still more unbearable. These divorces are a legal process and often turn ugly. Parents of these 'would-be-divorcees' are badly sandwiched.

How selfish can this young generation be? They neither bother about what would happen to their children nor do they bother about the turmoil and pain they cause to their parents.

This fifth stage of life is 'Dukh Dard' Ashram, which is pain and agony.

It is an old saying, '*Kharbooja chhuri par girey, ya chhuri kharboojey pay-katega to kharbooja*'.

It simply translates into this 'whether a melon falls on a sharp knife or a knife falls on a tender melon, it will be the melon which will get cut into two'.

Here the melon are the parents and the children of the would-be-divorcees, who are looking for happiness elsewhere to again live happily ever after.

Our four B's – Band, Baja, Baaraat and Boom!

Indian weddings are a big show-off and an occasion to display wealth and clout of the two families that are uniting through this extravagant bandobast. Tonnes of food and crores of rupees are wasted every year on weddings across the country and no one could be bothered.

Usually these are week-long weddings which become like a paid, five-star holiday for thousands of guests who congregate for this 'auspicious' occasion. Festivities start with dance, drama, sangeet and mehndi which usually last for a week. The wedding day is marked with 'Band, Baja and Baaraat', where the groom, along with his family and friends, descend on the venue which is all done up by the bride's family.

Both families meet and dine together. A lavish spread is laid out for dinner where thousands eat together. The stage is set for a happy union.

'Saat pheras', a ceremony which is the crux of the marriage, takes place to finally unite the couple in a sacred relationship.

The focus is more on dance, drama and rhetoric, where the actual spirit of the marriage and its sanctity is probably lost.

It is unfortunate that so much effort by both families, who spend crores in many cases, cannot hold the couple together for even a year. Where do all the rituals, promises and vows disappear so quickly?

In some cases, the entire thing collapses within months-and that is now becoming a reality across the country. Soon daggers are drawn and both families start a battle to disengage and undo what they so enthusiastically did, not very long ago.

And that 'band, baja, baaraat', ends with a boom! Yet there are sensible men and women, who understand the meaning of commitment and moving along together in life. They do make the best of it and for them that occasion; those celebrations, always remain fresh in their mind and spirit.

In every marriage more than a week old, there are grounds for divorce. The trick is to find, and continue to find, grounds for marriage
— Robert Anderson

The scent of a woman

A hotel room has all the comforts and facilities one needs. You get a comfortable bed, writing material, food on call, lovely bathrooms and hot water, but you still don't feel at home in a hotel room. It is synthetic, it doesn't have an identity and more so it doesn't reflect your character at all. A home is something which reflects your taste and complexion of a family. It also has a bit of history. Such a history is built of things you collect over a period of time. You are emotionally attached to these things. Home is a place for collective emotions.

It is not difficult, therefore, for anyone to discern between a bachelor's pad and a home? It is not mere cleanliness and keeping things in the right place, that matters. There are more subtle things which men wouldn't think about.

Women are the primary preservers of history which is, to a large extent, intergenerational. A home also reflects a women's taste and sensibility. It reflects her personal contribution too. The right fabric for the window curtain, certain things she crafted by hand are part of the woman's touch. Women are also good with plants and flower arrangements and many other delicate things which they pick up from the marketplace. When you come home you feel that there is a mother around whereas in a hotel you feel there is a housekeeper. And the difference between the two is huge.

> *What would men be without women? Scarce, Sir ....*
> *Mighty scarce.*
>
> – Mark Twain

In our case, we usually shopped together for 'major buys' and collectively decided on things that were big and expensive. What refrigerator to buy or what kind of sofas for the living room was a collective decision. Yet, I let my wife take the final call. I feel she had a better sense of price versus utility and would never settle for anything less than perfect. Generally, men lack this acumen. You cannot outsource your home décor to an interior designer alone. He may do a great job but it will still remain synthetic, without emotions. A lady's involvement is a must to fill this void. We changed almost twenty five houses during my stint with the army but each one of them was made into a home by my wife.

Being ladylike is something which men across the ages have admired and adored about women. In the armed forces, women are treated with utmost respect. Ladies also reciprocate with élan and show grace. Men in uniform never lack chivalry towards woman and are courteous as well as gallant towards them.

If somewhere men have lost out on their chivalry, women have also changed from being subtle to stark. Grace has its own appeal and can be captivating in a very different way. As some poets say, 'Veil has its own charm'. In the last few decades ladies became women and gradually transformed into females. A gentleman became a man and now a male. The niceties have probably disappeared. In the battle for equality, men and women lost their real identity, ladies and gentlemen. They collectively are referred to as guys.

Unfortunately, the culture has changed from subtle to stark; from shy to aggressive, from collective good to self; all in the name of freedom of expression and self-assertion. It has resulted in a false sense of equality. Do you need to use cuss words in public or even with friends to prove something? Do you need to get physical to prove that we have freedom; we have our right to do what we want? Oh, there may be better ways to achieve that, and must we achieve? Society is being goaded to speak out, what may be unnecessary. I was quite surprised and also amused at a comment passed by a celebrity guest during a TV show. The debate was on dressing sense and this lady said, 'If tomorrow I want to walk naked on the road, why should anyone have a problem?' The entire audience comprising mostly young men and women clapped, whistled and applauded! In fact they were being incited, goaded into pushing their own mental envelope.

What a bizarre statement to make on a national TV show! And with what purpose? I am sure that this lady would never walk on the road naked, and am also sure she will never appreciate it if any other women did so. The idea was to grab attention, raise the TRP of the channel and say something different, however stupid it may sound. That is what is 'pushing the envelope' for scoring brownie points. And maybe setting the stage to try to speak something even more bizarre next time.

Incidentally, there are laws against indecent exposure across the world, including Europe and America. What constitutes indecent exposure depends on the standard of decency of the community or society where the exposure takes place. But walking stark naked on the road will not be acceptable by any society.

> *Liberty means responsibility. That is why most men dread it.*
> – George Bernard Shaw

A woman will always appreciate a man who is protective, respectful and chivalrous and men across the world want women to be ladylike, well-behaved, polite and caring. Men are from Mars and women are from Venus, while men should not abandon chivalry and courtesy towards women, let the scent of a woman be the scent of a woman. Romance has a subtle meaning and has its own charm. Let it be.

Rock and Roll

Indian youth is on the roll and some say 'India is rocking'. More than sixty five percent of Indians are below the age of thirty five and all of them are exposed to the kind of luxury that is available in the market place. Availability of goods, great telecom connectivity, social media and a service-driven economy are the pointers of a great life. Three decades and the focus has shifted from 'survival to celebration'. Earlier it was 'save now and buy later' and now it is 'buy now, eat right now and pay later'.

People who are now in their fifties and sixties, grew up in a modest environment. Even in metros and large cities, their parents didn't have huge, disposable incomes and most had three or four children. Very few could expect their parents to leave behind assets which they could really bank on. Whatever was left by their parents was in most cases distributed amongst the siblings.

Therefore they worked hard to make a living, created little wealth, spent carefully and in the bargain, saved a tidy sum of money. Most of them invested wisely in real estate and created some good assets. They were prudent about procreation as well, and believed in 'hum do humare do'. Most, therefore, had one or two children. Today, these children are the youth brigade of India. Most would inherit a home, some other assets and a tidy bit of cash.

Liberalisation and Privatisation are pumping the economy and jobs and entrepreneurial opportunities are multiplying. With sufficient disposable incomes and inherited assets as a safety belt anybody would love to fly.

Marriage is a burden

With this kind of a rock and roll scenario, young men and women don't want to take any responsibility. They look at marriage as bondage and not bonding. 'I' is so much in the centrestage that they don't see anything beyond themselves. For a person so obsessed with his fun and enjoyment, having a child is a burden and a restriction on his/her freedom and independence. It is a herculean task for such a couple to produce a child. I heard a young woman complaining, 'After the delivery of my child, my world has gone upside down. My entire sleep cycle has gone for a toss'. What they don't understand is that their parents also did the same when they were born.

Mockery of marriage

In the last decade, couples seeking divorce are treating their marriage very casually. The wedding vows are forgotten quickly and in many cases, marriages last only a few months and in some cases only a few days.

In the earlier days, divorce which was probably the last option, has now become a popular expression of freedom, right, choice and independence.

Most appalling is the fact that the reasons for the split are very flimsy in many cases. Domestic violence or adultery are two reasons on which there can be no compromise and in such cases the ground justifies a split. Just because the society and law does not attach any stigma to a divorce, it doesn't mean that couples should take the easy way out of responsibility and sanctity of something as serious as marriage. Had this bond been so casual, there would have been no need to go through such long-drawn, legal battles involving allegations, counter allegations, claims for alimony and child custody.

> *Divorce is too complex a process to produce just winners and losers. People adjust in many difference ways and these patterns of adjusting change over time.*
>
> – E Mavis Hetherington
> Divorce Researcher

If it is hard to work through a difficult marriage, it is also hard to work through a divorce.

Several studies have been conducted on divorce in the west and many point out that a divorce generally does not lead to a better life. Four out of ten people, who built their relationships into a second marriage, had mostly the same kind of problems as they did in their earlier marriages. Almost a generation ago, people and lawmakers thought that easier divorce would help to strengthen marriage as an institution. They thought that if people were free to leave an unhappy union they could find a better partner in the next marriage. This line of thinking was flawed because divorce rates for second marriages were even higher than the first one and the break up rate faster too.

Brand Wilcox, a professor of sociology and director of the National Marriage Project US, firmly believes that the institute of marriage still symbolises core values which are important to intimate relationships.

Marriage conveys a sense of meaning, purpose, direction and stability that benefits children as well as adults. Expectation of fidelity tends to create a sense of security, trust and belonging.

> *'Your life begins to change the day you take responsibility for it.'*
> – Steve Maraboli

Why divorce rates have shot up in India

As mentioned earlier, men and women of marriageable age in India are having a ball today. They do not want to let this party be over. They have everything which 'I' in them wants. Therefore they don't want any interference in their lifestyle, they don't want to do anything for anyone except themselves, and that is a harsh reality.

In such a scenario, where does a marriage fit in? Huh! As far as society is concerned, it has started accepting divorce as 'fait accompli'. Families believe that a couple would be better-off staying separately as singles rather than as a married couple. Parents of a girl also feel that their daughter can have a life after marriage and can manage without a husband. The fast pace of life in bigger cities, leaves people with little time for gossip and bigger cities provide an ocean to disappear into and maintain anonymity. Therefore, a person who gets divorced escapes scrutiny from society.

A lot of debates have built an opinion that marriage is not a necessary evil. The work culture has changed and ambitions have skyrocketed. Early burnout for working men and women is nothing unusual; and that also impacts married life negatively.

A married couple, which runs into a problem, usually gets swayed by ill-informed people who are not well-meaning. These are self-acclaimed advisors who many times even incite both the partners to take a hard stand. They add fuel to the fire and young men and women take hasty and sometimes immature actions and ensure a premature demise of their marriage. Today many parents of the husband and wife both are made to believe that their son/daughter is going through hell and parents buckle under the emotional pressure and support a divorce.

Young boys and girls try to act as mentors. Here, more than training, education and degrees, experience is desired. Definition, of a mentor given in the dictionary is 'a wise, trusted', counsellor. Such people are neither wise nor can be trusted but become self-appointed counsellors. In many cases, divorce seekers go to divorcees who already have a negative perception of marriage. Obviously, such advice could be clouded by their own bad experience in marriage.

Rumani Saikia Phukan, writing on divorce in India, argues that women's empowerment is also a major cause for divorce rates going up. This also gives a misplaced sense of freedom and understanding of empowerment. Though women empowerment is to help women, this is also misused by many.

In a recent article, 'Stop misusing the term *Empowerment*', in Huff post lifestyle UK, Helen Reeves gives her candid opinion about women's empowerment. She says that the English dictionary meaning of the word empowerment is 'give someone authority or power to do something'. 'This word is being misused and over-used and it has really started annoying me', she writes.

Taking on how women should make money she says, 'Yes, on a continuum of empowerment, exposing your breasts for a fairly decent-albeit insecure-wage, probably affords relatively more power than some of other occupations women tend to disproportionately dominate in a profoundly unequal, capitalistic marketplace. Posing for Page Three may well feel more empowering than say, a low-paid cleaning job on a zero hour contract. Is this empowerment?' she asks 'No, No, No, it's not. It's just bloody frustrating', she says.

Quoting a feminist video album of Beyonce Carter she says, 'It was more about her arse than this elusive concept of 'female empowerment' – I was disappointed!'

Pseudo-spirituality

The idea of involving religion in a marriage was to give it religious sanctity, a sense of purity and commitment, therefore marriage has been a living example of spirituality for centuries. A couple was made to commit in front of God so that they both remain committed to each other and their offspring, forever. Both family and religion are therefore a serious affair and hence the connect.

I feel being loyal and committed to your spouse and your children is the best and the truest tribute to God. But this requires sacrifice, dedication, commitment and doing for others, which is the essence of any religion or spiritual belief.

People want an easy way out to even reach God and attain Nirvana. Spirituality has become a fashion and more of a symbolic rhetoric. People feign spirituality by quoting verses from religious texts, using symbolism yet not shedding their ego or evil minds. You can't become spiritual or godly by mere chanting without practising any good on ground.

A large component of your quest for spirituality will be attained if you are good to your own family and your near and dear ones. There will be no need to go to godmen because then godfather and godmother are all there at home.

I feel men and women must look at their marriage as a religious bond and a way to attain spirituality, as it has been constituted by every religion. They take the vows without understanding their meaning and the benefits it can accrue.

Be god-fearing, god-seeking through actions at home and you need not go to a 'guru or godman'. It's all there within you – within your reach.

> *To maintain a joyful family requires much from both the parents and the children. Each member of the family has to become, in a special way, the servant of the others.*
> – Pope John Paul II

Crux of the problem

While working on this book, I made it a point to speak and discuss with several of my friends, about the complex problem of withering relationships between today's young men and women. Most of them asked me a simple question, 'After all this research, what do you think is the crux of the problem?'

It is a very difficult question to answer, but I made an attempt to seek the terrible truth.

In my reckoning, the reasons for homes falling apart and marriages breaking down can be summed up as below. Seven mantras for demise of a modern marriage.

- No tolerance, no patience and no resilience.

- Taking full advantage of and often misusing the liberty given by society and law.

- Perverted perception of value system.

- Height of hedonism, extravagance and self-indulgence.

- Couples not prepared to take any responsibility.

- It is I, me and myself and that is the only thing that matters. Individual progress matters more than collective good.

- Not ready to listen to anyone's advice, parents or counsellors.

Today, young married men and women sometimes make life so difficult for each other during their wedlock and the divorce proceedings, that for them divorce becomes a celebration. 'Oh my divorce has finally happened!' and the usual response is 'Oh, congratulations'.

Church to court – A short Journey

When a wedding takes place, love, caring, bonding and God's blessings are in the air. Everybody seems to rejoice, and wish the couple as well as both the families great days ahead. The ultimate blessing in the Indian culture is 'Sada Khush Raho' which simply means, 'Be happy forever'. Most couples are blessed to live a healthy and happy life. Unfortunately, in certain cases where the union doesn't work out for long, relationships start breaking down. First it affects the husband, wife and their children and gradually it starts affecting their parents and their tertiary families as well.

When a couple tries to split, the atmosphere turns tense, threatening, ugly and comes under scrutiny of both the families and the law.

From churches having candles, the holy cross, fonts, pulpits, lecterns and stained glass windows for the holy union; you now have courtrooms, witness boxes, bailiffs, the jury box, judge's gravel, bar and benches for the split. Sermons, prayers, mandaps, hawans and church bells and prayers turn into arguments, counterarguments, allegations, false allegations, counter allegations, swearing, affidavits, witnesses and evidence.

Pundits and maulvis are replaced by lawyers, solicitors, registers and bailiffs.

God is out and the Judge is in. Just because two people couldn't get along with each other.

How long will the party last?

At the time of writing this book, men and women getting married in India are in the age bracket of twenty five to thirty five years. Divorce bracket would extend to twenty five to forty years. In today's context, this constitutes young India.

You are young, you are fit, you have money and you have means of enjoyment. If you are single by choice or singled out of divorce, you have only yourself to support. Therefore, you are even richer – no liabilities, no strings attached and no responsibility.

The stage is set for the party and guys and gals are having a blast.

Many of those who have left their broken homes behind and moved forward with the cliché, 'Let's move on', do not want to think about their past. They try to be happy and in fact, are very happy with their work, friends and colleagues.

'Even the darkest hour has sixty minutes', is a famous quote by Morris Mandel which makes us feel that 'This too shall pass'. The reverse is also true, 'the brightest hour also has just sixty minutes'. People, who unfortunately have to break their homes, have to cope with being alone or putting it another way, become lonely at some point in time. Friends are there at work or social gatherings, but at home you are alone.

Another challenge is that most of your friends are married and have a family and you become a misfit amongst that lot. They may welcome a divorcee but that person himself/herself may feel out of place amongst people who have a family.

This becomes more serious once you are a bit over the hill. When you are in your fifties and sixties, it could hit you the hardest. You need company, you need companionship, and you can't live on Bacardi and barbeque alone.

This is a hard reality for men as well as women. You need emotional and physical support as a human being. Such a support becomes more acute when one grows old.

The emotional effects of a divorce are a mixed bag of anger, fear, guilt, loneliness, anxiety, stress and grief.

It takes its toll on the health of men as well as women. Some debate that single women die seven to fifteen years before those who are married. Others say, divorced men have mortality rates which are 250 percent higher than married men. These may be backed by statistics and research. But at the end of it these are statistics only. In the firing line are those individuals who split and prefer to stay alone.

A wonderful wedding

As I pen down my closing remarks, I can make more sense of it. There can be no perfect marriage and there can be no perfect husband or wife.

Living together is something which leaves you with certain things in the credit and several things in the debit. I feel that all those who have 'lived happily ever after', managed their differences well, showed more tolerance towards each other and practised restraint during difficult times. Most importantly they showed maturity and were ready to compromise prudently. They saw more 'benefits for all' and in the larger interest of the family, managed to be happy with a bit of unhappiness, if it came their way.

In our forty years of married life, if I look back, it is not that everything was fine all the time. We had a fair share of our problems but we probably respected the lines drawn by society and played according to the rules of the game.

A wonderful married life is like a Persian carpet. The older it gets, better it becomes.

FRONTISPIECE

Human relations are very complex and most of them require commitment for them to last. Marriage is a relationship which exists across religion, caste, colour and creed. It is a 'culture universal'.

It is one of the oldest institutions, dating back to 2350 BC. Which means, marriage is a ritual around 4,350 years old. Roman Catholics started recognising marriage around the eighth century and the blessings of a priest were necessary for its sanctity. The Hindu marriage system is even older. For all religions it is now considered godly, spiritual, pure and binding. Hindus consider marriage sacred and so does every religion.

The institution of family, bloodline and inheritance stemmed out of marriage or wedlock. It acted as 'binding glue' between couples, gave their offspring legitimacy, certain rights, privileges and something around which a home was created. A home is made of emotions and people, where as a house is a mere brick and mortar shell. The idea behind the institution of marriage in Hinduism is to foster not self-interest but love for the entire family. Practice of self-restraint is the ideal of marriage in Hinduism. It is the love and duty cultivated for the entire family that prevents break-ups. It is similar for Christianity and others too. Love and bonding is like God. 'If you believe it, it is there; you don't, it doesn't exist.'

A family bond was the ultimate thing. Even the dons of Sicily gave family the first priority over anything else. One would be even prepared to die for brotherhood and family name. 'Blood is thicker than water' this saying did not come about just like that. 'Blood relatives' cannot be ignored as they are linked with our very existence. Both these have a deep-seated link with identity, loyalty, commitment and sacrifice for your own kith and kin. It was the raison d'être, an ecosystem for emotional bondage and living in harmony with a sense of belonging. Kings followed a family bloodline, the concept of blue blood existed and the Vedas and *shastras* of castes and *gotras* which all came into existence by way of the 'union' between a man and a woman. Marriage was a structured way of living which made us different, different from any other species on the planet. That is why when man realised the need to move from a 'free for all' society, to a saner, controlled living which would provide sanctity to the family system, almost 5000 years ago, he came up with marriage as an answer.

Society has changed drastically over the last few decades and the institution that lasted for centuries is possibly losing its sanctity. American society was the first to be bitten by the hedonism bug (maximize pleasure without pain), where people became very individualistic, somewhat selfish and started talking of personal freedom and rights rather than collective existence as family. 'I' became more important than 'we'.

Until 1970, live-in-relationships were not legalised in the US. The women's liberation movement started with a bang in the late seventies. It was described as a revolution that would affect every one, and it finally did. Gradually the storm of individualistic freedom; I, me, myself became so strong that by 1990 more than fifty per cent couples started having live-in-relationships before marriage. Some never got married and had children. This may have given freedom to the parents, what I call 'plug and play' relationships. But it had a devastating effect on the children. What came to be known as broken homes or devastated families, surged in numbers across the western world.

The western world looked at the East to learn about family bonding and lasting marriages. They started exploring India to find peace and understand spirituality. Indian Canadians and

Indian Americans came back to their homeland in search of a bride, 'who would last'.

In the last few years or may be a decade, we are moving towards the western way of thinking as far as marriages are concerned. Divorce rates have shot up and 'live in' arrangements are in fashion. People who go through a divorce, in the East or the West, describe it as a 'traumatic' experience, with spouses often ending up in depression when the bond would be broken. That is enough to prove that men or women are more emotional than rational. And marriage still has a lot to offer on the emotional front.

In the Americas, people started looking at marriage as a 'contract', whereas we in the East looked at it more as, commitment, devotion, duty, love, caring and most of all supporting each other in the time of crisis. It was 'Sanjha Choohla' or a common hearth. There was nothing like mine or yours. Everything that belonged to the two was *just for the two of us*. Therefore, contract is synthetic and commitment is at an emotional level, which is at the core of any human relation.

When the man of the house goes through ups and downs in life, he finds a strong shoulder, in his wife, to lean on. He can discuss with her what he cannot speak to others and pour his heart out. Similarly, a wife looks at her husband as someone she can depend upon through thick and thin. More importantly, children look at their parents who are theirs for a lifetime. They keep the nest strong and warm for their children. Let us not forget the grandparents who are an important part of the family. It is a family tree and not just the 'two of us'.

My Wonderful Wife

35 years – a flashback!

Hari Chaturvedi

Marriage is a phenomenon where a universe attaches to another universe and both become complementary parts of a new universe. From this new universe, no one can retract back to the wholesome status of his or her old universe, ever!

As if it happened only yesterday…

I was a young captain in the Indian Army. Trying to balance the ebullience of a carefree lifestyle, with the role of head of the family consisting of my mother and younger sisters, after my father's demise.

Army, however, would not recognise anyone other than a spouse as my family – and I just could not leave my mother and young sisters to live alone, without a male member's support. I had to quickly rig up an arrangement that would keep my family together, and for that I had to get a wife to make the Army give cognisance to my family. Therefore, with a sense of urgency, I set about arranging my arranged marriage in early 1978!

Match-making of eligible kinfolk is one task, relatives in India relish and I had help aplenty. Many tea and 'mithai' sessions were organised and prospects introduced, but nothing remarkable came off those meetings, mostly because I did not know what I was looking for and partly due to my scare of making a stupendous commitment affecting my remaining life, in a huff. I just could not bear to take a strategic decision for my tactical needs, to put it in military parlance.

My leave of absence was nearing its end and I was still far away from finding a solution to my predicament. Should I close my eyes and say 'Yes' to the very next girl my well-wishers line up for me? Or worse, let my mother or sisters fend for themselves and I abdicate my responsibility. The irony is that it never occurred to me that a girl also had the right to reject and the next girl might do that to me. But those were different times.

The day of reckoning arrived pretty soon, when I was called by a family elder to say that he was approached by someone from the Indian Foreign Service, on a brief family visit to India, with a proposal for his younger sister. He said the family was highly regarded and well-known to him and he had agreed that I should accompany the brother on his trip home the next day, to meet the girl and take a decision. He further revealed that train tickets have been booked and I would meet the gentleman at the Delhi railway station for an overnight journey to Kanpur! Fait accomplii?

It looked like destiny was playing me like a pawn on a chessboard. The next day I was heading to Kanpur to meet a stranger who would be my partner for the rest of my life. Her brother, en route, filled me in with glowing details about the girl and her family, and why he thought we were perfectly matched.

The meeting was fixed at her uncle's place and several family members were waiting for us eagerly when we arrived. It was quite visible from their demeanour that I had met their expectations in full measure and the family was keen that I join their fold. But somehow I could also sense some unease. As it turned out, no one had broached the subject of marriage with the other significant party, the girl. She was totally focused on completing her higher education and was rebuffing any talks of marriage. However, her family had high hopes that her reaction would be different this time. On their part, they had already made up their mind. And what the girl wanted did not really matter much.

She was brought there on the pretext of meeting her diplomat brother and was ushered in from the rear door. I could hear giggles and excited chatter from across other rooms, and suddenly there was silence followed by pleading voices. The embarrassment of the family elders attending to me in the drawing room was palpable when they were told that Manju (the girl) was inconsolable and refusing to talk to anyone, after she was informed that her marriage was being arranged and a boy was waiting outside to meet her.

I was already affected by the Stockholm syndrome and began sympathising with my hosts, thinking of finding a way of easing them of their predicament. I volunteered to meet Manju alone and to try convincing her that I was not a scary monster but a presentable and even pleasant male specimen.

I was led to the room she was in and found a creature, coiled like a rope with head hidden between knees and hands tightly clasping toes. All I could see was her back heaving up and down keeping rhythm with her unceasing sobs. Well I had no chance whatsoever of charming her into opening a dialogue. All I could do was mumble to her that no one would force her into marriage and also that I would be happy to meet her again, if she wanted.

I returned from Kanpur utterly confused. Here was a family that had readily accepted me as one of their own. It also was loving, supportive and strong – who could provide me the patronage I longed for so much, shouldering the family responsibilities after my father's demise. On the other hand, how could I hitch my life with someone who had exchanged neither a glance nor a word with me?

Soon the assurance came from the girl's side that everyone including the girl was fine with this alliance and an early date could be set for the marriage. I took a great leap in the dark and gave my go-ahead for the marriage with a caveat that I must get the endorsement in person from the girl.

I had to have a word with her to ensure that she was not being forced into this marriage against her will. What if she had someone else in her life? While for me marriage was the exigency demanded by my immediate family responsibility, I had no right to use her as a pawn in my scheme. That is why, I laid down the condition that I had to have a one-on-one meeting with her before we brought the 'baaraat'. Uncertain, I met her again in her parents' home only two days before the marriage.

I was led into the room where she was sitting on a cot – this time neither crouching, nor hiding her face like our first meeting. It was immense relief to discover that she was beautiful indeed!

In a flash, my looming marriage to this girl whirled from a self-imposed penalty for me to my ardent wish. I wanted her to say yes to our marriage and would employ all my charms to win her over. But she still would not look up and talk to me face-to-face. All my efforts to begin conversation with her went nowhere as she just did not respond. Finally I decided to put it to her as a plain choice and told her that notwithstanding ongoing preparations, the marriage would be called off if she felt that she was being forced into this alliance. To this she responded by vigorously shaking her head to say 'No'. And to my next question, 'Will you marry me?' she nodded to say 'yes'. I could discern a faint smile in her face and that sealed the matter!

Unlike conventional wisdom that love is kindled ever so slowly and nurtured through the process of prolonged dating, I experienced love like the switching of a light bulb. All it needs is a flick to brighten your life forever. I am happy to say that the glow from that day has not diminished for me even after several decades.

Our marriage was a low-key affair. Our customs do not entail dowry or extravagant ceremonies. Moreover, only two days were available to make arrangements after the final confirmation was obtained from Manju. We set out for the marriage with immediate family and some friends, but even amidst festivities and frolic, there was a lingering doubt that the bride could well be speech impaired as no one had heard her talking yet. Therefore the highlight of the marriage was the moment when my sister came running to me in the marriage 'pandal' to inform excitedly 'Bhaiyya, bhabhi ji can talk! I have just heard her speaking with my own ears!'

Marriage ceremonies over, we headed back to Delhi the next day. My new bride, my mother and I were in the back seat of the car. To my amazement, Manju's demeanour gave no hint of unfamiliarity. She behaved as if she always was an integral part of our family. All along the journey she was tending to my mother, who was having bouts of motion sickness, as a dutiful 'bahu' would normally do. Cradling my mother's head in her laps and massaging it lovingly. However, no such courtesy was extended to me.

Back in our transit quarters in Delhi, Manju was escorted by other ladies for completing ushering-in rituals and in no time she became part of the contingent doing home chores. She was serving guests and family, without a hint that she was yet a stranger.

After evening meals, the menfolk settled back for a session of cards and I was dragged in too. Soon the party started playing for stakes and I grabbed Manju's handbag stuffed with currency gifted to her, to pay up my losses – my very first exercise of husband's heady rights. We might have played two or three rounds; suddenly Manju came in sauntering and took the handbag away. There was a deafening silence for a moment and then the room burst out in laughter. Very quickly, I was shown my place in the hierarchy, without a word being spoken. All within couple of hours of the beginning of my married life!

With the change of marital status I became entitled to family accommodation and other perks from the military and was allotted a government house in Pune, my duty station. My dependents, my mother and sisters, could now live with us and a huge load was taken off my chest. The arrival of Manju, my life partner, dissipated all my anxieties in a jiffy. My ostensible act of self-sacrifice turned out to be a huge blessing instead. I now had a strong pillar of strength to share my burdens.

I had taken a huge gamble by marrying a whimpering girl just on the basis of her family credentials but she turned out to be poised, stoical and a most fitting person to share my responsibilities. She took to running the household like a fish takes to water. Though, often, with mixed results. Like when she gave away all the pairs of trousers of my olive green uniform to the washerman and laid out a pair of khaki trousers for me to wear with my brass and ribbons adorned OG shirt. I had to skip my office that day. She did not know what constituted an Army uniform! Obviously I was at fault; I should have trained her in Army ways rather than taking things for granted.

Manju adapted herself to her new role as an army wife spectacularly. Her transformation from a small-town schoolgirl to a dignified lady with élan was total. While she enjoyed her new-found status, she never compromised with her duties towards her new charges, my mother and younger sisters. She was worried that my sister's education was disrupted by my moving them to Pune. On her prodding, arrangements were made to send them to school. Then a bombshell was dropped that she herself would complete her professional course which was disrupted because of marriage. She told me that she was dead against marriage only because it would disrupt her education. Her protests were ignored by her family. Now she expected me to right the wrong by letting her complete the unfinished course.

In a way it was poetic justice, indeed. Here I was for whom the charade of marriage was only a means to bypass regulations, so that I could keep my wards with me. Now, that hurdle was removed and I got what I wanted. I therefore did not really have any locus-standi to object to her dumping me so soon after the marriage to pursue her dreams ... so I didn't.

She returned to her institution in Kanpur to complete her degree course in teaching. I was back to my bachelorhood, but something had changed profoundly in these two months. I was not the same person anymore. I never thought earlier that there was anything amiss in my life. My universe was my job, my friends and numerous fun things a young army officer indulges in. But this time, with her departure a void had set into my life. I felt incomplete.

Marriage is a phenomenon where a universe attaches to another universe and both become complementary parts of a new universe. From this new universe, nobody can retract back to the wholesome status of their old universe, ever!

After a shotgun marriage, Providence was taking us back in time to reboot again with an all new courtship phase. This forced separation helped us a lot to nurture our relationship by making us appreciate the value of our bond. She had a felicity with the written mode of communication and did communicate a lot through letters, which otherwise could have remained untold in the restraints of the spoken mode. Again, it was not just a typical romantic chat between newly-weds. She also remained conscious of our responsibilities and tried to do all she could, to guide the care and upbringing of my younger sisters remotely. She also revealed to me why her resolve to get the professional qualification post-marriage was reinforced, even after discovering the thrills of army life. It was because she had concluded that we had to have two incomes to manage the household.

We resumed life together after one year's pause. She was now qualified and took up a teaching job, managed the extended family and participated enthusiastically in the social activities demanded of an army wife. Her versatility often baffled me. She would effortlessly switch from one challenging role to the other without showing any strain. Life in the army was no bed of roses. Field Marshall Sam Maneckshaw called it a life of dignified poverty. We were paid a pittance and yet were expected to flaunt elegance. Often, it was the army wife, the 'Memsaheb', who would face the brunt of this impossible pretence. Hosting frequent parties, organising frequent social events and keeping the house in impeccable order were all her obligations. She would mostly do them single-handed since we could not afford to hire outside help.

The positive spin-off of her learning to juggle so many different roles was the confidence she gained in handling difficult tasks beyond her age. We had to perform the role of family elders in finding suitable matches for my marriageable sisters. Manju took up this task energetically. She was instrumental in finding right matches, negotiating marriage and finally staging the events for both my younger sisters in quick succession. What an exhilarating feeling it was for me! I had taken a huge gamble by marrying a mute and passive girl but she turned out to be such a great communicator and performer! Having satisfactorily resolved our larger family responsibilities, we could now devote more attention to our own lives. We were blessed with a daughter followed by a son and our family was complete.

Then, a transformational change occurred in our lives when I was selected to go to the University of Manchester, England by the government to pursue my master's degree in Computer Engineering. In the eighties, going abroad, even for a couple of weeks, was quite a rarity. For us, going for a prolonged period, with family, was a quite a prize. However, alongside the excitement of the stay abroad came the worries of setting up home in a foreign environment. The challenges were much bigger for Manju as she would be cut-off from the support base the familiar cantonment life provided. Also worrisome was the prospect of rearing two small children in an alien setting. Luckily, my brother-in-law, the same Foreign Service officer, who was instrumental in arranging our marriage, was posted in Oslo. We drew solace from his proximity and started packing for the big journey.

We headed for London in the first week of October, 1983. It was Manju's first travel by air and first visit abroad. Yet she showed no thrill and gave the impression as if this was her nth trip overseas. I could never exactly fathom this behaviour of hers. Her reactions to happenings around her were invariably inversely proportional to their importance. Just this past month I had excitedly conveyed the news of my significant successes on two successive days to her; one, that I was selected for Staff College (a prized military course) and the other that I was nominated for doing masters in England. On both occasions her response was a shrug and a yawn! In retrospect, this probably was her coping mechanism that helped her deal with big issues so stoically and I needed to be grateful to her for that virtue.

We reached London on a cold and wet day with two small kids in tow. I was told by officials in Delhi that a representative from the Indian High Commission would receive us at the airport and make arrangements for our onwards journey to Manchester and our stay and expenses there. But nobody turned up to receive us at Heathrow airport. I was anxious because I was allowed to bring only fifty pounds in currency from India and had no clue what to do next. I called the High Commission in panic. After several attempts I managed to get hold of a junior staffer at the High Commission in London. He wasn't much of a help as he said he lacked any financial authority. All he could do was to suggest that we take a train to Manchester and call the office the next day when senior staff would be present.

Manju, in the meantime was busy taking care of our children and the luggage. She engaged the kids with toys and visits to shops in the airport lounge and kept them occupied allowing me to sort out the problem at hand. Thankfully, she did not compound my problems by showing any anxiety.

I had the phone number of an army officer from the previous batch, who was already in Manchester with his wife. Nervously, I contacted him from the airport and told him of my predicament. He welcomed us warmly and said that they too faced a similar problem when they arrived in London. It was futile to expect the High Commission to arrange our travel or lodging, they extended such courtesies only to senior officials or politicians. He guided me on how to get to Manchester by train and assured me that he will receive us there and take us to his house to be their guests until we find a place. This was a huge relief as otherwise we would have been stranded at the airport in an alien land without any money. This also underscored the kinship intrinsic in the military fraternity. We had never met before, yet they, as it transpired later, the newly-weds, were ready to vacate their only bedroom to accommodate our family. The contrast was too stark with the apathetic treatment from the High Commission, who were duty-bound to assist us.

We took the train to Manchester, it was chilly and wet when we arrived there late in the evening. Our saviour, Satish, was at the station to receive us. The moment he took our charge, our anxieties just vanished. He took us to his apartment not far from the station. Once home, we were treated like family members by him and his wife and they took utmost to take care of us. Manju established an instant rapport with his wife and soon they were in the kitchen together, preparing a meal for us.

Satish, accompanied me to London the next day and introduced me to the Military Attaché and other staff there. I was given the much-needed monetary advance in pound sterling to set up house in Manchester and start my course in the university. We quickly overcame the initial shock and started planning for our extended stay, with our host's generous help, of course. House-hunting and all other preparatory tasks fell on Manju's shoulders as I was too busy adjusting to academic demands. She quickly overcame the language barrier and it was flattering to see her dealing with natives without getting intimidated.

She had definite ideas about the kind of house we should settle for. It needed to be in a good neighborhood, with good schooling facilities, which translated to paying high rentals. My allowances did not permit such luxuries and I was reluctant to strain ourselves. Moreover, it was imperative that we did not overstretch our host's hospitality beyond reasonable limits and give them back their space. We needed to quickly find something affordable. Manju, managed to do just that. She found a spacious house in a nice locality and negotiated the rent down to manageable amount, all by herself!

It was exciting to move to our new home. Though the house was furnished, there were hundreds of sundry things we had to do to make it fit for us and the children. As I would be gone for the whole day to the University, Manju had to take care of all these necessary chores and to my relief, she actually relished doing them. Every day she would take the bus to the city centre for her shopping expeditions, with the kids in tow. This was the first time she got the opportunity to set up a home all by herself, unlike after marriage when she came into a crowded household, being managed by my mother and sisters.

The new house was now fully functional and Manju set out to find the school for our elder daughter and a playschool for our son. She established rapport with helpful neighbours who had young kids and obtained their recommendations and all necessary information on children's schooling and other facilities in the neighbourhood.

And then she surprised me with the news that she had met the headmistress of the school and our daughter's mid-term admission was approved as a special case. Imagine, a small-town girl raised in a most conservative atmosphere, accomplishing this feat single handed, within few weeks of her coming to United Kingdom. My wonderful wife did that and made me proud.

With important issues taken care of, we settled down to the staid life of an English suburb, peppered with the occasional excitement of visiting nearby attractions and variety of events in and around Manchester area. We were constrained to indulge in penny-pinching because of the meagre allowances paid by our government. So much so, we had to limit the heating of our home to just the kitchen and one bedroom. The house rent was paid directly by the High Commission to the owner, but we were supposed to pay the heating/electricity bills from our living allowances, which would have taken away most of the allowance if we heated the whole house. The landlady was furious when she found out, as the fungus in unheated rooms in the house would surely have ruined them in due course.

However, our financial situation changed soon when Manju's diplomat brother visited us. He was aghast at our frugal living. He enquired about the allowances I was getting and he could not believe it. He found out that it was a case of gross underpayment. We were eligible for almost double the amount we were getting and, in addition, were authorised to claim heating expenses. He went to London the next day and confronted the concerned people in the High Commission. Within a week our allowances were jacked up and we transitioned from penury to affluence. Thanks again to my wonderful wife and her clan.

Life in England had its own challenges for Manju. In India, one is seldom alone at home. There are servants, helpers, relatives and friends around you all the time. One has help available for household tasks and for escorting kids to school.

In England, she had to manage everything all by herself. In retrospect, I should have shared some of her household chores and helped with the kids. But it never occurred to me that our circumstances had changed. As for me nothing had changed, except now I went to my classes instead of my office and I did not wear a uniform. But for her it was a seismic change, which I did not appreciate then. Now I wish I had. To my readers, I would like to say marriage is a partnership and to make the partnership work, both need to share burdens and rewards.

She never complained and never revealed the stresses she must have been facing in coping with the unfamiliar circumstances in a foreign land. And her tenacity knew no bounds, let me cite an example.

I had three weeks free time after the first term break in the University. This was summer time and a great opportunity to see Europe. We planned an eight-country rail tour on a shoe-string budget. Most of the stays were in youth hostels or bed and breakfast places. Visiting so many places in three weeks with two young children was an ambitious adventure indeed. But we took the plunge and through sheer grit and deft handling of kids by my wife, we managed to pull it through.

On our second day into the trip, we were in Amsterdam. We headed out from the youth hostel in the outskirts, to downtown museums. We were taking a tram for our journey. When the tram arrived I pushed Manju and the kids into the tram compartment but realised that I had to get down and go to the driver's side to get the ticket. The moment I got down, the tram pulled ahead and I was left stranded. We did not have mobile phones then and I had no means of reaching my family. I took the only alternative available. I boarded the following tram hoping to catch my family at the next stop. But after a few minutes run the tram halted on the tracks and the announcement was made that the preceding tram had been stopped for some reason. I was extremely worried but could do nothing except wait.

Eventually the tram resumed its run and in a couple of minutes I was at the next halt. To my utter relief I saw my wife and children waiting on the platform and I ran to them. Manju showed no emotion when she saw me, other than waving towards me. The kids were ecstatic of course. Then I saw some policemen with Manju and my anxiety increased. What I heard from policemen was an incredible story. Manju had caught a thief on the train!

When the tram pulled off without me, Manju was not perturbed as she was sure I would board the following tram and catch them at the next station. As she was trying to settle the kids in their seats, she felt a tug at her purse and on a reflex caught the hand that was tugging it. The thief, a burly, black guy, tried to wrench his hands free but Manju would not let him go and raised the alarm. She only let him free when the cops arrived and escorted him away. Incredible tenacity and level-headedness, right?

Her reactions to situations like this proved that she was capable of handling difficult situations on her own. Often, I had to go out of town for prolonged periods like for my project work in Cambridge. I could do so without worrying about her or the kids. Safe in the belief that she could handle any situation.

We returned to India after the completion of my post-graduation after which I was posted in a research position to the Military College of Telecommunication Engineering in Mhow. After our extended British upper-class living experience, this new place turned out to be quite an anti-climax. We got a two-room tin roof tenement in a dilapidated barrack. We had no place to unpack the variety of ultra-modern gadgets we had brought as trophies from England. And there was hardly any furniture in the rooms. This looked liked the Army's deliberate way to bring you down to by freeing you of any wrong notions you would have acquired about yourself after acquisition of prestigious degrees. We learnt that there was a three-month wait before we could be allotted our authorised accommodation. There was a long wait for buying a transport too. Finally, I had to settle down for a moped, the only vehicle available off-the-shelf. It was not easy for a family of four riding around on a moped. It turned out to be disastrous. One day Manju's sari got wrapped around the rear wheel and our vehicle turned turtle.

These were trying times for my wife. Just recently, in England, she had built us an affluent home, up from only two suitcases which we had brought from India. Now she had to scale it back to fit our new humble abode. But she took it in her stride, as is her wont.

In time, we got better accommodation and a bigger transport. The children also began to enjoy their new school and new friendships. Both for me and Manju these were great times. We had financial stability, no encumbrances, amazing colleagues, incredible superiors and assured career progression. In totality, life was great. But then everything changed in an instant, when I got a stroke.

We had hosted a small party the previous night. Some friends had come over and we retired late in the night. In the morning, while getting out of the bed I could not hold steady and was feeling somewhat groggy. It could not be drinks I thought because I was always a moderate drinker. Anyway I went on to get ready for the morning run. I could not tie my shoelaces and called my wife. She too could not figure out what it was, but advised me to do a brisk run and assured me that exercise would take care of the problem. My morning run actually was more of a hobble as I could not put weight on my left foot. However, I decided to soldier on and told my wife on my return that I was feeling much better and drove to office as usual.

Once in the office, I realised that I could not even type on the computer. It was time to consult the doctor. I drove my scooter to the Military Hospital and told the doctor on duty about my situation. I was surprised to see him become very serious. He shouted for the nursing staff to got a stretcher. I was made to lie down and told not to move at all. Soon the specialist was summoned and he confirmed that I had suffered a stroke affecting the left half of my body. I was very confused with the prognosis and my new status; from an athletic me – just back from my morning run to an invalid, flat on the stretcher!

I was taken to the emergency ward and my wife was called. She was ashen-faced but fully in control. She cheered me up saying it was surely a transient phenomenon and I would be up and running in no time. She maintained her courageous façade throughout the next several months of my hospitalisation and recovery. During this period, when I was shuttling around between faraway specialty hospitals, she was single-handedly managing the home, kids and my elderly mother; keeping a tight lid on her own anxieties.

After nearly full recovery, I returned to Mhow. But the scars remained both on my health and my career prospects. I was on track for a great career in the Army but now with my sub-optimal medical condition, those avenues were blocked. We had to reconcile ourselves to an unexciting future. The effect of this change should have been more telling on Manju, because the credence a lady commands amongst her peers in the military is always relative to her hubby's future prospects. But she was impervious to such slights. She never worries too much about the future, the present is what matters to her the most. She was happy that I was back and in good health.

My next posting was to Secunderabad. There, Manju got a chance to be a history maker. Here is how it happened..... The army division I was posted to was asked to go to Sri Lanka as the Indian Peace Keeping Force. I was responsible for organising communications for the expedition. The first wave of the expedition was being airlifted from Hyderabad airport to Jaffna on the night of July 31, 1986. We said goodbye to our families and were heading towards the airbase, when I got a message that I needed to talk to Army Headquarters, immediately. I returned to the office and took the call. Head of Army Signals, Indian Army was on the other side. I was told, Army Chief General Sunderji was dictating a personal message for the troops, as we spoke. The chief wanted printed copies of his message to be delivered to all force commanders, who would then personally read it out to their troops before they boarded the designated aircraft to Sri Lanka. The message would arrive on our teleprinter shortly. I was asked to make seventy copies of the message and get it distributed to waiting commanders.

I was in a huge dilemma. This was an impossible demand. We had no photo copiers in our inventory, and there was no chance we would find a photo copy shop open at midnight in Secunderabad. Also as an aside, we had no official funds available for such expenses. Then an idea struck me. At home, I had my personal computer and printer which was a rarity in those days. I had brought these from England. I rushed home, woke up Manju and asked her to help me make seventy copies using our home computer. So while I quickly typed in the chief's message, Manju got the printouts. The mission was accomplished and within an hour I was on my way to the airport and shortly thereafter the Indian Army was on its way to Sri Lanka. This is how my wonderful wife was instrumental in the launching of the Indian Peace Keeping Force (IPKF).

After the gruelling experience in Secunderabad, my next posting was in Delhi. This came at a most opportune time as our children were now grown up enough to need stability in their education. However, living in Delhi also meant more expenses. We had to buy a car and I also booked a flat on the prompting of relatives for securing our future. But I had over-committed myself, inadvertently. My army salary was not enough to sustain ourselves. I would not admit it openly but strains of the financial distress started showing on marital harmony. I exploded at most trivial issues and each episode would be followed by a long period of mutual apathy and silence.

Manju probably diagnosed the problem and after a gap of many years restarted her teaching career. The addition of her income took care of our financial woes and we were swinging once again. One thing is certain that financial stability is the bedrock of a successful marriage!

I realised that in order to secure our future, I needed a course correction in my career. There was neither money nor a career for me in the Army. So I started looking around. It did not take long, as in an industry seminar where I was presenting a paper, Mr. FC Kohli, head of TCS, offered me a senior position in TCS. I took up his offer and we moved to Mumbai. It was a quantum leap for us, moving from the Army to the apex of the corporate world. A new realm had opened for us; it was almost a re-run of our UK experience, but in much better circumstances. We had the company flat waiting for us in Mumbai and for my daughter and son, the promise of best schools. Money was not a problem, either.

Manju, adapted herself to the new environment without a hitch. Her people-skills came in handy for her networking with other ladies in TATA towers and navigating her way around. She again took up a teaching job, this time it was not for supplementing family income but more as an expression of her independence.

Her spirit of adventure and adaptation skills helped me take some major decisions in life. Like, after two fruitful years in TCS, an exciting opportunity presented itself, requiring us to move to USA. It was a difficult choice to make because it entailed giving up a promising career in TCS and embracing the challenges of relocating to a different ethos, relatively late in life. On the plus side this was a chance to open up tantalising prospects of a great future for my children, taking them away from the fierce competition and barriers they would invariably face in India, being an upper caste and thus on the wrong side of the divide. I let the decision rest with Manju. She endorsed the USA option without any hesitation.

Starting a new life in USA was not that difficult. We had gone through this process before in UK and were better off money-wise this time around. We also had family members well established in USA and they helped us ease into a well-knit Indian community.

It was a pleasant surprise to discover a vibrant and self-assured Indian diaspora in United States, unapologetic in the practice of their culture and ethos. It was heartening to see that the children in their homes grow up imbibing what their parents and community elders practise as the tenets of Indian culture. Contrary to popular belief, USA actually celebrates diversity and allows its inhabitants to flaunt their origins. It is a country of immigrants after all, who have learnt to co-exist and collaborate without diluting their own cultures. It is strange but true that children of Indian parents in USA are more influenced by India's heritage, than Indians in India, who try to ape the pretentious westernized, cultural ethos prevalent all around them, ridiculing their own values. In fact, youngsters in India are in many senses more 'modern' than those in US. There is a backlash towards the old ways and culture in Indian kids that those who are raised in Indian homes in the US do not have. In USA, both cultures integrate well and there is an openness with parents and children that may not exist in India.

Coming to USA unleashed our children's potential as this is one place where merit alone counts. There are no barriers to impede your growth. No restraints are placed before you based on your race, caste, age, sex or domicile. We are not penalised for our forefathers' purported sins and asked to yield our place to the less deserving only on the basis of accident of birth. This, in any case, was the reason we had decided to move out of our dear country. Our story is no different from a majority of other immigrant families here in America. All of us came here with just two attaché cases, containing our clothes, memorabilia, tokens of our culture and of course, a determination to work hard. We knew well that in this land of equal opportunity there is no place for complainers, here nobody is interested in your excuses if you fail. Yet it is a level-playing field and rewards are yours to take, if you strive for them with determination.

Being in the Army, we had to continuously move across India, schooling for children in Army schools was no problem but once I left the Army and became a civilian, the scenario changed and our children lost their privileged status. On joining TCS, our biggest worry was to secure a good school for our children in Mumbai. I remember vividly how my boss, Mr. Y.P. Sahni, then the COO and President of TCS, took me to Mr. Deepak Parekh, the illustrious chairman of HDFC for help in securing my son and daughter's admissions to sixth and seventh grades!

We shuddered to think of the future when they would be denied admissions to professional colleges for not having a domicile certificate. They were rolling stones which did not qualify for permanent resident status anywhere in India because there 'army officer' dad worked pan-India and had only one identity, an **Indian**. Once, in USA, we did not have to worry about any of such uncertainties. Everything moved here with clockwork efficiency, everyone was cheerful and eager to help. Admission to schools was a breeze and our children adapted to their new environment with ease. So much so that when my son was asked by a neighbour how different he was finding living in USA, he replied 'not much except the electric switches are wrong side up here.' He was referring to the need for flipping the switch up rather than down as he did in India for flicking the light on.

Once again it was my wife, who shouldered the responsibility of running the show. I worked for a 'Big Five' consulting firm and had to travel all over the globe on consulting assignments for extended periods. She took all the decisions concerning day-to-day running of the house. She managed finances, paid the bills and arranged for repairs and supervised the education of children. She had the onerous responsibility of steering the children skilfully to be achievers. Bringing up the children squarely rested in the hands of my wife.

She had to be stern with the children sometimes and be vigilant so that they do not get sidetracked by pitfalls teenagers are regularly exposed to without supervision and guidance. At the same time she was a friend to them so they had no hesitation in confiding in her. She loved them unconditionally and her love was reciprocated. She taught them the right values that helped them grow into well-adjusted confident adults who love and respect their parents. From early on, she instilled in them the notion that they were responsible for their own lives and were expected to steer it in the direction they chose. Both our children followed this principle religiously and took control of their affairs from an early stage.

Our daughter won a prestigious internship with a top corporation just in her first year in college and was further rewarded with a stint in the company in their Europe office in Brussels. This helped her finance her college on her own and got her transference as a regular corporate employee immediately after her graduation. She was already three years senior in the company on her first day of regular employment! She capped her achievements further with an MBA from a top-notch institute, a tenure with an elite consulting company and now a promising career in industry.

Our son made us proud as well. He too won an early internship and paid his way through college. After college he became Management Consultant at a global consulting company, did his MBA from a top-ranking business school. He now works in Wall Street.

Even as the children were carving out their identities, getting ready to fly away from the nest and move out of town for higher education, Manju decided to jump back into a professional career herself, not in education but this time as an IT professional. This required re-educating herself, and she joined a local college to acquire the necessary professional certification. She made good use of her lonely time at home as I was away mostly on my consulting gigs and the kids had already moved out. It goes to her credit that she re-invented herself as an accomplished IT professional and continues performing her multi-faceted roles of being a full-time government employee, responsible for crucial social services IT projects, a skilled guide to successful children and also a devoted house wife, impeccably.

Manju has managed to keep the Indian-ness of our family intact even after two decades of our stay in USA, through her personal conduct. She strictly follows the rituals, does her morning and evening puja, and celebrates all the festivals. She strives hard to participate in family events in USA and in India, and now uses social networking effectively to strengthen family bonds. Her efforts are not limited to the family either, she frequently organises community get-togethers locally, and helping members to experience a large family feel and provides guidance to the new arrivals in the locality. She is the embodiment of essentials of Indian-ness viz, respect, adaptability, humility, simplicity and confidence. Many a times, her self-denial irritates other family members who see no reason to be frugal but financial prudence is a cultural thing, perhaps, and has nothing to do with your material prosperity.

We have a generalisation about USA that everyone here adapts to a uniform Yankee culture – in dress, conduct, eating habits and a typical nasal twang. The perception that we need to give up our own identity to be a part of the rest of America, is a fallacy. It is not a melting pot anymore but a kaleidoscope where different cultures mix but remain distinct. The mixing mostly happens at work and rarely at social levels. This is generally the case with first-generation Indian immigrants, mostly the affluent, professional class living in suburbs. They have created a sanitised version of India in all its diversity and richness almost everywhere in USA. The success of this segment showcases the wonders that can be achieved if we mix uncorrupted Indian heritage with stellar characteristics of the West viz, honesty, integrity, hard work and philanthropy.

The insulated culture zone that the Indian diaspora presently lives in, has its own puzzles. They face one of the most challenging sociological quandary when their children come of age. On one hand there is a strong urge to preserve your heritage through future generations and on the other hand there is the compulsion of accelerating a seamless assimilation with your adopted home. Our generation, already past its prime, could manage compartmentalisation of our professional and social lives but it is too much to expect the same from our children. It is well-nigh impossible for them to live the double lives of their parents. Their outlook, worldview, upbringing, exposure to traditions and perspectives are fundamentally different; and any attempt to force our values and expectations through emotional blackmail leaves them utterly confused.

Finding life partners for her children is the most vital undertaking for an Indian mother and Manju was no exception. However, the tried and tested match-making recipes that parents in India apply, do not work for NRIs. Firstly, arranging a marriage through intervention of the family back in India is a logistical nightmare and more importantly, expecting your child brought up in the western milieu to submit blindly to your dictates and marry a stranger, is wishful thinking at best. In pure statistical terms the sample size amongst second generation NRIs is not big enough to yield a match locally, meeting desirable caste and regional criteria. So something has got to give.

In the case of our daughter, she solved this problem for us rather neatly. No sooner had Manju started her search for a suitable boy than our daughter announced that she had found someone, who she had no doubt would meet all our expectations. Which indeed was the case when we met our son-in-law. He exceeded our expectations in all parameters. Respectful, cultured, well-qualified and a North Indian like us. They had known each other for some time and took the mature decision of getting their parents' blessings after evaluating all aspects. From then on the parents took over, all rituals were followed and they were married in India. In her marriage, we gained a loving son, who has been with us through thick and thin. He is actually the crown jewel of our family, doing spectacularly well, career wise.

After a couple of years it was now our son's turn. Manju took to the task in real earnest. But how to find a girl who would be a perfect blend of tradition and modernity, would be at ease both in a club and a temple, and most vitally would play the catalytic role of strengthening family bonds? By definition this had to be an arranged marriage.

My wife's game plan was to find such a girl in America through marriage portals. Filter them based on their location and find someone in New York or a neighbouring vicinity. Once the right candidate was found, the next step would be to coax the boy and girl to meet frequently to get to know each other and hope to God that eventually they would decide to tie the knot. Parent facilitated dating in other words! Chances of this strategy succeeding were pretty slim based on the reasons I have already enumerated. But parents must try. She would spend long hours at night and weekends hunched over the laptop, send her selections to our son and get back a bunch of excuses from him, every time. His contention always was that he was too busy with his job and not ready for marriage yet.

Then, the day came when he informed us that he had found the girl he wanted to marry. He knew what our expectations were and assured us that this girl fulfilled them all and more, which none of the prospects we were looking in matrimony sites could match. And the bolt from the blue – that she was white American!

Manju was crestfallen and infuriated with our son for keeping her in the dark all this while. She felt guilty for her lengthy exchanges in marriage portals with so many girls and leading them up the garden path. It never occurred to her, however, that she should have taken her son's views into consideration as well, while determining a life partner for him. In a way it was déjà vu, repeating the past pattern when her own marriage was decided by her parents without her consent.

It was an awkward situation to handle for other family members, who were not deeply committed to the match-making odyssey. One saving grace was our son's revelation that the girl, Courtney, had laid out her precondition for the marriage that it will not happen without the parents' whole-hearted blessings. Thankfully, we had the luxury of time in our hands.

Once the initial shock was over, the process of reconciliation started albeit tenuously. We learnt later that our son and Courtney had considered all the ramifications of marriage and had a clear plan for addressing cultural, religious, language and culinary issues. She loved Indian food, watched Bollywood movies, dressed in saree, salwar kurta and had enough Hindi vocabulary to startle any 'desi' with her native accent. In fact, there was nothing to distinguish her from a traditional Indian 'bahu' other than her fair skin.

Manju gave up her diffidence eventually and agreed to visit our son in New York and meet Courtney there. We were invited for lunch by Courtney to her apartment. She welcomed us with correct Indian greetings making a great first impression. She said she was cooking an Indian fare for us and requested Manju to help. It was really a master stroke. How many westernised Indian girls today would desire their first encounter with future 'Sasuji' in the kitchen? In an instant they became a team and have remained so ever since.

However, there were major issues to be settled upfront before we could give a go-ahead for the alliance. Our main concern was the perpetuation of our heritage and traditions through coming generations, what we call the 'samskars'. We explained to Courtney that our brahmanic lineage demands every generation to perform 'shraadh' for deliverance of our departed forefathers and we owe it to all generations, past and the future, that those traditions are maintained. She readily gave her commitment and it was enough for us.

Manju's acceptance was whole-hearted and she insisted that the marriage be done in India with the participation of all friends and family. That was done and Courtney wowed everyone with her humility, graceful demeanour and all the more, with her Indian-ness. None of it was artificial as she maintains the same persona in US. As a fashion designer, she enhances Indian attires to match western styles and wears them regularly at work and home.

Looking back, the phobia we have about maladjustment because of different cultural upbringing, is highly misplaced. Ultimately its success depends on the maturity of the spouses and how they resolve cross-cultural differences by respecting each other's perspective. Both our son and Courtney exemplify that assertion amply.

Manju has played a crucial role in Courtney's smooth integration into the family structure by mentoring, encouragement and appreciation. She invites her daughter-in-law for all festivals and we celebrate them together. Her approach is that of an osmosis process whereby traditions and culture are imbibed without coercion but slowly and surely.

It is amazing how my wonderful wife has coped with her expanded role within family and beyond. As our children excelled in their education and careers, their mother was behind them as a bulwark, cajoling them, guiding them and comforting them. And when our family enlarged with children finding their life partners, she expanded her ambit to provide them the loving embrace. And now with our grandchild coming on the scene she is that young man's best friend. The stellar role Manju plays in our lives has not changed a bit with the passage of time. She remains the pivot around which our family moves.

At this juncture – when I look back to our first encounter many decades back, I shiver at the thought – what if I had rejected the dumb girl that was brought before me! There was no hint of the tremendous potential that girl possessed, at that time. Given my circumstances, she alone was my perfect match, and how providence guided me to her!

There is an old adage that 'marriages are made in heaven'. I am now a firm believer of that saying, and the trials, tribulations and triumphs of our long year's partnership amply exemplify it.

'Once again it was my wife who shouldered the responsibility of running the show. I worked for a Big Five consulting firm and had to travel all over the globe on consulting assignments for extended periods. She took all the decisions concerning day-to-day running of the house. She managed finances, paid the bills, arranged for repairs, and supervised the education of the children. She had the onerous responsibility of steering the children skilfully to be achievers. Bringing up the children squarely rested in the hands of my wife.'

Song of my Soul – our Marvellous Journey

Sohag Sarkar

You are the song of my soul
In my life, you have the most promising role
I always find you near, up-close and hold
It's the spirit of Love, I have never told

'Her caring is so touching and deep that she would impress
anybody and get informal with him or her in no time. I still
have not found a soul like her in my life. She had all the
qualities, which an orthodox mother-in-law would yearn for; yet
she had a modern outlook. She would be loving and respectful,
yet be stern and aggressive when it came to professional work or
otherwise. Pooja would make her first impression similar to a
cricketer who hits a ton in his debut match.'

Prelude

The growing-up years are perhaps the most carefree and uncomplicated. Our thoughts are not biased with the dogma of society, religion or the inherited beliefs of others. And our actions are pure, genuine and instinct-based. Therefore, in adulthood, if a guy encounters a situation where he finds the perfect girl, who doesn't speak the language of his parents, who is a complete opposite when it comes to food habits (either vegetarian or non-vegetarian), who is somewhat older in age and earns more than the guy, what should the guy do? Well, I encountered such a predicament and without a doubt I married the girl. After all love is the reaching of that eternal state that makes you carefree and matters, an uncomplicated lot.

The beginning

Before narrating the starting point where it all began, let me pen down a few things about myself. After completing my MBA, I was on a new high. My seniors used to tell me that none of the college toppers had ever got the best placement so far. And here was I, working for the Big Blue (IBM), a Top Ten Fortune company in 2005. Bharti Airtel had become the torch-bearer and proved to the telecom fraternity that outsourcing was the business game-changer. And I felt proud to be a part of this strategic Business Transformation engagement. I still recall the India Town Hall meeting when, Mr Sunil Bharti Mittal was invited as a special guest and he said 'Such is the relationship with IBM, that at times I feel IBM stands for 'I, Bharti Mittal'. Each passing day was so eventful, there were new learnings, new interactions and new challenges. Many a milestone our team achieved and many a celebration we partied on. And one fine day, a strange realisation struck me that it was perhaps my last day on that project. Suddenly, the comfort factor was all but gone. And with a mixed feeling, I proceeded back to the Oxford of the East, Pune (earlier, where I had the best time of my life during my MBA) in the latter half of 2007.

The transformation experience gave me a real fillip. Especially my credibility as a key member of another Telecom Business Transformation that was about to begin. It was the Project kick-off and the stage was all set to present the end-to-end transformation journey to the client team members. I was trying to rehearse some good quotes or anecdotes so that I could leverage during my speech to an unknown audience. And I made good use of the (now clichéd) inspirational quote from the movie 'Spiderman' where Peter Parker's grandfather, Uncle Ben says, 'with great power comes great responsibility'. I proposed to the audience that the project could achieve greater success if they all contributed their might and applied their varied experiences. And suddenly, my mind raced back into a flashback mode to reminisce this interaction with a female client amongst others (just minutes before my presentation). Someone introduced me to her mentioning that she had telecom as well as airline expertise. As an opportune example, I quoted her so as to excite the larger audience. Now that I recall that moment, I often ask myself why I took just one example of the whole crowd? It was a paradox, it wasn't the project kick-off after all. It was the beginning of my love journey, something I still wasn't aware of.

Not just breaking the ice

Consultants are like nomads, smitten by the wander lust, every time they have to start afresh after reaching a new destination. I had already abjured all the comforts when I left my previous project, my colleagues, my seniors, my well-wishers, and above all, my clients with whom I had strengthened my trustworthiness. And then it was like starting from scratch. Some of my present colleagues had the position of advantage. They had already interacted, travelled and made friends with the client team during the Pre-Transformation phase. I felt like a kindergarten kid, nervous and sceptical, getting ready for the first day at school. Immediately after the project kick-off, we were dispersed into respective project tracks. Given my past experience, I was offered one of the larger tracks (by scope). I experienced the ostensible joy of acquaintance, when the client I had quoted in my speech joined my track as the Client Lead. That was the first time I learnt that her name was Pooja (a Hindi name that connotes adore, worship or pray).

The business planning and discussions followed suit as I was consciously reminded that my colleagues still enjoyed a better rapport with the client team than me. This was an unsettling feeling, and any favourable gesture from the client meant the world to me. It was then that the moment arrived. We were to travel back from our business workshop sessions to the project office. My colleague's car was parked bang in front of the gate. It was a given that the client team would sit and go in his car. Damn! My car was a distant far. With drooping shoulders I reached my car, only to see Pooja and her colleague follow me. I was elated. Alas! I have earned the parity that my colleagues enjoyed with the client.

My first trip abroad

The project was in full swing, and I had developed a good rapport with everyone in the client team, including Pooja. My brother's marriage was on the cards and it was decided that he would get married in US on 28 February, 2008. As the case maybe, the last person I messaged while going for the International Airport was Pooja.

It was my first flight abroad and I was truly enjoying the experience. Hopping through Charles de Gaulle Airport (Paris), I finally landed in Dallas, Texas. It was really wonderful to explore the country. I wrote about my arrival to my office colleagues, select client members and close friends. The reply back from Pooja was surprising as she wrote, 'The business workshop went well. Good session. Missed you'. At times it is so reassuring to hear that you are being missed.

My brother's wedding took place in a Hindu temple in Raleigh in North Carolina. On the night of the wedding, I attended a reception of a different kind. Typically, in an Indian wedding reception one would expect a flowery stage where the groom and the bride would have a back-breaking experience while taking the blessings of all the elderly invitees. And the invitees would be hovering around the food stalls in no time to bring their attendance to a closure. But according to the US tradition, you would invite only a select few. My brother tied the nuptial knot as per Hindu tradition. But, the evening reception was held perhaps more like the American way. There were round tables with nice placards mentioning the names of the invitees. There were people from mixed cultures and nationalities. One of my brother's college friends took over the responsibility of being the master of ceremony. And one by one, he would call upon the close friends and relatives of the groom and the bride. The entire event was magical and fun-filled. To my surprise, the eventful day just seemed to go on and on. After the reception, we headed straight to a party hosted by my sister-in-law's friends. It was carousal with drinks and music; and by the time I reached my hotel room it was almost five a.m. My sleep was gone by then as I began surfing my e-mails. One of the unread mails was that of Pooja. She had replied to my previous e-mail asking me when I would be joining back and my fingers started to type a reply almost instantly.

Actions speak louder than words, and my e-mail had several high points. Words like, 'wish you were here too', 'miss you' and 'please let me know what I can get for you'. Did it go a little too far? I had no clue where I would land up with this letter. Nevertheless, let's come back to this e-mail a little later.

The Frisking Incident

The 9/11 happenings were surely horrendous because its aftermath affected our freedom. After the wedding, I was slated to join my school friend in Nashville, Tennessee. She was my school friend and had also come to attend the wedding. This was for the first time I was travelling in the US all by myself. Outside the airport, a baggage collection guy examined my passport that featured my schoolboy photograph. He instantly taunted that I looked like a Moroccan or a Paki. Mentally, I might have instantly banged him hard for even mentioning that to me; not for the fact that I hate being a Moroccan or a Pakistani but because I could make out that his racist remark meant something else. The story didn't end there. He scribbled something on my boarding pass. And when I was entering the security check queue I was politely asked by a cop to step aside into another queue (where there was no one else apart from me). They took my passport and went on to show it to another senior. My bag was taken and was being scanned over the ionic scanner. I tried to pretend that I was calm and kept a positive disposition, though inwardly I was getting goosebumps. After almost ten minutes, the officer came and said, 'We are good. Thank you for the co-operation'. That to me was a big relief and I started towards my departure gate like a lion king.

A typical syndrome that I have witnessed amongst shopaholics like me is that whenever one of our kind goes abroad they shop a lot for their friends and family. Getting a return gift for my friends was always at the back of my mind. So I entered one of the CNBC Airport Stores. I flipped through some articles until my eyes froze on a rack that had some beautiful feminine gifts. There were brooches, earrings, lockets and what not. All of them had this eye-catching fossilised look with a brilliant display of colours. I read through the price tag and immediately dropped it. It ranged from $25 to $35. A mental calculation told me that it was outside my budget. And a big red signal was sounded by my mind as any item would cost upward of thousand bucks. But my heart said otherwise. What's the point if you don't buy it with an open heart? To add more to my dilemma, the female shopkeeper came and softly whispered, 'Pretty expensive ones they have got here, she should be really special if you are getting these for her!'

Nashville is called the Music city and if you happen to go down town, for sure, you will enjoy the live music. Each store on the street will have a live band performing, and one can see the crowd dancing to their tune and merry-making. I have no clue as to when the streets would actually go to sleep. The trip was truly amazing as another schoolmate joined us for a really incredible time. I returned back from Nashville with memories that I would cherish throughout my life. It was an energising realisation that one needs to enjoy each day and every moment of their lives for fulfillment. And last but not the least I carried with me a pair of earrings, a locket and a brooch (in ascending order of price) purchased from the CNBC store. Damn the price tag!

Coming back to reality

Returning back to the country after a trip from a first world country can be a bit of a letdown. Perhaps I was too charged up, energised and fresh. I was intoxicated with the politeness, the enthusiasm and the spirit of freedom that I experienced in the US. But here I was, making an understanding of the literal meaning of the words, 'reality bytes'. On the very first day in office, I was told that one of my colleagues had permanently replaced me from the Track that I was so dearly leading. It meant two things, one, that I might be a co-lead in another track and also, that I would have to build my rapport with the new client members of this track right from scratch. And then I came to terms with a third nightmare. I was given the worst performing track to lead as another colleague was struggling hard to control the client members and get the project on track. The sessions used to be tense, and I could make out that the client members were having no fun doing it. It took me a couple of sessions to make peace with the client team. Once we had taken off smoothly, I set the auto-pilot mode to steer it through the remaining deliverables.

Earlier, one snowy morning I had walked to the Walmart store near my brother's apartment and brought more than a dozen small, gift bags. I used those bags to present the nice, little gifts that I got for everyone. Everyone was really happy to receive their bag and was curious to see what the other person had got. I gave the earrings and the locket to two of my friends, while Pooja got the best of the lot, the brooch.

Not just casual shopping before the date

Exuberance was overflowing within me, as I wanted to go out and enjoy the way I used to in the US. But I found my office friends a bit dull and nonchalant. And then when I asked Pooja, she almost instantly agreed. I cannot recall why, but I desperately wanted to buy a pair of new shoes before the next working day. My best guess might be that I had left my formal shoes in the US. So I asked her if she would mind coming with me to buy shoes before we went out for the dinner. She agreed and we headed straight after office to this shopping arcade near the International Convention Center (ICC). While trying I really liked one of the pairs of shoes and I asked Pooja if it was good. She nodded and without wasting a second I announced that I wanted it. Only to realise later that I had purchased a five-grand dollar worth pair of shoes (the costliest so far), and the reason being that I had declared it a bit too early.

People familiar with Pune would know what ABC Farms would mean (way back in 2008, if not in the present). It meant 'it's a happening place', always bustling with a young crowd. One of the restaurants that I used to truly cherish not for the food but for the ambience was *Sheesha* (which also meant Hukka). Set on a terrace, with dropping or hut-like high-rise covers placed over bamboo sticks, the place is near perfect especially when it is raining. Greenery surrounds the restaurant all around. Many a moment did I share with Pooja and the evening ended without any of us realising that it was our 'First Date'.

The Journey that just wouldn't come to an end

After my return from the US, the biggest worry that haunted me day-in and day-out was that of Jessica. She was all alone in my parent's place in Bhopal while they were still there in the US. If you are still guessing about Jessica, let me tell you that she is the fondest member of our family. She is a beautiful German shepherd with an understanding more than a best friend. Her affection is unparalleled to any other relationship in this world. Apart from being a true sweetheart, she was also a brave soul for staying all alone while we were away. We stationed her in my parent's house (as she hated being in a kennel), with our neighbour and one of our family friends providing the necessary meals and human interactions.

So I was faced with this daunting task of bringing her from Bhopal to Pune. I had no clue as to how to manage that. The only planning that I did was to book a First-AC railway ticket from Bhopal to Mumbai with the thought that I would manage to get her in the railway coupe. Pooja was very anxious when she heard about Jessica, as she too had a German shepherd named Tiger. Some of our likes and interests were starting to match. The first sight of Jessica, after reaching Bhopal worried me as she looked pale and lethargic. But after seeing me, she got charged up and returned to her usual bubbly character.

The first bad news that I got was that my train tickets were still unconfirmed though I had booked them a long time ago. So I called Jet Airways to check if I could carry my pet on their airlines.

Thankfully they said, 'Yes, provided you get a cage for your pet'. Jessica was a big dog and I approached a furniture shop to design her cage. By evening I was all set, with the newly-made cage and went to the airport. On reaching the airport, the crowd looked at me, as if I was carrying a tiger with me. Jet Airways politely denied me permission saying they did not allow pets on ATR (smaller airplane) flights. The only alternative was Air India and they came up with another innovative excuse, 'we cannot run the cage through the screening machine (of course the cage was bigger considering the size of my dog)'. After repeated requests one of the Air India personnel told me that they never screened the pet's cage and that I was being denied admission as the Jet Airways flight had got delayed and most of the passengers had rescheduled their booking with this Air India flight. It meant that given my big cage they would be left with little space to accommodate their passenger luggage. Disheartened and disgruntled I had to return back home with only one piece of advice: 'Take her by road'.

Without wasting any time, I arranged for a cab and gathered the necessary things for my road trip to Pune (which was just about 800 km). By 10 pm, I was already on the highway. I messaged Pooja about my plight as I headed towards Indore. She replied, 'Good lord, have a safe journey. Wish I could have been of some help'. It was really nice to hear that from her. We exchanged a few more SMSs, mostly chatting about Jessica. Around 12.30 am she messaged that she was sleepy, and I didn't bother her after that. Around 4.30 am, the driver parked the car near a roadside *dhaba* for tea, and just then my mobile alerted me of an SMS. I managed to check it through my sleepy eyes, and was surprised to find that it was from Pooja. She had messaged asking as to where I had reached. My natural reaction was to ask, as to why she wasn't asleep? And her reply was the turning point in my life when the change in course happened, 'Am not able to enjoy sleep thoroughly. No one who cares would, till the time you reach back here safely'. These words felt like golden words to my ears and sent a shiver right through my body. In the middle of the highway, when it was neither night nor morning, when every known soul was fast asleep in their cozy beds; someone was awake and concerned about my whereabouts.

The journey was supposed to take nothing more than twelve to fourteen hours. At around 4.30 pm, the driver declared that we might have taken a wrong route. Pooja had earlier messaged that she would like to meet Jessica and me in the evening. Though, I must admit that by then it was me who was looking forward to meeting her. At 7pm she messaged me to enquire if she could start from her place. I had no clue as to where I was and when I would touch down to Pune. As it was getting late, she messaged saying that I might be tired and we could meet some other time. I was really desperate to meet her, and insisted on meeting her that night itself. Finally, around 8.30 pm I stepped out of the car and was able to stretch my aching body with the satisfaction that I had brought home my little accommodating sweetheart. I was too exhausted and mentally drained. But more was in store for me as Jessica entered my apartment. She started huffing and puffing. She started to run left-right-and-centre, inside my apartment. The place was new for her and she would go on and on to measure every nook and corner of the apartment. I was in no position to control her. It was then that my angel entered through the door. Pooja sensed the situation and held Jessica close to her heart. And within few minutes Jessica's super excitement and palpitation stopped and she returned to her normal demeanour. With it rested my desperation to meet the person who had showered so much love, caring and empathy all along my twenty two-hour, non-stop journey.

In middle of nowhere

Jessica was the bonding factor between Pooja and me. In no time, we realised we were like a family. After office, we would run home to feed Jessica before going out for dinner or otherwise. In no time we realised that we are head-over-heels in love, without even saying anything to each other. Like an SRK romantic movie, this is the time when mellifluous songs travel through your ears and make you intoxicated with their meaning. I often remember and recall my school-time favourite and beautifully scripted prose called 'Crazy True Love'

I find no words to tell you how
A flame is kindled when your eyes glow;
The way I feel when you fix your stare,
Happiness more than my heart could bear.

Splendour in your form stirs feelings so tacit
The warmth of your breadth, so sweet, so placid,
The nectar in your eyes tends to intoxicate.
Unparalled beauty so immaculate

My body quivers by your gentle gaze
As you pass by, the fragrant tresses undulate
Hypnotised I turn around to behold,
Overwhelming grace draws near to captivate

Give me the moment my soul desires
Promise me a life full of you.
Pulse near to pulse as our hearts beat together
Make a way of my dreams come true

We were looking forward to the weekend when one of her friends visited us in Pune. So I roped in one of my good buddies, Anuj, who was a 'forced bachelor' as his wife had gone to her parents' place. I was thankful that both of them were able to get along pretty well, which gave us enough time to discuss and settle things between us. Pooja was elder to me, and she wanted to ascertain whether that would be of any concern for my parents. It was really thoughtful of her. However I really cursed the Indian knack of complicating things and giving undue importance to things beyond love. Four of us planned a trip to Mahabaleshwar, which is also called the 'Jewel in Sahyadri's Crown'. After reaching there, Anuj suggested that we visit this place colloquially referred to as the *Chhota Kashmir* (Little Kashmir). On reaching there, we found a lake with still waters reflecting the blue skies and the mighty Sahyadri range. It was more romantic than picturesque. On one side we had two bustling lovebirds and on the other side were two married people (of course not with each other but away from their respective partners). We hired a boat, and the boatman lured us to go a bit farther ahead to one of the temples on the banks of the Sahyadris. On our return, the boat stopped in the middle of nowhere. On asking the boatman, he replied, 'Diesel is over, let me fetch it from the village'. He manually rowed the boat towards the shore that was relatively close as our friends got down to leave us to ourselves. In this middle of nowhere, on the placid lake, near the magnificent Sahyadri's, under the pleasant blue skies and inside a boat which had no fuel; we finally promised to each other a happy life together thereafter.

Meet the parents

We had discussed amongst ourselves that the next stage was to inform my parents. As the case maybe, I had already informed my brother that I was going around with one of my office colleagues. I gave the first hint to my parents while they were still in the US. Their plan was to come down to Pune, and take Jessica along and then go back to Bhopal. When I used to go to office leaving Jessica in my apartment, I would leave my webcam on so that my parents could see what she was doing. To my surprise, my parent's informed me that she would nicely jump onto my bed and have a nice sleep there.

My parents finally arrived in Pune and the very next day I introduced them to Pooja. I was a little nervous though. But soon, she gelled well with my parents. She is like that only. It would really take an effort to keep her away. Her caring is so touching and deep that she would take no time to impress people and get informal with them. I still haven't found a soul like her in my life. She had all the qualities which an orthodox mother-in-law would yearn for, yet she had a modern outlook. She would be loving and respectful, yet she would be stern and aggressive when it came to professional work or otherwise. Pooja would make her first impression similar to a cricketer who hits a ton in his debut match.

To take the interaction to the next level, I invited her to join us in taking Jessica back to Bhopal (this time thankfully via train). She threw a real tantrum when we put her inside the pet cell inside the signal guard's coach (usually the last coach in the train). I left an adequate quantity of water and food for her while she howled and barked at me. I am sure she wouldn't consume even a drop of the water, forget the food. On reaching a major Junction with sufficient stoppage time, Pooja and I ran to meet Jessica. She was excited to see us and expressed it amply with her varied sound tracks. We also took her out on the platform for a stroll. It reassured her that we were also travelling with her in this strange and mammoth looking car (the only other vehicle she ever had a ride on). The reservation for the pet cell was only available in the Indore-bound train and we had to alight in Indore and drive down to Bhopal. Nearing Ujjain (which is almost equi-distant from Bhopal and Indore), Pooja got an idea as she thought of cutting short the travel time as she dialed some numbers. This is another of her excellent traits, she is a quick decision-maker and makes things happen in a jiffy.

In no time we were out of the train. That day, Jessica might have really thanked Pooja for that early reunion. The cab was already in the parking lot when we came out of the Ujjain platform, as we started our journey towards home. Jessica was my father's favourite. No one can understand the meaning of true love and affection like a dog can. And I witnessed this in real, when I saw Jessica leave my father's lap to go and sit with Pooja for the rest of the journey. Believe it or not, Pooja had already become a part of our family by then.

My First Drive to Mumbai

In the middle of 2008, Pooja had to shift back to Mumbai as she was on temporary deputation in Pune. My trips to Mumbai could be counted with the fingers of a single hand. I used to feel nervous whenever I went to Mumbai. I used to imagine it to be a mega-city; quite similar to what an immigrant worker from the rural hinterlands would think about a city. It used to give the same New York-like feeling to me. After Pooja joined work in the Mumbai office, I travelled in one of the inter-city Volvo buses for the first time to meet her. When the next weekend was approaching, I wondered how to travel to Mumbai. I had never driven my car to Mumbai before and was not familiar with Mumbai roads. It was then that she boosted my confidence and asked me to give it a shot. And against all odds, I decided to take the plunge. It was an exciting drive through the swerving roads to cross the Lonavala and the Khandala *ghat*s. I entered into Navi Mumbai thanks to the directions given by my friends. My final destination was Hiranandani in Powai. I still don't know how it happened but the only place I made my final halt was in front of the building where Pooja was staying. Today, the entire thing looks so silly after having made limitless trips between Mumbai and Pune. Mumbai city is no longer an alien land to me. But, it was her inspiration that made me take the plunge and it was her love that made me reach my destination.

The Not-So-Good Times

Good times do not last forever. Like anybody would, we kept our romantic relationship to ourselves and maintained an absolutely professional relationship during office hours. Though as a responsible employee, I had raised an online query on 'BuzzHR' (a confidential, online HR query system) asking if there were any client-dating policies for the employees. And thankfully I got the response that, 'As of now we do not have a policy that stops any employee from having any personal relationship with a client'.

But something that came as a shocker was when we learnt that one of the representatives from the client project team was going crazy after Pooja. Pooja is good-looking with a very pleasing personality. She has a pleasant smile and attractive hair. These qualities are good enough to attract enough bees around you. But, this time it wasn't a bee but a fly. It was a stalking fly that just won't leave her. Not taking names though (let us call that character Mr Bad Guy), I must mention that he was married and also had a daughter. As luck would have it, observing our out-of-office activities, he soon discovered that something was going on between us. Realising that she was already going around with someone added fuel to the fire and he started harassing her. Her natural reaction was to ignore and keep doing her work, which any decent person in her place would have done. But things went from bad to worse.

Therefore, Pooja gathered enough courage to complain to her People Manager and in the process she also had to mention our relationship. To our surprise, Mr Bad Guy had already gone and told many a lie about Pooja and me, so much so that her Manager (with whom she had more than five years of professional relationship) just ignored Pooja's complaint. Her Manager's immediate reply was that every beautiful girl thought that the other guy was after her. It seemed like the end of the road for us, as things were really getting out of control as all of us were on the same project. I even tried to message her Manager, so as to provide an independent view and convince her otherwise but in vain.

Such things are pretty commonplace and most of the time while such cases might be straight forward, they get complicated in the absence of the right responses from people whom you trust. It felt that the sky was falling on us, as we were under extreme stress. But in this state also, I saw Pooja still going strong (as she was the one who was being cornered within her own organisation) and that gave me strength to survive this testing time.

We finally didn't become the Aksinov of the famous Leo Tolstoy's short story titled, 'God seeks the truth, but waits'. Blame it on social media, we were saved by the social media. One fine day, I get a call on my mobile from a guy asking for Pooja. Gullibly thinking it might be an official call, I passed on her number to the guy. Later, I learnt from Pooja that she too got a call from a guy who said he wanted to make friends with her (like a cold dating call). When she questioned the guy sternly, he got nervous and informed her that there was a social media profile page mentioning her complete name with our official mobile numbers. After doing an intelligent search we did find the profile with a sleazy picture. Creating a fake social media profile might not generate any buzz as there would be no hits to a newly-created profile page. Therefore, in a desperate attempt, the culprit had published messages on dating forums inviting people to call on our numbers. Thus redirecting unwanted users to the profile page. Without even talking to each other we guessed who might have done this heinous act. My mind raced to refresh the learning's from the IT and Cyber Security elective that I had pursued during my MBA programme. I went and raised a 'false personation' ticket with the then popular social media site, and the profile page was immediately put off the site. But before that we had taken all the necessary screenshots for record purposes. We searched the internet and got the site for Cyber Crime Investigation and wrote a complaint letter while attaching those screenshots. I still remember it was a weekend when we made the complaint and Monday morning we got a call from sub-inspector Vijay (who later turned out to be our Amitabh Bachchan, playing the cameo role of Vijay). Together we went to the police headquarters to submit our written complaint. He just enquired if we suspected anyone, and we named Mr Bad Guy. Though he had the screenshots, he told us that one shouldn't block the profile before making a police complaint. Nevertheless, he was able to investigate it in collaboration with the social media site and the Internet Service Provider (ISP) to zero in on the culprit within forty eight hours. All our doubts about the efficiency of the police department vanished into thin air. Mr Bad Guy was called to the Cyber Crime Investigation Headquarters for questioning and we were told that they had all the necessary proofs to press charges against him in the court of law. I again wrote to 'BuzzHR' detailing the turn of events, and received a reply telling me whom I should inform regarding the same. I informed all the stakeholders about the incident within my organisation and Pooja to do the same at her end. The case was reported to the Managing Director of her company, who without a moment's notice recommended the sacking of Mr Bad Guy. Red-faced, he made an exit from the company, but not before all his colleagues and his family had come to know about his unpardonable crime. In the entire episode, Pooja came out to be the strongest as she put up a brave face, protesting against something which has become commonplace in most of the organisations today. People who did not listen to her earlier, came back and expressed their heartfelt apologies. The forgiveness that they received from Pooja was something that they would never forget. The entire episode reinforced the saying that 'good times never last, but good people do'.

Drama during my brother's Wedding Reception

My brother and *bhabhi* made a planned visit to India in the December of 2008. Perhaps it was their first visit after their marriage. It was also the opportune time to meet Pooja. So we invited her to come and stay with us for a day in Bhopal before we left for Kolkata (my *Bhabhi's* hometown) for their India reception. The same was arranged primarily to appease the relatives who couldn't make it to the actual wedding that happened in the US. I felt the first meeting with Pooja was a bit more formal than the one that happened in the Jehan Numa Palace Hotel in Bhopal over lunch. Though they had a good impression about Pooja, they wanted me to take sufficient time before making the final decision (like any other parent would have naturally done). Little did they know that I had already made my decision during the Mahabaleshwar trip and that there was no turning back for me.

As I had mentioned earlier, she is very quick to impress anyone. And soon she got another opportunity she did away with the formality and got closer to the family. After we bid adieu to Pooja, we were slated to travel to Nagpur via train and then take a direct flight to Kolkata. As luck would have it, the train started running behind schedule. Pooja was tracking the progress of the train and informed us well in advance that we would miss our Kolkata-bound flight. The reception was the next day and reaching Kolkata in good time was critical. What's the point of having a wedding reception without the bride and the groom? Pooja's prediction did come true as by the time we reached the airport the flight had left. We should thank our lucky stars for Pooja's meticulous planning, excellent networking and God-gifted luck factor came to our rescue. As always, she was there to bail us out of this fix. She arranged a flight booking from Nagpur to Kolkata via Mumbai (by speaking with the Airport manager, with whom she had earlier worked during her previous stint in the Airline Industry) and also made bookings for our overnight stay in Mumbai. It was almost ironical that while she was not one of the invitees for the reception, it was she who made it possible for the bride and the groom to be there in good time.

Home, Sweet Home

In early 2009, our search for a new abode finally ended as we zeroed in on a beautiful flat closer to the Pune Project office. Before Pooja came into my life, I was pre-occupied with my merry-making ways and had become a true shopaholic. So much so, that I couldn't dream of a flat so early in my career. And, while I was still living with my bit of excuses, Pooja made her second home a reality. It was me who was the business consultant, but it was she who was the better financial planner. I could never understand this logic. She used to spend lavishly on herself and people, including me, and still end up with handsome savings. It's quite natural to see a guy getting a home for his wife or family, but then in an exceptional scenario, I was shifting to her apartment.

The Wedding Bells

In the later part of 2009, I quit my job and shifted to one of the big four companies in Mumbai. Soon, I was deputed to a large programme management engagement and had to travel to Gurgaon for the same. Pooja was very supportive even though the engagement had left us to be a weekend couple. Gurgaon has its share of infrastructure problems, one of the critical ones being the problem of public transport,especially local cabs or autorickshaws. Seeing my daily plight of travelling to and fro from the guest house to the client site in calling cabs, she proposed that I should take the car to Gurgaon. And on New Year's eve, when the entire planet was partying, we two started our journey on NH-8 (National Highway). While hopping through Ahmedabad and Ajmer, we finally reached Gurgaon covering the entire length of 1,375 km. If not for the initiation that came from her, I would not have this wonderful experience of driving through the states of Gujarat and Rajasthan.

Having taken enough time to understand each other, we were in a state when our parents were eagerly waiting to see us get married. Pooja was very practical, she didn't want to waste too much money on the marriage as she felt it was an unnecessary expenditure. For some months now, we have been regularly saving money as we didn't want to burden our parents with the marriage expenses (which can be a black hole account in itself). It was in spring when Holi festivity filled the air. Set in the traditional backdrop of the Sonar Bangla theme and under the night stars we tied the nuptial knot.

For You

Thinking about Pooja, one of her distinctive attributes is her ability to successfully complete any plan. After taking voluntary retirement, my father invigorated his deep desire to pen down his life experiences in the form of poetry. Despite his preoccupation with his profession and service he nurtured his passion for poems. He has been scripting poem after poem in his secret diary, which he later typed on his computer. To give his writings a proper form, Pooja got his anthology of English poems printed in a beautiful hard-bound book titled, 'For You'. The journey didn't end there. Some year later the same book was up for publication with Outskirt Press. And Pooja thought of making it really big and really special. So she contacted a few of his office colleagues and reached out to a famous celebrity. Believe it or not, the book was later published with the endorsement of mellifluous singer and Bharat Ratna recipient, Lata Mangeshkar. Pooja would go all out to do something no one else would have imagined or thought of doing, leave alone making it happen.

After completing her first mission, she shifted her focus to my mom who has an excellent painting talent. In a day's time, my mom could come out with a masterpiece. So Pooja organised a photo-shoot for all her paintings with the plan that she would organise an exhibition where the world would see her creative art.

Pooja is considerate towards her parents as well. In more than one possible way, she has gone beyond herself to support them. Be it her mother's bypass surgery or financially supporting her father after his paralytic attack. Till date she has ensured that they enjoy a life of luxury and comfort and live everyday with the feeling of abundance.

Every Diwali she would prepare hundreds of snack packets for the village kids that would be distributed by her office doctor and friend who runs an NGO. Her intense love and affection doesn't culminate with her parents, sister, relatives or poor kids. She would actively contribute to organisations like WWF, PETA and is an avid pet and animal lover. I still recall the incident that happened during our brief stay in the Pune flat after our marriage. Pooja found him under the common staircase area near the building lobby. Yes, a very cute-looking dog. We learnt from the society guard that his name was Pepsi. While Pepsi was very cute, he would abnormally keep shaking his head and was very restless. Pooja took him to our flat and patted him and fed him with a bowl full of milk before it went to sleep. His shakiness subsided but after he woke up the symptoms reappeared. Pooja asked me to consult a veterinary doctor. The vet later diagnosed distemper virus infection for poor Pepsi. The doctor had given up hope for his survival. But she kept him under her care and even asked me to take him back to the doctor where they administered intravenous medicine. Pepsi survived and got better by the day and that gave us hope. Meanwhile, Pooja also enquired with a kennel and an NGO if they could take Pepsi into their custody. One of the college students staying in the adjacent flats volunteered to take care of Pepsi. After many a month, I got a call from one of the guys informing us of Pepsi's death. I wonder if the poor soul would have survived that long had it not been for the fighting spirit shown by Pooja.

Another trait that I often see in Pooja is that she pays attention to finer details and this gives her the ability to connect with people. This incident happened with my Project Manager. During one of their initial interactions, he had casually mentioned that he liked a book. A year later, when Pooja went to a book fair, she saw a movie CD which had the same title as that of the book. Almost instantly she picked up the CD and got it gift-wrapped for my Project Manager. He got emotional as he received the CD, that in a choked voice he said, 'This is the best gift that I have ever received'. Pooja had a magical way of relating with others. I really don't know how she got this ability, but it is truly a God-gifted one.

Testing Times

Pooja had started to work very early in life. The fact of the matter was that her parents never believed that she would do well professionally as she wasn't that great in her studies. But she was very outgoing, presentable and enterprising. She was the Secretary as well as the Editor of the Rotary Club. She is very good in HR management considering her stints in the Airlines and the telecom sector. She has a 'never-say-die' attitude and has this amazing ability to absorb truckloads of work. And sometimes heavy duty work can have a negative impact on an individual's health and physical well-being. In the middle of 2011 she started getting some medical problems which was later diagnosed as a skin-related auto-immune problem. And the only remedy for the same was to take immune-suppressants and steroids. I was at a juncture where I was slated to go for a Philippines project and this untimely discovery was really a shocker. She convinced me to go ahead and we discussed the same with the doctor. After an assurance from the doctor I did take up the overseas project. But things went from bad to worse and she suffered a major health issue owing to the heavy-duty steroid dosage. She got an abscess and had to undergo a surgery. One can really get demoralised with such medications which come with multiple side-effects. But owing to her positive outlook, she did everything possible to get back on track. A very usual side effect of steroids is weight gain; and to her doctor's surprise given her exercising and physical activities she reduced her weight while on heavy steroids.

Accolades at work

It's hard to believe the number of awards Pooja has been getting over the years. I must admit that for me as a Management Consultant, handling one project becomes difficult at times; while she can would multi-task and oversee twenty five to thirty big to small projects simultaneously. This was one of the prime reasons why she was chosen for the Chairman's Award and distinguished herself in the Talent Pool of her organisation. During the disbursement of Excellence Awards, while handing her the fifth award during the same function the guest of honour had asked her jokingly, 'Hope you are not coming back on stage for another one?'

The Journey so far

If I look back at bygone days and reminisce about my journey with Pooja, I feel I have come a long way. I must admit that like any other couple, we also had a lot of melodrama, a lot many fights, a lot many broken utensils and earthen pots. They are all part and parcel of married life. The true experience is the 'journey of discovery' and we are still demystifying new things about each other. When it comes to common interests, we both love pets, scuba diving and we de-stress by going to the Spas. We enjoy throwing New Year parties for our friends and relatives and watching movies. The list goes on forever.

During difficult times, when we encountered a heath setback, we both called it quits at work (unthinkingly sacrificing our professional review cycles) and took a long break for a US trip while visiting some amazing places like the mighty Grand Canyon, frozen Niagara Falls, skyscraper NYC, unbelievable Las Vegas, filmy Los Angeles, Hollywood and had a wonderful stay at my brother and *bhabhi's* beautiful abode in Dallas. It gave us the strength to bounce back to life and also keep pace with it.

Pooja is a Marathi and gives my mom immense pleasure when she converses with her in Bengali. On realising the fact that my protein intake was getting affected owing to a vegetarian diet at home, she started cooking delicious chicken meals every Sunday, while still being strictly vegetarian.

So to say, what's worthwhile to mention here is that I am looking forward to the future. My marriage with Pooja has been an exciting journey and it has significantly changed my perspective and outlook towards life. I have a deeper understanding of the little nuances in life and a lot deeper realisation of the way the world sees you.

I now know that joy is not just in giving, but giving it beautifully, giving it with a personal touch and giving it whole-heartedly. I now understand that the only way you can touch someone's heart is not just by knowing what brings him/her the greatest joy but to go and make it happen for that person. I now know how important it is to plan for a contingency as there are no forewarnings before an untoward event in life. I now realise that life is what you get when you have planned for something else, but there is no point in cribbing and ruining your present. I now feel what value a family brings to an individual. While one would play many roles that wither away with time, it is the role of the family towards you and your role towards the family that never changes.

While I was penning down my love journey I realised that I would never be short of interesting events or anecdotes which involve my better half. And I am equally sure that by the time you become familiar with our journey, together we would have scripted new moments and new discoveries, worth mentioning.

Pooja makes me happy, she makes me better, she scolds me badly but she loves me madly. She holds me tightly but she makes me stronger. She guides me further but she calls me back when I am so lost. At times she takes the lead and takes me along. She is like the song of my soul that brings out the real me, nothing less and nothing more.

I now feel what value a family brings to an individual.
While one would play many roles temporarily that wither
away with time – it is the role of the family towards you and
your role towards the family that never changes."

Song of my soul

You are the song of my soul
In my life, you play the most promising role
I always find you near, up-close and hold
It's the spirit of Love, I have never told

You whispered your love with an enigmatic sigh
Oceans across, I write to you with Spirits so high
I die to meet you, and take you out
So much in love, I silently shout

You are awake for me, with your silent care
I recline my head, as you stroke my hair

You love the ones', I love the most
To thee I shall always raise the toast

Closer it comes, the closeness in us
Envy the others, can one dare to fuss?
Sacred at heart, we ride the tide
The God, the World, all by our side

The festivity of colors during the Spring of Joy
That's when the Girl marries the Boy
By the Sun and the Sand, in the Baywatch we meet
Drive through the beaches, up-close and up-beat

Life's a journey, it's never complete
The voyage is enticing; when I have you by my seat
I always find you near, up-close and hold
It's the spirit of Love, No...I have never told

Our journey together through thick and thin

Mustafa Raj

Before I met Mukta, my wife, I had lost all interest in life. I was living each day as it came and hardly looking forward to anything. Mukta inspired a new interest in life and she taught me how to treat life, and people, with respect.

My introduction to Mukta happened by chance! I had come to Pune after passing my 10th std in 1985. I took admission in Wadia college and was living in the hostel. Her brother – Divyajit (Dimpy to his friends) was in the same class. There was a hockey match between India and Pakistan and he invited me to his house so that we could enjoy the match together (there was no TV in the hostel!). And that is how I met her. The memory of our first meeting is still fresh in my mind. She had just come back from school and was still in her uniform, hair neatly tied in ponytails! Dimpy and I were sitting in the living room, watching TV. Suddenly their dog, Julius – a full-grown Labrador, walked casually in. Being a dog-lover myself, I naturally raised my hand to pat him and she shouted, 'Don't touch him!' I intuitively knew that I shouldn't touch him! Later on I understood that he was extremely possessive of her and could attack anybody if he felt that she was threatened by somebody else in the vicinity. I also realised that she had yelled at me because she didn't want me to get hurt, just in case…

A couple of years later, we both became classmates in college; undergoing a B Com. Course. She was in girls' hostel and I in the boys' hostel.

Our 'courtship', if I can call it that, started when we used to walk from Wadia's to the Kendriya Vidyalaya in Southern Command for learning Accounts. It was during these walks that I truly got to know her as a person. The admirable traits which I could see in her (and which I admire and respect even today!) were self-belief, courage, love for animals, and physical stamina. I warmed up to the fact that here was a person who could understand me and with whom I could talk freely.

Continuing on our life-journey together (albeit separately), we came to realise that we liked spending time with each other. In fact we realised that we wanted to spend the rest of our lives together. However, I was too shy to share my feelings with her. Eventually, and I think after waiting for a considerable period of time, she decided to 'break the ice' herself and told me in her typical, no-nonsense manner that she knew that we both had started loving each other. When I agreed, she quickly got down to brass tacks and listed out what needed to be done.

I think the most important action we took was to inform our respective families about our feelings for each other and about our decision to marry. All hell broke loose! They (Mukta's parents) basically could not digest the fact that a Muslim boy could become their son-in-law. I still remember that one of the reasons for them not accepting me was that being a Muslim, I could marry more than once! Her family strongly objected to my presence in their life, and abandoned Mukta. I tried talking to Dimpy, but he also did not support us. I still remember that he had locked me out of our room as a sign of his protest! As far as my family was concerned, my father only said that they would be OK with whatever we decided to do. My mother was silent as usual. The only observation he made was that both of us should be concentrating on our career at this point-in-time.

Mukta's father is a renowned dermatologist and has served in the armed forces before retiring as a colonel. Actually, we had thought he at least would not oppose us since he and I used to spend a lot of time discussing issues of mutual interest. He came across as a man with a modern outlook. So his reaction came as a shock to both of us. Mukta was so angry that she wrote to her father suggesting that he burn all his books. As for my family, my father is an electrical engineer having worked with PSUs such as Bharat Aluminium Company (BALCO) and National Thermal Power Corporation (NTPC).

Mukta and I realised soon enough that we were on our own. And since her family had stopped sending her monthly allowance, our first (and only) priority was to take up some job somewhere so that she could sustain herself. She started working in a hotel as a receptionist while I took up a job as a delivery man with a courier company. Unfortunately, we could not earn enough to afford her college fees and she had to leave her studies midway. I continued with my studies as we had decided that at least one of us should complete the course. However, I had to leave my job with the courier company because I suffered a slipped disk due to excessive biking. Nonetheless, our struggles continued. Mukta continued working in hotels and I took up a part-time job with an auditing firm. Our collective income, however, was not sufficient to make ends meet; so I started a tea stall (with help from one of our friends) outside the college.

All this happened in a span of less than one year. And we were still very young – Mukta was nineteen and I was twenty.

I must now introduce Mr. Khetaram Choyal (Khetaram sir to us).He and his family came to our rescue in our difficult times. Mukta and I used to go to sir's house for studying Accountancy. Of course, Mukta knew their family since her school days, I just tagged along! Being the wise man that he is, Khetaram sir gave us the much-needed moral and emotional support. And it was thanks to him that it dawned upon us that we should marry to give our relationship legal sanctity. Mukta and I got married the day after I turned twenty one. I clearly remember the occasion (obviously!), more so because it was the time when the Babri Masjid was demolished and the whole infrastructure in that part of the country had come to a halt. So, my parents could not come (and I am not sure whether they actually wanted to come!). However, one of my college friends – Venky, somehow managed to come all the way from Calcutta! It was a court marriage under the Bombay Marriage Act. The venue was Mobos Court, opposite Wadia College. And since I didn't have the money to pay for the expenses, one another friend – Shekhar, managed to convince the lawyer (who was elder brother of his classmate) to take care of everything with a promise that we would pay him as soon as possible. And we haven't been able to pay him till now! Not because we can't afford it (the amount was Rs. 500/-), but simply because he didn't want to take any money from us after he got to know our 'story'. And he is a corporator now.

If we look back this was the state we were in – financially.

Date: 26th October 1990
Age of Bride: 19
Qualification: Second Year B Com
Age of Groom: 21
Qualification: Second Year B Com
Combined cash-in-hand: Rs.12/-
Combined cash-in-bank: NIL
Assets: Bike – KB 100 RTZ

And the struggle continued.

From an approximately 50 sq. ft. room in the LIG (Lower Income Group for the uninitiated!) housing colony in Nagpur Chal, which I used to share with a friend of mine, I shifted to Mukta's 'room-with-a-view' at the Somsukh Lodge in Vishrantwadi. We used to call it a room-with-a-view because it had a balcony from where we could see the Mula-Mutha river! We thought it would ease our financial situation since instead of paying rent for two dwellings, we would need to continue to pay only for her room. But it was not to be so! The owner of the lodge demanded more monthly rent since it had now become a double occupancy!! We boldly understood his reasoning (as if we had any other choice!) and smartly 'negotiated' a deal – within the same amount of monthly rent, we got to use one of the sheds in the premises where we could do our cooking. It was a great feeling of accomplishment! The only issue was that we didn't have any utensils, cutlery, stove, fuel etc. etc. So, the quest began to acquire whatever we could afford from our joint income, which was around Rs. 2,000/- at that time.

I don't remember how much time in terms of days or weeks it took to fully set up our kitchen. I only remember that the stove was the old-fashioned one which comes 'alive' after a good amount of pumping! And obviously, I had to activate all my local contacts to procure sufficient quantity of kerosene to keep the fire burning! I also have a vivid memory of the first meal that Mukta 'attempted' on our beloved stove – it was the occasion when I was getting my bike back from the mechanic. In fact, it was after my accident on the same bike that I had made friends with that mechanic – he had helped me in getting enough money from the insurance company to cover the cost of the repairs. I had felt so grateful to him that we decided to invite him over while bringing the bike home. I also remember that I felt so grateful to the insurance company that I actually wrote them a thank-you note! And now that I remember this, I wonder whether somebody at the insurance company actually got to read my letter.

Anyway, coming back to the dinner, Mukta decided that she would make vegetable 'pulao' in honour of our guest and to celebrate the home-coming of our bike. She told me that by the time we reach the lodge from the garage, the pulao would be ready. I couldn't wait to reach back, and when I did, I found her in tears inside the make-shift kitchen. First I thought that it might be because of the smoke from the stove (it was actually quite smoky inside). However, I realised quickly that she was actually crying. When I asked her as to what had happened, she could only point towards the stove. I could see that a container was placed on the stove and lot of smoke was coming out, not only from the container but also because of the rice and vegetables which had spilled over and fallen onto the flames! Although I didn't have a clue at that time how the 'pulao' is cooked, I could see that something had gone fundamentally wrong with our own 'pulao'. Mukta later confessed that she didn't realise that the rice, while in the process of getting cooked, starts occupying more and more space within the container than when it does when it is in raw state! Our collective learning was that we must first get a clear understanding of the right measurements of rice and water so that we could cook plain rice first and then make an attempt for the pulao!

We stayed in that lodge for a few months and we needed to augment our monthly income on an urgent basis as we were finding it very difficult to make the ends meet. The monthly budgeting went something like this –

Expenses:		
	Rent -	Rs. 1,600/-
	Kerosene -	Rs. 200/-
	Ration -	Rs. 500/-
	Petrol -	Rs. 300/-
	Others -	Rs. 200/-
	Total – approx Rs. 2,800/-	

Income:		
	Mukta's salary -	Rs. 600/-
	My allowance -	Rs. 1,000/-
	Income from tea stall -	Rs. 400/-
	Total – approx Rs. 2,000/-	

So, obviously, we had to go on a fast on almost all days of the month. Enter Nasir! Nasir had joined my gang of friends during my hostel days. He was doing his graduation and he used to work as an apprentice in the Ammunition Factory at Kirkee at the same time. Since he used to live in Yerawada at that time, he used to drop in to our room on his way to the factory. After a few such visits, he realised that there was no food to be seen or offered in the house. Without asking anything further, he simply started bringing food from his home for us. Thank you, Nasir! We will forever be grateful to you.

In any case, we knew that we had to do something to enhance our monthly income. So, Mukta took up a job at a hotel as a cashier and her salary increased to Rs. 800/-. Both of us were quite thrilled when we got to know that she was selected for the job! On my part, I started working with an audit firm on a part-time basis along with running my tea stall. Our daily routine was –

0500 Hrs – drop Mukta to the hotel
0515 Hrs – open the tea stall
1200 Hrs – report for the audit job
1800 Hrs – pick Mukta from the hotel
1830 Hrs – reach the lodge
1830 onwards –cook something or eat a 'vada-paav' and go to sleep

After completing my graduation, I went back to the courier company to see if I could get a better job which would not require me to be on the road and drive around the city so much. Thankfully I got the job of an Operations Supervisor. However, we soon realised that our collective income was still not sufficient to meet our basic needs. So, I left this job and went back to college to study Personnel Management. Throughout those two years of studies, Mukta continued to work and manage the home front as well. I still remember the kind of distances she used to travel (by bus obviously). Once she even went to Delhi to procure export surplus jackets, sweaters and blankets, which you get on the roadside, and put up a stall in the neighbourhood.

I must mention here that throughout our ordeal, Mukta **NEVER** complained about our financial condition. She never got frustrated and nor did she let me get frustrated. Now that I look back on those times, I realise that by doing so, she actually gave us a lot of hope.

The journey of life continued.I did not get any job immediately after completing my PG. So Mukta continued working. Eventually, I got my first job with a family-owned manufacturing company. My own salary was still not sufficient, so Mukta continued with her job as well. After working for almost three years, I got a career-turning break with a start-up company Lever Johnson Limited (LJL) – it was a Joint Venture of HLL and SC Johnson of USA. I was with this organisation for five years and it was here that I got exposed to the best HR practices. From here, I shifted to Mercedes where I got another boost to my learning – thanks to Mr. Mallier, the then HR Director. And it was during this time that Mukta got an opportunity to start working in the field of wildlife – her area of passion! Fortunately, now she did not have to work for money!!

There are some very interesting things I remember when I got selected in LJL. The company where I was working at that time was Oriental Rubber Industries Limited – a family-owned business. It was here that I got to learn the ropes, mainly in areas of personnel management, statutory compliances, office administration etc. – thanks to Mr. H P Srivastava, who was my first boss and one of my mentors. Under his tutelage, I learnt all that is to be learnt in the areas mentioned above. Coming back to my selection in LJL, I remember that my gross salary while in Oriental was around Rs. 4,500/- per month. And when I was finally selected in LJL, I was asked as to how much salary I expected and I promptly said Rs. 1 lakh per annum! Neeraj Jain – Head of Commerce & Finance in LJL, one of the interviewers on the panel, raised his eyebrows and said that it was almost double of my current salary! I said yes I know that and also said that I think I deserve at least that much!! Now, the reason for me to ask for that particular figure was actually quite simple – whenever I used to go for interviews during that time, Mukta and me always used to say (because we simply believed!) that I must get the magical figure of Rs. 10,000/- per month because we deserved a better life now!! And so it happened – the day I joined LJL (1st October 1995), my monthly salary came to a little more than Rs. 10,000/-. And it was actually more than what I had asked for! The reason being that the allowances for my grade had just been revised by HLL, so I got an increase by default. When I came back and broke the news to Mukta, her joy was boundless..

And there has been no looking back since then.

Back to Mukta and her work in the area of wildlife. During her 'occupation' with her passion, I saw a new Mukta emerge! Her passion and energy drove her, literally!! She used to go to her workplace by bus which used to take her almost two hours, one way!! And when she used to be back in the evenings, she used to be more energetic (rather than feeling tired)! And then she developed an interest in wildlife photography. She used to sit for hours and shoot the birds with her handycam. I still remember her excitement when she had gone to Kanha National Park and she got to capture live footage of a tigress going in for a kill. I think she just turned younger during those days!! This was her first 'transformation' witnessed by me.

Mukta's second 'transformation' happened when Joshua was born (and I was lucky enough to see him first as I was present during the delivery!). As Dr. Boudhankar – our dearest friend, says, 'With the birth of a child, a mother is also born'. I have been a witness to Mukta's 'birth' as a mother. As a mother, she is as fiercely protective as a tigress! Yet, she is the first to discipline him!! She can be as child-like and play with him the kind of games played by children of his age. She can also be very mature and engage in adult-like conversation with him when it comes to subjects like values and principles. The best part is that even Joshua's personality changes vis-à-vis Mukta's role! And his friends just love 'Mukta aunty' since she knows how to create fun and joy from almost anything and nothing!! Her Christmas parties are famous.

Coming straight to the here and now, I simply want to say that our small family's happiness is only because of Mukta! She is the pivot around which our life rotates. And she efficiently manages two portfolios – Home Ministry as well as Finance Ministry! Plus, she also enacts her two roles very effectively – Lady-of-the-House as well as an Entrepreneur. She runs a music academy affiliated to the Rockschool of London and is currently busy with preparations for opening her own café! Personally, I have learnt some of the most important lessons in life from her – family comes first; you get what you believe in and ask from the universe; two-way communication is the essence of any relationship, especially marriage; play as a child with children; be kind to animals; respect our elders; and above all, be thankful and appreciate what you have!

By way of concluding (so that 'the moral of the story.' angle gets covered!), I just would like to say this – there is nothing like right or wrong when it comes to marriage. However, please bear in mind (and heart and body and soul) that the wife is always right! What I mean to say is that as a husband, I must understand (and respect) that she has a rightful place in my life. She has a right to express her thoughts and feelings the way she knows and does best. She has a right to ask questions (which doesn't necessarily mean that she does not trust me!). She has a right to take time off (it is amazing how most husbands take their wives' role for granted). And above all, she has a right to be heard! One more thing – nobody can give you a cure-all type of advice for a happy married life. Both spouses have to embark on the journey together and discover the key notes to be played together so that life's symphony is in perfect harmony – most of the time if not all the time! The only thing required of the husband is patience (especially when you are feeling very impatient and want to voice your own thoughts/ feelings) and let your wife complete her 'download'. And you need to compliment your patience with respectful acknowledgement so that she understands that you have understood what she was making you understand! Please don't be under the impression that she needs you to solve her problems. She only needs you to listen to her! In any case, if she finds you worthy enough to help her out with something, she will simply ask you to do it!

As a parting note, I only want to say that instead of wondering whether you have a wonderful wife, just make an inventory of what all she does in a day. I am sure you will realise that it is no wonder that she is partnering with you so that both of you lead a wonderful life!!

Our journey together through thick and thin

A Tale of my Two Wives

Afzal Kader

I have no grudges against Nazneen. She stood by me whenever I needed her. She loved me a lot but I was equally responsible for her deeds. The only thing that was not under my control was my fate.

It was the last year of my graduation and I just had to dance. Dance had always been my passion since my childhood. My cousin Ramzan was the one who introduced me to the stage when he participated in the cultural programme in his final year. He lost his parents when he was five years old. My dad adopted him and we all grew up together. For four years I was an active participant in the cultural programmes. But this year I was falling short of good dancers.

I got three dancers. By end of the first week, we managed to get five more from the junior class and other groups. I was still falling short of one female dancer who was supposed to be the lead dancer with me. I wanted the best dancer. A friend suggested Nazneen's name. She was from my college but a year junior. I decided to meet her directly and ask her if she would be my dance partner. Just a week was left for the final day – 29 December. I could meet her at 11 AM after her practicals, she said.

'Nazeen, are you Nazeen?' She was standing with her back towards me, talking to her friends. Then she turned and time stood still. Her shining hair flowed gracefully around her. The cold wind blew on my face freezing my expression. She had the most beautiful smile

I had ever seen. My mind stopped and it seemed that that there were just the two of us in the entire universe.

'Yes' she said. 'Hello, yes I'm Nazneen', she repeated. I recovered my senses and told her that I had got her reference from Mohan and asked her whether she would be interested in dancing with me for the cultural day. She had a confused expression and was about to say something. That is when I remembered that I never introduced myself.

'Hi, sorry, I didn't introduce myself. My…?' 'No, but I know you', she interrupted. 'You are Afzal from final year aren't you?' I nodded with an expression of wonder. 'You are famous in our college Mr Prabhu Deva'. 'Oh!' I thought to myself. I mainly choose his songs for dancing. I smiled and said 'Well, so what do you say? Are you interested?'

'I am but I will have to get permission from my parents. I will let you know by tomorrow.' I asked her if she could confirm by five in the evening so that we could start our practice immediately. She agreed and said bye and started walking away from me. For that one minute; I felt a strange emptiness and a sense of being left alone. I had my brother and sisters, but I wasn't so happy being with them. I wasn't close to anyone in my family except my grandmother and father. My grandmother had been with me since my childhood. She taught me everything like cleaning the house, cooking, ironing my own clothes and so on. Ever since I was eight years old, I used to take care of everything in my house for everybody along with my studies. My elder sister Sajjda was timid and very shy and not good at household work. My younger sister Raziya was very good at her studies and a meritorious student. Hence she was kept away from household work. Apart from this; my mother during her childhood days went through many sufferings as she was born as a girl in a society where sons were given more preferences and privileges. She taught her girls that they were not born to just look after the family as a housewife but had a right to have their own ambitions and realize them. My father was working for a government organisation and remained on tour throughout my childhood. I never blamed him and could understand his predicament. I therefore spent less time with him but whenever I was with him; I used to be very happy. Sometimes he used to take me with him on sites where he worked and I spent hours with him and his colleagues. Hence, my vacation was the happiest of times. No school, studies and being with dad. Well, to talk about my mother, we didn't have a good rapport with each other. So my childhood was very lonely.

I experienced the same loneliness standing there looking at her walking away from me. 'Hey, buddy, what's happening?' I heard my professor 'Shaikh' saying. 'Nothing Sir! I...I was asking her if she is interested in dancing in my group for the cultural day.' Our city was a very small one and so was our college. A boy talking to a girl outside the laboratory looked odd. 'Your eyes tell something else, Afzal. What's it?' he asked with a mischievous smile. Professor Shaikh was a cool man. He could get along with any generation and was the favourite of every student. He was our organic chemistry professor. He gave examples to suit our generation and he really believed that every human in this world will have chemistry in their life at least once. This was the statement made by him in our first lecture.

I blushed and said good morning and left for my practicals. I couldn't stop thinking about Nazneen. I noticed that everyone in the lab was looking at me as if something terrible had happened to me. Yes, I felt that. I had few friends as I was happy with my loneliness. Chetan came to me and asked what happened and if I was OK. I smiled with a blank expression and started doing my practicals. I was waiting for the clock to strike five and each hour, minute and second seemed like a decade.

I was waiting for her sitting on the stairs. She didn't arrive even fifteen minutes after five. My mind was telling me to move on as she would not come. However, my heart was fine with waiting. It was more than an hour and it was dusk. I forgot that almost everyone had left the college and in sometime it would be closed. I cursed myself as I hadn't taken any telephone number or address. I got up and started walking towards the gate. I saw someone entering the gate. As it was a bit dark, I couldn't recognise the person. Then I saw that it was none other than Nazneen. 'Hi, I thought you might have left but still felt I should check. I stay nearby hence…' She said. 'Thank you; I was just trying my luck. So did your parents agree?' I asked. She nodded with a sweet smile and asked why I had waited for so long. 'I was…just like that…was hoping that my dreams might come true….I mean…I was hoping that if I get a partner I will be able complete my group for the dance performance.'

'Oh!' she exclaimed. 'I should leave now, will start tomorrow. What time will you start the practice?'

'Well we started our practice a week ago and I will have to cover all that first with you so that we can synchronise with the others. I was wondering if you could meet me tomorrow at 5 a.m. We can practice at my home.' I was thinking that this way I would be able to spend more time with her.

Surprisingly she agreed. I couldn't sleep the entire night thinking of her and how it would be the next morning. I was listening to romantic songs the whole night and finally it was 4 am. I got ready and went to college, waiting for her near the gate. She arrived fifteen minutes late and was looking like an angel. We walked seven km as in those days middle-class boys rode cycles. I will never forget that walk for the rest of my life. After reaching we danced and danced to a romantic song. For the next seven days, that is, till 29 December, this was our routine. We practised alone in the morning and in the evening with everyone else. During these days I managed to impress her by saying and writing a few poems. She liked all the poems and used to say 'you should write these poems… sher-o-shayari janab, you are very good at that'

A verse in the Bible states that God created the day and night, the sky, plants, animals…even man in six days and on the 7th day he rested, blessing and making it holy. Yes, my life was going to become holy…I decided to ask her if she could be my life partner forever. It was 29 December and I went to pick her up from college. She was wearing a saree and looked like a mature lady. We went to the auditorium by rickshaw and on the way I asked her if she had any boyfriend. She smiled and shook her head. I had a wicked smile and looked away. 'What about you?' she said with a naughty expression. I said 'Till now I didn't have one, but I think I have started liking someone but don't know how to proceed. Hey will you help me. You are a girl and you should be able to help me in letting me know how I can express my feelings to her'. She said 'Yeah, sure! I will. But may I know who she is'. Here's where the interesting game started between us. I said with a smile 'No yaar, I can't disclose her name now. I am not sure how she would react or feel if she comes to know that I am discussing about her with you'. 'Okay, then tell me how she looks. Is she from our college, a few more questions and I will guess who she is,' she said. I was sure that she knew that I was talking about her but wanted to make sure she knows but not directly.

I started describing about my girl looking at her 'Well, she has fish shaped sparkling eyes. Without saying a word she says everything through her eyes. Her eyebrows look as if an artist spent all his life just to carve them. Have you ever seen rose petals that are sprinkled with honey creating a shining effect kept one above the other, that's how her lips look. I could read my future on her forehead and wanted to plant a kiss on her forehead to show how much I love her. Brownish golden hair...ah, feels like an evening in heaven.' She was listening calmly looking straight into my eyes. I couldn't take my eyes off her. After a few moments we realised and felt a bit embarrassed. She smiled and asked 'Hmm… seems you have been seeing her for a long time.' 'No, I just saw her a week ago and since then I have gone crazy.' I commented. 'Oh! Is it? But after listening to you, I feel you have lived with her the entire life' she said. 'That's the strange part. Sometimes, I feel that for her I could sacrifice everything except my life as I want to live a life with her' I added with feeling.

We had reached the auditorium. For the first time in our college there would be an event which was a mixture of salsa and Jive. We also wanted chemistry between partners. However, for Nazneen and me, we didn't have to act, as it was happening on its own. The whole day I answered many of her questions, giving hints about my girl. She had named almost every girl from our college and at the end got tired and asked me to disclose her name which I didn't as I had my own plans.

The day was coming to an end. She said that it was getting dark and she had to leave. 'Hey…wait we will go together. I have my cycle parked at the college and don't you want to know her name' I replied. 'I don't think you will tell her name as you have been playing around since morning. I took so many names and none of them is your girl.'

She was very confused and I could see her restlessness. I told her 'Sure I will let you know on the way.' We left the auditorium and reached college by 10 PM. I took my cycle from the parking and asked her 'Do you mind walking with me this way? We will go till there and by the time we return you will know about her.' 'OK! Hope to know the name' She said and we started walking.

For a while, we both were silent and I could clearly hear my heart beat. It was beating so fast that I felt, I would faint. 'Yeah! Tell me…' when she said, my mouth went dry and I couldn't speak. Stammering I said, 'Let's walk till there and I will…' Of course I was scared. This was the first time in my life I was with a girl whom I loved and I was going to propose to her. After a few steps, I asked her 'what kind of guys do girls prefer? I mean if I were to ask you, what kind of a partner would you like?' She answered 'first of all I will not be choosing him, my parents will. They are the reason why I am here and they would definitely know my choice.' 'Oops!' I said cursing myself. I should have directly proposed rather than asking a stupid question. I thought for a second and managed to re-phrase my question and stated 'Ok… let's say your parents ask about your liking or the man that you are looking for.' She continued 'the man of my dreams should be at least six feet tall.' 'Well I failed on the first criterion itself…,' She continued, 'He should possess good computer skills and earn well. He should frequently visit America and should take me along with him.'.'Vow!' I said and thought I should move in now as I would never make the cut. 'Well, it's too late, I think we should move' I said. 'Hey. One more thing. He should love me like there's no tomorrow. ' she added. 'And this is not fair, you said you were about to tell me about your girl and now you are breaking your promise.'

'It's you Nazneen, I love you and I want to be with you forever, forever, and forever' I went closer and closer to her and said with my hand sliding from her forehead towards her cheek. I don't know how I got so much courage. That's when I realised that its needs only twenty seconds to pull out all the courage and confidence within you and make that moment a success. With the other hand I was pulling her close and was looking straight into her eyes and continued 'I know I am just five six in height, and not good with computers either. But I love you very much, I can keep you happy forever. I have been alone all my childhood and can't bear it anymore. You walked into my life like a sunrise.' My words were followed by complete silence. We both were mesmerised. We could hear each other's heart beats and could feel the warmth of our breathing. All this time she was in my arms and so close, without a movement. It's been years but still the moment is so alive that I can still feel it.

I was hypnotised by her and she was with me. That was the moment I could taste the honey on her lips. We moved apart after a while, not knowing what to say and stood side by side holding hands. Her eyes were avoiding me and I was too confused to speak. 'Will you marry me?' I stammered. 'I don't kiss anybody just like that.' she said looking away from me. 'I suddenly took her in my arms....and said 'What about the criteria?' she said 'Well, I don't think even I fulfil all your criteria....there might be something missing in me as well.' That is when I understood her understanding nature.

I went home and saw my grandmother sitting out in the cold, waiting for me. I entered the gate and the first thing she asked me was if I had had my dinner...I lied to her parking my cycle. Mom came out of the house and started abusing me for coming late and hit me. Hearing the sounds, dad came outside and asked my mom to be patient and consoled me saying 'Go to sleep and take rest. We will talk tomorrow.' This was my dad. He never reacted; rather stayed calm and quiet and would discuss and close issues. My mom was just the opposite and hence my dislike for her. My grandma, always tried to make her understand but she never understood.

I was in a world of dreams. I was thinking about my first kiss and was still in her arms. This morning was different for me. Everything seemed beautiful.

It was an off-day and there was no way I could meet her and was finding reasons to get out from my home. I gave her three missed calls on her landline and got back one. I understood that she was waiting for my call. I managed to call her. She wanted to meet me at any cost, sounding very scared. Though I asked her what happened she didn't answer and said 'Will meet and discuss'. I told her that 'Today I can't come as it's an off and last night there was a scene. Will meet tomorrow at five am at the same spot' I had to wait till that time, and I couldn't concentrate as she was almost crying on the phone. I used to go to the gym during those days and hence I told her to meet at five. We met the other day. She had brought her scooter, and asked, 'Do you know some safe place which is a bit away from the city. I need to talk and can't risk being here.' I remembered a place near a river, where nobody came. I parked my cycle at college and took her there. 'Tell me what happened. I couldn't sleep the whole night.' 'Same here' she said and her eyes were filled with tears. I went close to her and she continued 'We are not made for each other; we cannot get married, please forgive me and forget me.....' I said, 'What nonsense, what are you saying and it's just a day that I proposed and I couldn't....'

'That night, my mom was mad at me as it was too late and asked me where I was? I told her that you had proposed to me and that I was with you, 'she interrupted. I stopped her and asked if she was mad. 'Why did you....I mean you could have lied. You told her that I proposed to you....what do you think that your parents will easily agree to your getting married to a person who's at his final year of college. Nazu, I don't have a job ....I ....I'm nothing how would they agree.' she was crying. I took her in my arms and consoled her. 'Ok, you didn't do anything wrong, that's fine. Anyways some day or the other they have the right to know. Let me think...wait. Let's do this. But before that, can I ask you something?

'She nodded. I continued, 'do you love me?' She nodded yes.' do you trust me?' She nodded yes. 'Don't discuss anything about me with your parents. Once I complete my final year, I will hunt for a job and will send my parents to come to meet your parents with a marriage offer. Is that fine? 'What if my parents bring a proposal before that? I can't oppose my parents. 'she asked. 'Well, if you love me, if you want to be my better half, you have to .... not with hatred but with love.' I said.

She thought for a while and said, 'It's not that easy, Afzal...let's forget everything and move on. I don't think I am strong enough to protest or commit something that I can't. I can't...please forgive me.' I told her, 'My love is like a mayfly or sandfly that cannot live for more than twenty four hours. That's all, isn't it. Allah never allowed my happiness to last longer. The moment I feel like living in the world he makes something go wrong and the next moment I hate this world and want to die. But one thing Nazu, you are my first love and you will be my last. I may be able to forget you but not your presence. You will be there...in my heart forever'

She moved away from me with tears in her eyes. I too turned around and started walking, not knowing where to go. Can someone love somebody so much in a few days? I felt the pain of my soul being plucked from my body. I stopped and said, 'Nazneen, I was thinking that this New Year was going to bring a new happiness into my life, but tomorrow is not a new year for me. I would wait for forty days for you. On 10 Feb I will be waiting for you here for the whole day. If you get a chance to think things over, and want to change your mind, I will be there for you. After that I will stay with you forever in my thoughts and will not think of anyone throughout my life. I believe if my love is strong enough that day would be the first day of my new year. But please, if you come here on 10th Feb there's no way I would permit you to go back.' I continued

I never cried till date but that day was different. I burst out and cried a lot. Just imagine a life where nobody loves you at home, no friends, no love. God had gifted me with strong willpower else, I have seen people who commit suicide after a broken love affair.

Seconds, minutes, hours, days passed. I was a living like a dead body.. Forty days had to pass. The thought of giving a space of forty days came from a belief that after death the soul dwells on earth for forty days. Each evening just after sunset the soul is brought to its home and is asked to see how many of them remember you and how many are still crying. It's a fact that everyone forgets the dead and continue with their lives. On the fortieth day the soul returns to the grave forever. Hence if she loved me, she would return to me. I couldn't concentrate on my studies and this was the final year. Only two months were left. These forty days we did not meet at all.

And the day arrived. I went to the river side spot in the morning and was waiting for her from dawn to dusk. I said ....

'Jee to rahe they hum, yun akele hi
Jasbaton ki aadat lagayi tumne,
Chal rahe the kaanton pe, mushkil hi sahi,
Phoolon pe chalne ki aadat lagayi tumne,
Nafrat ki aag mein jalte rahe
Pyaar ki aadat lagayi tumne
Ab jab jeene ki tammana jagi
To maut ki aadat lagayi tumne
Na intezar kiya paida hone ka kabhi
Intezar ki aadat lagayi tumne
Aakhone se wada karke mukar gayi
Beizzat hone ki aadat lagayi tumne..,

I felt somebody's presence behind me. I thought it might be one of the forest officers and turned around. It was her. She suddenly took me in her arms holding me tight, crying and said, 'I am sorry Afzal, I couldn't forget you. I am being selfish now as I can't live without you. In these forty days, there wasn't a moment in which I didn't think of you.'

'Well, you came for yourself and not for me' I asked with a cunning smile. She smiled and asked how to go ahead with our marriage. We sat there for long discussing about our future. We decided, that once I finish my exams I would get a job as a medical representative which was easy to get those days and then send a marriage proposal through my parents. She agreed and we started meeting every day.

I didn't get a job because the job market was bad. I didn't wait for an opportunity and started working as a teacher in a school. My first salary was just Rs 500 and a few tuitions helped to get additional 500 bucks. But this was not enough. Her parents would never agree for a groom earning 1000 bucks a month though I had a house that my father built. I started looking for options and opened a dance school. I somehow managed to arrange 5,000 bucks for the deposit from the money that I was saving during my graduation. I rented a shop and got a few students for my dance class. I also used to do event management which didn't help much commercially but brought me recognition. But even this wasn't sufficient. Days were passing swiftly and Nazu was finishing her graduation. She suggested that I get admission into a post-graduation course. I agreed and discussed the same with my father. Though he agreed, he wasn't sure if he could manage that much money. My mom argued that Raziya's education and Sajjda's marriage would get disturbed. I tried convincing her in vain..

This conversation led to an argument that was heard by my Dad. I was saying to myself, 'Why did he keep quiet. The next day, my father agreed. However, things soon went bad. Owing to the fight between my parents I decided not to write anything in the CET Exam and planned to enroll for a simple computer course and get a computer.

One day my Mom came to know about me and Nazu through someone and abused me a lot. I talked to Nazu and told her that I could not continue with our relationship.. This disturbed her a lot but then she consoled and reassured me. I was thinking how I could leave such a wonderful life partner. For the next six months everything went according to routine.

Sajjda received a marriage proposal and was going to get married. We were supposed to leave for Sangli for her marriage. A day before, my mom told me that she wants to meet Nazeen. I was shocked. I replied, 'But mom I don't meet her, we are not in touch. Why do you want to meet her?' I asked. I was worried that she may rebuke her in front of others. But my mother insisted on meeting her.

Nazu arrived in the evening. My mom welcomed her and asked Raziya to make some tea for us. After a few minutes of silence, I decided to break the ice. But my mom spoke first.

'So Afzal said that he loves you and you too love him. Is it true?' After a thirty-minute chat, mom said, 'Fine, tell your parents that we will come to meet them on Sunday.' She agreed and left. I was on Cloud Nine. Bhabhi came near me and said,' Devarji, are you happy now? 'I blushed. She continued, ' You should thank Guddima'(our granny.) 'She is the one who convinced mummy.' I immediately went and hugged her tightly. I don't know why but I cried in her arms saying, 'Thank you Guddima, I love you so much.'

On Sunday, my parents and my sister-in-law went with the proposal to Nazneen's home. After an hour or so they came back. Everybody seemed to be happy. This was a sign that they had agreed. I called bhabhi aside and asked her what they said. By the time she spoke I heard my mom talking to Guddima. Mom wasn't happy with the status of the family but she agreed. They planned the marriage for the next year. I was still insecure. Days passed and I could see Nazu's relationship with my mom and other family members, strengthening. She used to take my mom for shopping and at times cooked at my home during weekends. I started extra tuitions to make more money.

One day Nazu suggested that I start my own web designing business. But buying computers and setting up a shop was way beyond my financial capability. She advised that I take a loan for setting up the business. This idea was fine by me but I was totally unaware of any kind of banking and still opted for it. I took a good amount of loan and set up a shop with the name 'Miracle web designing and software Developers'. In the first few months I hardly got any contract and couldn't pay the EMI for almost six months. Bank representatives started coming home and were even rude to my family members. This disturbed everything that we had once managed to streamline. I was worried as they even started coming to my shop. Though I got a few contracts it wasn't enough to pay my EMIs. Nazneen advised me to take another loan from a co-operative bank and pay the previous bank. I was really dumb as I accepted this also and borrowed some more money at a very high rate of interest. My mom cursed me for everything. Still my business was not making any profit. The interest accumulated heavily and the principle was as it was. All this started making me feel more and more frustrated. Arguments between Nazu, my mom and me happened everyday. Her parents kept adding fuel to the fire by constant backbiting and condemned me as a 'good for nothing' person. This resulted in fights with Nazneen too. I started feeling that our marriage was under threat. Such was the scenario at my home. My mom used to curse Nazneen blaming her for everything. When I discussed about the loans, nobody from my family bothered to guide me. Instead the blame was put on Nazneen. I used to get angry easily. This was the first psychological problem that I went through. I even tried to hit Nazu. I never thought that behind a cool-tempered person like me was an animal. Nazu never even protested to my physically abusing her.

I started running away from bankers, from my family, from my life, day-by-day. I forced Nazu to get married with me. This created pressure on both sides. But the main problem was money. And that too when I had financially collapsed. There was an 'Istima' arranged from 27 to 29 March. Their parents approached mine with an idea of our marriage in Istima. My dad agreed as he was religious too and it is said that whoever gets married here is blessed by Allah and his angels and prophets.

Finally we were going to get married but don't know why we were not that happy. On 29 March we got married as scheduled. The next day her parents visited us to invite us for the evening reception. After this they were supposed to follow the five Friday rituals. My mom was not ready for this ritual and by refusing to accept this, she insulted Nazu's parents. This created a rift between me and Nazneen and we both had a big fight.

In the evening we attended the reception. My cousin Shakila created a scene. Now I realise how wrong I was. I never thought of Nazu's feelings but always about my family. From the next day a new routine started. Nazneen was a teacher in a school with a monthly salary of Rs 2,500 only. I was struggling to bring my business on track for me to pay out the EMI's. Nazneen's school started at 8 am and ended at 2 pm. However after that she took tuitions for extra money for three hours. Then she walked to my office and we took evening tuitions till 7 pm. By the time we reached home used to be 8 pm. This was our routine. So we left home together and reached home at the same time.

One day my mom asked me to come home in the afternoon as she wanted to discuss something. Mom told me that Nazneen was neglecting the house and that she was just bothered about me and her job.

I had different priorities but mom's priority was the house. Our discussion soon turned into an argument. I told Nazu everything and asked her, 'So will you take care of this. If you want I will help you. We both will get up by five in the morning. You sweep the house and I'll take care of the garden. I'll help you in the cooking as well. After dinner, you clean up the utensils and I'll wait in the bedroom.' I smiled at her, pushing my shoulder against her. She started laughing and agreed. We implemented what we discussed. Things didn't go that well.

One day when I came back from office, there was pin drop silence and my mom's face looked as if she had cried a lot. I went to my bedroom and saw that even Nazneen was crying, After I left there was a fight between my mom and Nazu. My mom accused Nazu of hitting her.

Nazu denied this and said, 'Mummy came to hit me and I stopped her and she is now accusing me.' Hearing this I lost my mind completely and asked my mom, why she had lied and the argument took a wrong turn. Mom said, 'She is lying, why would you would believe me?. OK I will say sorry. 'Saying this she fell on to her feet and started apologising. Nazneen moved back and said, 'Mummy why are you doing this to me. What wrong have I done? Am I not like your daughter? Please don't.' Nazu tried her best to save the situation but my mom kept accusing us both and went to her bedroom and closed the door.

In the evening, we went to Nazu's house as she wanted to meet her parents. When my mom came to know about this, she was angry. She expected us to inform her of everything we did and that we shouldn't have any privacy. She used to start an argument even if Nazu came to sleep early. My dad never knew half the things that were happening here as he was working in a different city. My siblings supported my mom all the time and never bothered to consider what was right or wrong. Even my sister Raziya never showed any respect towards me or Nazu. This hurt me a lot.

This was our married life for three months. Every day some new issue would come up. One day, my mom said that she was going to Chennai with Raziya to visit her relatives. She was planning to go for about twenty days. Bhabhi would go to her mom's place. Even dad was not going be there. I was happy that I would be relaxed for a while and I agreed. The day came and it was only me and my love. That night was the only night we were so happy and loved each other without any worries. I call that day our first night.

The next morning her mom called and said that she wasn't feeling well and that there was nobody to take care of her. Nazu wanted to go and stay with her mom for few days, when no one was there at my place. This led to an argument between us.

As mentioned earlier, I was too dominating at times and would not listen to others. I got angry. 'See Nazneen, I have decided that you are not going anywhere and that's it. If you want you can call her here. I have to go now. Inspite of my stopping her, she was getting ready and this angered me further. I used abusive words and hit her badly. Finally I dragged her and threw her out of my house.

I came home and called up my mom and asked them to come back as soon as possible and added that I wanted to divorce Nazu. Mom said she would come. I went to office but I couldn't stop thinking of her. I was worried wondering whether she would have reached home or decided to commit suicide. My mom reached after two days and wanted to know what had happened. The worst part was that my mom asked our neighbors before discussing this with me. You know people love to gossip and that's what they did. Dad was back the same night and called me to his side after dinner. I told him what had happened. He asked,' I have been hearing everything from your mom all these days. See I don't know if you are still sure about what you want from life. Have you thought about everything in detail? 'I said, 'Yes, dad.' He continued, 'Well if you are sure then I think the discussion is over and we will take this ahead.'

I was uncomfortable that night. I decided to meet her the next day. I went to the school where she was working. I told her that I needed to talk to her. She refused in the beginning but later agreed. We went to the hotel where we often went. She asked, 'What do you want to talk when everything is over? My parents will visit your home for completing the divorce formalities. This is what you wanted. Right?' I replied 'No, Dabbhi (*pet name that I had kept*). I don't want this. Look I am sorry. What I did was wrong. But it was a reaction to what you uttered.'

'Oh! Reaction? Is this your explanation or excuse? If that was your reaction, then what I said was my reaction to your words. You don't bother how your words hurt others. Have you ever thought of that?' Before I could speak, she continued, 'Why would you think about others, you only think of yourself. I think this is how it had to end Afzal.' She interrupted.

'Don't say that Dabbhi. I don't want to lose you. I love you and I can't live without you. Let's sort this out between us. Let's go and stay away from both our families. Please give me a chance. I promise I will not let you down. Even my parents want us to get divorced. We don't have time Dabbhi. They will be calling your parents this evening. But before that we need to take quick actiom so that I can stop my dad. Please Dabbhi. Please'. I said.

'Well, I first need you to get settled within a month. Then probably I can think over this.' she replied. I asked 'Why, for what? Why this condition?'

'Afzal, please understand. If we had to stay away from both our families, we need money. We will have to pay for the rent, groceries,

A Tale of my two wives

electricity bill and other daily needs. Do you think the money that you and I are getting is enough?' She said. I was convinced and said fine 'Well, today itself I will start hunting for a MR (*Medical representative*) job and get it in a day or two. Then we will start our new life. I went home and asked my mom where dad was. She said that he had gone for performing Namaz. I waited and once he came I said 'Dad, I want to talk to you.' He had an expression like he knew what I was going to say. I continued 'Dad, I need time to think things over. Please don't call her parents. I can't forget her.' Dad didn't say anything and packed his bags to go. Mom abused me again and again and said that she had spent money on her trip back from Tamil Nadu in vain.

Dad had left by evening without saying a word. I felt bad for letting him down again. I got a job through Ramzan's reference. I thanked God. I had to leave for Mumbai for training for a month. I went to Nazu's school to show the offer letter. She wasn't so happy and said, 'This is just an offer. You have to clear your training and get the job. Unless you get the first salary I can't be sure. Let's see. Anyway all the best.' Fifteen days of my training were over. In between I used to call Nazneen. Even she was missing me. I asked her to come to Mumbai on Sunday as I had an off. She agreed and met me at Haji Ali Dargah. I was happy and discussed the possibility of renting a house and starting a new life. It was amazing. The day came to an end and she had to leave. I cleared all the tests and got the hiring letter.

I came back and told my mom that I was going to stay with Nazu in a different house. Once we developed our relationship and understood each other well, we would come back. She didn't speak anything and was listening quietly. I cried sitting next to her and my head was on her shoulders while saying this. I packed just a few clothes and things that I needed and left my home. I was crying on the way not bothering about the people looking at me. I reached the house that Nazu had rented. We didn't have many things in our house; a mattress, two pillows, our clothes, a stove and a few utensils; that's it. A week went off well.

It was a Sunday 13 July. My birthday. Nazu asked, 'Dear, this kerosene stove is not working fine and it is difficult to cook. My mom told me to take her gas stove and cylinder. Can we bring that in the evening?' I asked her 'When did you meet your mom? We had decided that for a while we will not be in touch with any of our family members.'

She replied, 'No I didn't go to meet her. She had come to my school to see me. That is when she said this.' I interrupted 'So if she comes to meet you, will you discuss our issues with her? You have betrayed me. Isn't it?' 'No, I haven't. It was a general talk. It's not as if I am not happy with you.' she replied. I wasn't happy and started accusing her of being disloyal. This led a huge argument between us.

I got angry the moment she called my mom a fool and went to hit her. She said, 'hit me, come hit me, you want to kill me right? Fine, don't take that pain. I will kill myself.' Saying this she picked the stove and tried pouring kerosene from the stove on herself. I said, 'Oh, you are blackmailing me. Let me show you how it's done.'

I opened the kerosene can and poured the oil on me. I lit the match stick and burnt myself. I was on fire as I was wearing satin clothes. The fire engulfed me easily. She got scared after seeing me on fire and came and hugged me, 'Afzal, what have you done? Allah. Please' As she was also wearing a satin dress and kerosene was on her too, she was too on fire' Seeing this I tore her dress off and pulled her into the bathroom. I poured a barrel full of water on her. Thanks to Allah… the fire got extinguished. But then I realised I was still on fire. I could feel the unbearable heat in me. I too stripped and started searching for water. There was just a pot of water now available in the house. I took Allah's name and poured it on myself and the fire got extinguished. This was a miracle as the water had not been sufficient. We both were standing in front of each other seeing how much we had got hurt. Many things were burnt. I put on loose clothes and asked her to put on a nightie. I went to my home as my brother was an MR and my bhabhi was a nurse and they could help us. I had put on a cap. My mom saw us coming through the window and came out asking, 'Why is Nazneen in a nightie?' I said 'Mom, lets' go inside. Don't get scared. We had an accident' and I removed my cap. The moment she saw my burnt hair she cried saying 'Allah, what happened to your hair? Are you burnt? ' I removed my clothes and all my family members were shocked to see us.' I said 'Mom, please don't ask us what and how it happened. We need treatment, please help... its burning Mom... It's paining a lot, please help or give something to kill myself. I can't bear this pain mom. Please mom. Please look after Nazneen. Bhabhi, please take her inside and check her.' My Bhabhi took us both inside and gave us first aid.

Dad decided to take us to a doctor who was his friend as this could become a police case. On the way we met Nazu's relative who informed her parents. The doctor told my dad and that if I would have been on fire for one more minute, both my kidneys would have got damaged. Nazu had just a few blisters and could recover in a week. But I would take at least a month's time. He came to me and said that I was lucky to be alive but the pain in the coming days wouldn't be that easy.

On the way home I asked Nazu, 'Why did you hug me? You could have left me to die. I was cruel to you. You had got a chance to get away from me.' She kissed me on my forehead and smiled with tears in her eyes, 'Because, I love you. I can't afford to lose you.' I thought to myself, 'Are we made for each other? We can't stay happily with each other nor can we leave each other. What kind of love is this?'

Nazneen's parents were waiting for us. They sat beside Nazu the whole evening and then left. My mom came to me and said, ' Today is your birthday and this day could...' Bhabhi stopped her 'Mummy, don't. By Allah's grace nothing happened. Forget it. Everything will be all right.' I was on bed rest for a month. My manager visited us and approved a month's paid leave on special approval. Everything was going fine for a few months until one Sunday my dad asked me, 'Afzal, so when are you and Nazneen moving to your new house.' I was shocked and said, 'What...I mean... I mean everything is all right now dad. Even Nazneen has changed. She takes complete care of the house and the family. Mom and Bhabhi are also happy. We all are...'

Dad replied 'See, we allowed you to stay here as you were under treatment. When you had once left the house for her, I can't permit you to stay here messing our family. Who knows after a few days, something else may come up? So please start looking for a home. I will give you a month's time to get settled.'

'Dad, is that you speaking?' and I looked at my mom. Dad replied 'Yes, whoever has guided me is not wrong and to some extent I agree. So by evening let me know your plans' Hearing this I left home angrily. I mentioned everything to Nazu and asked her to take the day off to look for a house. We got a house close to her school and finalised it. She had brought her scooter from her mom's house when we moved back. We went back to my home and what I saw was unbelievable. My dad had moved all our things into my room and had locked the door. When I entered the gate he asked me to stop where I was. He got the keys and said, 'We have locked the door of your room from inside. You can use your room from the other door until you find a home. These are your keys.' I felt lost and couldn't think of anything. Nazneen and I were looking at each other in shock..

I was sure that my dad would never do this to me. There was somebody else behind this and was 100 percent sure that it was my mom. I took the keys and opened the door and my room was a mess. Dad alone couldn't have moved all the things. He hardly was aware about the things in our house and that too he could not differentiate between our belongings and the rest of the family's. I asked Nazneen 'Dabbhi, how much money do you have. We are moving now.' She had 500 Rs and suggested that she could take her advance salary from school. We got the money, hired a tempo and started loading the things. It was only the two of us who moved all the things. Nobody from my family helped us. After moving to our new house, we sat and cried in each other's arms in despair. Nazu was pregnant. I took this as an opportunity and asked her if we could meet our families and inform them. There was no one with us to share our happiness. After hearing the news, my mom didn't react and there was no trace of happiness on her face. We left and met her parents. At least someone felt happy.

The next patch was worse. The money was never enough. She had to leave her job as it was her ninth month. My brother took back the bike he had given me. For my job, a bike was very important as I had to travel a lot. My manager said that they could not afford me without a bike.

Eventually I lost my job. Nazu gave birth to a handsome baby boy that month. We named him 'Afzaan'. We left the rented house and started staying at my parents-in-law's house. They were poor and the house was small but I could see their heart wasn't. Nazu suggested that I go to Pune and get a job and that her parents would help us financially. I agreed and went to Pune. After two weeks, even Nazu came to Pune with her mom and our son. We both started hunting for a job. She got one first as she had good communication skills. Her mom used to take care of our child. We rented a house and the agreement was in Nazu's name as I had no job. After a month's time I too got a job but with just Rs 7,000 a month whereas her salary was Rs15,000.

A few months passed and I noticed that Nazu had changed a lot. She was not the Nazu I once loved. She started ignoring our son. She worked throughout the night and came home in the morning. She slept the whole day and didn't spend time with Afzaan. There was little communication between us. I used to visit my family once in a month. After sometime; even Nazu's dad and brother came to stay with us. There was hardly any privacy between us. We spent very little time with each other. I felt that we were drifting apart. She took loans in my name and paid back all our previous loans. She bought furniture, a TV, DVD, a refrigerator and lot many things on loan.

Whenever she was on leave, I noticed that she was getting calls even in the middle of the night. When I asked, she said that it was from her office. I wasn't feeling comfortable about it. I started tracking the mobile bills and saw that she was paying a heavy phone bill. I saw a few foreign numbers in those bills. She said that those calls were made to Dubai for official purpose on company expense.

I believed her. Six months passed and our relationship was going from bad to worse. I could see that Nazu's mom taking charge of everything. Nazu used to handover a part of her salary to her saying that she was taking care of the house and hence she needed it. Nazneen had totally changed and she hardly bothered about me. I started losing my temper on small issues. I started fighting with everyone from her family as I couldn't tolerate them taking control of everything.

I was on a weekly off for two days and went to meet my parents. On Sunday I dropped my dad to the bus stop. My dad seemed worried about something and asked 'How are you?' I replied 'I am good dad. Why are you asking this all of a sudden? Is there something you want to tell?' He replied 'No, nothing.' He was worried about something that he didn't disclose.

The next morning we received a call at 7 a.m. saying that my dad had a brain stroke and he was paralysed for a few hours. His right side was paralysed. We brought him to our city and admitted him to hospital. He lapsed into a coma. The doctors wanted to keep him under observation for 72 hours. I called up Nazu and informed her. She said she could not take leave and would come later. After 72 hours he came out of coma but had lost his memory. This wasn't easy for us. After 13 days in the ICU, we took him back home.

I asked for more leave which was not approved. I stayed back and I lost my job. When I called Nazu she spoke in a callous manner and cursed my dad for what he did with her.

I went to Pune and her mom asked how my dad was. I said, 'Still alive.' She said 'How could you reply like this?' I said 'Well, thanks for that but I think you would be happy if he is dead.' She reacted sharply and this led to a fight between her brother and me. Nazu asked me to leave the house and her life forever.

I packed my clothes and left. I thought 'Good I left the job at least nobody can say that I earned because of her parents'. This was her turn to throw me out of the house. Tit for Tat.

I reached home and my mom reacted angrily after learning that I had lost my job. I felt bad but couldn't do anything. I had once again lost everything but this time my dad too. Day by day I started losing control over myself. I started hallucinating. Bhabhi realised that I needed a psychiatrist. For the next four months I was under treatment. Nazneen's loss was so deep that I forgot that my dad was ill. I only prayed for my love and life. I got cured after four months. I needed some money to travel and give the interviews and my mom gave it to me reluctantly. I got a good job with a salary of Rs 13,000 a month. Nazneen even today was earning more than me. After getting a job I tried contacting her but never got a response. I tried sending her mails. That is when I remembered that when we had met I had opened e-mail accounts for both of us which we hardly used. I had her password.

I went to the office during the weekend and I tried accessing her account using the password. I came to know that she was having an affair with Shaikh Abdul who was one of her relatives. He was her past love from school. However, he moved to Dubai for his college studies, got settled there and later got married. These mails started from the time we had moved to Pune, almost a year ago. I started reading the mails from the very first mail, which was addressed by her to him as 'Abdul Bhai' Bhai means brother. Eventually the relation of brother and sister was changing. Now the signature from each other said

'Love, Nazneen...' and 'Love Abdul'. I started linking each mail with the experiences in the past.

There was one such incident which formed a proper link. I read a mail that was from him stating:

'My Love, how are you? I just can't wait to meet you, especially now when the time is so close. Just two days to go. Accha listen. This is the plan. Ask Afzal to go and meet his parents. Book a hotel that is on the way to your office. Book it as Mr and Mrs Shaikh Abdul so that nobody will doubt us. See I am taking a big risk. I don't want my family life to be screwed. Hence no mistakes, please. Be good with Afzal so that he will not create a scene. OK? Chal I have to go now. Packing is pending yet. I have a flight tomorrow mid-night 12 AM. Will meet in person.

Until then Lots of Kisses
Love you Abdul '

This is exactly the weekend when I had been to my city and on Monday my dad had a stroke. After this mail there were few mails that contained photographs of both. All this time she was fooling me. This is the reason she reacted to my questions so aggressively. I got her bank account numbers in her mails and the passwords for net banking that she had shared with him. I logged into net banking too and saw every month he used to send a good amount of money starting from 10,000 to 50,000 Rs. He paid for her post-graduation too. I spent the entire night reading all the mails. After reading I changed the password of her mail accounts and took print outs of her bank transactions.

I called her after a week. Even I wasn't the same Afzal now. I took time to think. You know whatever happens in your life is never wasted, be it people, relations, or even non-living things. When I used to take tuitions there was a twin whose father was an advocate. I went to meet him and discussed everything with him. He advised me not to react at all and take steps with maturity. He said 'Afzal, till now you have taken all decisions through your heart which is not wrong, but you failed to listen to your head. First talk to her. See what she says and then let's see what happens.'

I called her home and said 'Nazu, there's something that I have come to know and I want to hear it from you rather than believe it blindly.' She said 'What's it?'

'Who is Shaikh Abdul? What is going on between you and him' I asked. To which she replied 'What nonsense? What are you talking about? I had already told you about him and there's nothing between us. I told you he is married and now has a kid too. But who told you about such....or is it something you who have imagined by yourself?'

I smiled and very smartly said 'Well, now you have learnt to lie and that too without any hesitation. Good! Like your name, you are still proud of yourself. Amazing. If you don't want to speak the truth, I will have to go to court with all the evidence that I have. I give you two days' time to think over it. If you don't come to meet me at 9 AM, I would assume that you are ready for the consequences.'

She asked 'What evidence do you have?' I interrupted smiling and said 'You may leave now.' The other thing that I learnt in the past when I was going through psychiatric treatment was to read people's psychology. My doctor was not only treating me but unknowingly he also taught me. I could see her face turn red and that there lots of questions haunting her mind.

She came to meet me the next day. I offered her tea and asked, 'So is the horse going to speak from its mouth?' She started crying but this time I could feel that it was not from her heart. I asked her what happened. She said, 'Afzal, I never loved anyone like I loved you. I know I have committed a sin but don't you think even you are equally responsible. If you would have taken care of me, why would I have done this to you?'

She went on 'But Afzal you were more worried about your family and you didn't spend time with me.' I interrupted her and added, 'Not only this, you lost all your jobs. You were an irresponsible father too.' I laughed loudly and continued 'this is what you will say next, right? You are so smart Nazneen. But I am far better than you. Your smartness is a reflection of what has been taught to you but mine is by birth. You haven't seen my other side. Now you will.' She had a confused expression. I smiled at her 'You were smart enough to open a new e-mail account, but dumb enough to keep the old password and old e-mail ID for password recovery. I read how he taught you these dialogues, from your new account as well.'

Inspite of all this I was ready to forgive her and tried to take her in my arms. But she protested, wiped her tears and said 'No Afzal, I want a divorce. I don't want a life with you. Please let's be realistic. As I know you well, you are not the one who could ever forgive anyone. In the future, at some point of time I might, have to listen to your shit. Its better we end it here rather continuing and destroying each other's life.' For a moment she cried and now she is…. different. I asked 'What about Afzaan? 'Don't you think he needs a father and a mother?' She replied 'No, he doesn't need a father; I am capable enough to take care of him.' Saying this she left.

I met her mom and dad and discussed her extra-marital affair with them. But they were happy that I was not going to be a part of her life. Her last words were 'Do whatever you want.'

I discussed this with my advocate. He suggested filing a petition through court and requesting the court to place an order for her to come and stay with me along with my son. This case went on for six months. She had spent all the money that she had earned. My side was strong as I had enough evidence against her. During the court case, I made sure about one thing that whatever happens, the affair or any of its evidence, should not be produced in court. I didn't want my son's future to be spoilt.

The case didn't stand for long as both the parties were sticking to their opinions and asked to file a separate case through the Muslim Marriage Law. Her advocate suggested to convince me to divorce her. In return she would waive the alimony. My question was 'What about my son?' My advocate suggested divorcing her and letting her keep our son, thinking about her future.

I agreed to what my advocate suggested. I made up my mind. After seven years; our relation was going to come to an end. I drafted the divorce papers myself and got them validated by my advocate. The last line of which said

'Nazneen, maine tumhe talak diya,
    Nazneen, maine tumhe talak diya,
        Nazneen, maine tumhe talak diya.'

I posted the divorce papers to both her addresses. The divorce papers reached her home on 29 March, the day when we had got married. *Unbelievable…*

I have no grudges against Nazneen. All this while; when I needed her she stood beside me. She loved me a lot. Yes, I was equally responsible for her deeds. The only thing that was not under my control was my fate.

Yes, she took a wrong path but she was *'A Wonderful Wife'*. Even after so many years, the memories are still fresh in my mind. I still love her and think of her. Today I don't know where they are. But wherever they are I will keep praying for them and their happiness. Amen!

Failure is not the end, but it's the beginning…it's a stepping stone to success. With the learning from my failure, I am going to start a new life. This is where the second part of my life begins.

I started a new life. I started hunting for a new job as the night shifts started troubling me and I was unable to sleep throughout the whole day. Secondly, I was looking for a stable growth where I could make a career and make some money to pay off my debts. Along with my friend I started hunting for a job. I got selected for a well-known MNC company that had just stepped into outsourcing. I was hired as Senior Customer Support for an International Process wherein it was an afternoon shift. Hence by 10 PM I could reach my room and take some rest. I was happy with my salary. It was a batch of thirty members who joined on the same day. Though by now I was smart enough and had an aim, I was also searching for a life partner. I never wanted to live alone…Old habits never go easily.

On the first day of induction, I saw a girl from my batch. She was beautiful with a round face and sharp eyes. On the first day itself I had got attracted to her. From the attendance sheet I got to know that her name was Maya, (a Hindu girl). Shit! I said to myself, the first one was a Muslim and I faced so many issues, now if I plan to marry her what would be consequences. I had a bad habit of inviting problems. I went to her and introduced myself. 'Hi, I am Afzal. I suppose you are from my batch.' She said,' Yes, I am Maya'. She was an open-minded person. Probably I was shy. We got to know each other. We finished our discussion and started leaving for the day. I saw her in the parking lot and went to her. I asked, 'Let me help you in getting your scooter.'. She laughed and said, 'That's not mine. Here's my bike.' I was shocked, she had a Pulsar. I didn't speak a word and helped her in getting her bike away from the parking. She asked, 'Which is your bike.' I said, 'There the red queen Karizma'. She replied, 'Wow, you have a Karizma, I always wanted to ride it. Hope you will give me your bike to ride' I said, 'Sure, if you had that scooty, I wouldn't have but now, I will.' She said bye and left. I too started my bike and left for home. On the way, my bike's battery got discharged and I had to go to a battery shop. There was no one in the shop. I was trying to search for the owner or the mechanic and by that time I heard a very sweet voice from inside the shop saying 'May I help you?' I went inside the shop and saw a girl at the counter. But her face had a Nakab. She was a Muslim girl in a 'burkha'. Just her eyes were left unveiled. She had beautiful eyes with long eyelashes. The eyes were sharp and tapering towards the end, with black eye balls. I was speechless as I looked into her eyes. I asked her 'Where is the mechanic? My bike's battery got drained and I have to charge it.' She asked me to wait for sometime. I broke the silence 'How much do you charge?' She said 'Fifty Rs.' I smiled, and asked 'If I give it now, can I get it charged by tomorrow 12 PM as I have a shift at 1 PM.' She said, 'Yes…it will be done.'

The mechanic came and removed the battery and took it for charging and said, that I would get it by the next day. I thanked the guy and girl and left. The next day, I came at the said time and asked the girl, if it was done. She said 'Yes, Imran Bhai, can you please fit the battery that we had kept for charging last night.' I tested my bike and was about to leave. By then, I came back and asked 'May I know your name and phone number?' She had a confused expression. I continued, 'If I face some problem with the battery, I will call and intimate you.' She relaxed and gave her number. I asked 'By what should I save this number?' She said 'Uffra.' I continued, 'Nice name, what does it mean.' She said 'It means the dewdrop on the petals.' I said, 'Wow, nice meaning too'. I smiled and left.

Maya and I had become close friends. Within two days, I had told her my entire life story. She had no words after listening to my story. I told her about Uffra and that I liked her. What do you say?' Maya replied, 'What could I say? If you like her then go ahead.' I interrupted, 'No yaar, It's like, I met her three days ago and how could I propose to her. You are a female, what would you do if I proposed to you as even we met just three days ago.' She blushed and said, 'I don't know, I could say yes or may be.' I was shocked to hear this and asked, 'Do you mean to say that you would accept my proposal.' She smiled and said, 'I don't know, I said. I might say yes or maybe later. Go and ask her.' Saying this she left the place.

I thought through the night and decided to propose to Uffra. The next day, I called her and asked her to meet me near a bakery. She hesitated in the beginning but agreed later.

I picked her up from the bakery knowing where to go. I took her to the Katraj Tunnel. I made her sit on the desk near a temple. I took a document from the file and gave it to her and said, 'This is my Talaknama. I was married and had a son from her. But things didn't go well and I divorced.' She was confused but then I told her that I wanted to get married with her. She replied, 'Ok, talk to my dad.' I asked, 'Does that mean a Yes, from you?' She said,' Yes,' I couldn't believe what had happened. I told her, 'Now that you have agreed to marry me, can I see your face.' She nodded and removed her Nakab and her eyes were shy. After seeing her I couldn't take my eyes away. She was so beautiful, round face, carved pink lips, a cute nose that was placed exactly at the centre of the face. There wasn't a trace of any make-up on her face. She asked, 'How could you propose to me without even seeing my face?' I replied, 'I liked your eyes.' She blushed and I continued and asked about her family details. 'My father is an auto driver. I have a younger brother. He doesn't do anything. My mom passed away when I was twelve years old and my father got married again. I don't like my stepmother though she is nice. I couldn't accept anyone at my mother's place. My dad loves me a lot. He never allows me to miss my mom.' 'Oh, well do you have time till evening may be till 6 PM.' I asked. She replied, 'For what?' I said, 'I would take you to meet my parents'. Luckily she agreed. My family members were happy seeing her and agreed to our marriage.

Uffra and I reached Pune by 7 PM. The next day, I met her father. 'Excuse me, are you Imtiyaz Shaikh?' He turned around, and said 'Yes, who are you.' Damn! At the first sight I got scared. He was six feet tall, with broad shoulders and beard and wore a cap. I said, 'Sir, my name is Afzal, I wanted to talk to you.' He silently, came near me and said, 'Sure, let's have some tea and talk.' He was accompanied by his friend who was the owner of the battery shop. I showed him the divorce papers and introduced myself. I briefed him about my past and continued, 'that's when I met your daughter at the shop and I liked her. I wanted to ask your permission for marrying her.' I implemented the twenty-second-technique that I mentioned in my first story. There was silence as he read the divorce papers. I also forwarded the court papers and other documents. I told him about my job and salary and that I could keep his daughter happy. He was still quiet, took a sip of the tea and said, 'I would like to see your parents and other family members and then decide.' I agreed and asked him to fix a time.

He agreed and I picked him up from the rickshaw stand. On the way, I told him the past in detail. He met my parents and family members. He was happy and I saw his smile for the first time. His father had plans to get the engagement done by the coming Sunday. Bhabhi replied, 'Sure! We will come for the engagement on Sunday.' I was happy and confused, I mean; think...I met a girl on 10 February, 13 February I proposed to her, 14 February I met her father, 15 he met my family members, and on 18 February,our engagement...Doesn't this seem to be very quick and that too with my kind of luck.

Uffra and I got engaged on 18 February. On that day, I came to know that Uffra was just seventeen years old and her father wanted the marriage once she turned eighteen.And after six months we got married. Those six months were amazing. Guys, let me tell you, the period between engagement and marriage, is something that you can never forget. This is the time when a bridge is built between two people of different culture. This period should not be less nor should it be more. I came to know that she is a very possessive and sensitive girl. Her memory was amazing. We used to talk over the phone and hardly met for one or two times in those six months.

On 27 May we got married. After our marriage we went to Mahabaleshwar for our honeymoon. It was an amazing moment. I had never thought that my prayers would be answered. This was the life I had always wanted. We were back and next day I had to go for my job. Uffra was crying the next day as she was going to be alone the whole day and I consoled her.

So I was now a working professional with a beautiful wife. A very normal and a cool life. During weekends, we travelled and enjoyed. Uffra got pregnant after four months of our marriage. I used to take good care of her. Everything was going smoothly, until one day when Maya called me and said she wanted to talk. She proposed to me and I was shocked though she understood that nothing was going to happen. We planned not to meet.

For the next few days, we didn't meet at all. She couldn't travel abroad as her project was shut down and she was given another project. I said to myself, 'If she would have left for abroad, these things would have never happened.'

Well, sometimes I don't understand God's game. A few years ago, I was in love with someone and she left. And now when I am happy with my wife and family, somebody loves me. Why? You know this brain that God gave us, is not just a brain. It is responsible for many things in our life and yes, the question is 'How could you just not think of something you know?' Whenever, I saw Uffra's eyes, I felt that I am fooling her as I was thinking about Maya. Yes, it was true that I liked her, but because Uffra was Muslim; I selected her. Somewhere I felt that I was selfish. After a month I called up Maya and asked her how she was. She replied that she was happy and asked why I had called her. I told her, 'I wanted to meet you, just like that. It's been a while since we met'. We met the other day. Things started changing. I looked at her with different feelings. Was this Infatuation or love? I couldn't understand. Our relationship strengthened in the coming days. One day, we went to a trip along with our office colleagues. She was sitting beside me throughout the journey. Our picnic spot was near a lake. I asked her if she still loved me and whether she wanted to marry me. She said yes and I decided to take this up with Uffra and her dad.

We came back from the trip and one day, I took Uffra to a nearby garden. It was her seventh month of pregnancy. I said, 'Uffra I have something to say. I am not sure how you will react to this but, it's important. I can't hide it anymore.' She got scared and asked me what happened. I told her 'Uffra, you know Maya right?' She nodded yes. I continued, 'She has been in love with me since the day we met. I wasn't aware about this earlier, got to know a few months ago.' Tears started falling from Uffra's eyes. I didn't know what she was thinking but I could see she was very upset. I continued, 'Since last few months, even I have started liking her. That doesn't mean I don't love you. I love you too. But I don't know I love her too, maybe.' After hearing this she broke into sobs. I tried consoling her but it was of no use. She said, 'Please drop me at my father's house. I don't want to discuss anything.' I was speechless. I had hurt her and thought, that's it. I have lost my other life as well. I told her, 'Let's go home.' But she refused and insisted that I drop her to her father's house. That night her dad called me and said, 'Uffra is not feeling well and now because this is her seventh month let her be at our house.'

This was the mistake I made. I was trying to sail in two boats at the same time. I called up Uffra and she spoke to me as if nothing had happened. What should I understand from this? I had discussed this with Maya and even she was confused. After a few day's, Uffra called me and asked me to come home. Her father wanted to talk to me. I was scared to death.

I went to her house, nobody was there except her father. Uffra had told everything to him.. He said, 'See son, I don't have any control over your thoughts but I don't want my child's life to be spoilt like yours. I have no issues with you getting married for the third time, but my child shouldn't be left alone.' My jaw dropped, not knowing, what exactly he meant.' I have no objection nor has Uffra, provided, equality is maintained till the day of death.' Saying this he left the house. I was left alone to process my thoughts. I was now afraid to take up the issue of marriage with Maya. What if I couldn't manage the equality between both the wives? By that time Uffra and her mom came home. The moment she saw me she asked, 'Oh Ji, kab aaye, ruko haan chai banake diti hun.' She went to the kitchen, made some tea and asked, 'So dad had a word with you?' Her normal behaviour was hurting me a lot. She took me aside and said, 'I am not angry now. Papa explained to me about our shariyat. I don't want you to kill your desires only for me. Just a request, please don't leave me. I will care for you and your family forever, and will never give you a chance to get upset with me.'

Hearing this I couldn't control myself. I burst into tears, took her in my arms and said, 'I am sorry Uffra. I didn't know that you love me so much. I have hurt you a lot by sharing my feelings. I was being selfish and didn't think of your desires. You have won me by the respect and the love that you have shown to me.'

I left the house immediately and was about to call Maya to meet me but I received a message on my cell from her stating that she wanted to meet me urgently. We met and she said, 'Afzal, sorry but I can't marry you. My parents came to know about our love through messages and my dad hit me. They have told me not to meet you and to resign from the organisation. They want me to get married with a guy who is a relative.' She said all these things quickly and left just as quickly. I couldn't process the words so fast.

I always get carried away with my emotions and am not a very practical person. I lost face in front of Uffra and her father and Maya was least bothered about her.

Uffra, a girl who is so much younger than me; but so mature and understanding. It's been seven years now. In these seven years, every single day she has been getting up in the morning, cooking my breakfast and packing my tiffin. She irons my clothes when I go for a bath. She has been very supportive. When I am depressed, she consoles me. When I need some advice, she helps me discuss pros and cons. Many a times due to a heavy workload I don't take care of our home, but she has never raised any concerns, in spite of me asking her.

With her support and love, I climbed up the ladder in my career. I could complete my ambition. In six and a half years, from a Senior, Customer Support I have now become a Project Manager in IT.

She gave birth to a smart and wonderful son. I named him Darakshaan which means 'to shine above everything'. She is not only a wonderful wife but a wonderful mother too. She groomed my son in every aspect. I see my son growing and getting the love that I never got from my mother.

She is also my Finance Minister as she manages to run the house… in fact she saves a good amount of money in that. Till four years of marriage, I tried my best to pay off my debt and she helped me by selling her gold ornaments. I paid these debts off but I couldn't pay the debts that Nazneen had taken. Due to this my credit score went down. With growing expenses I am falling short of the same amount that I used to seven years ago. But now I don't feel that pressurised anymore.

I would say Uffra is a complete woman. She fulfilled all her responsibilities towards my parents. About three years ago, just ten days before my dad's death, we had taken him to his birth place in a car and he almost collapsed on the way. He started losing his consciousness too. We could see that he was not going to survive for long, but taking him to the place where he was born, where he spent his childhood, got married, lived a life; was something that we felt was important. Maybe that was his last wish. On the way, many a times he couldn't control his ablutions and Uffra used to clean him and the car without any hesitation. After seeing this I started respecting her more than ever. My relatives too appreciated her.

While returning from our journey, my dad's breathing was unsteady. The next day early morning, I heard everyone crying and my mom calling my name, 'Afzal, get up, get up, see your dad is leaving us…' I ran to the bedroom and saw Bhabhi with my dad's head in her lap. Dad's eyes were closed and he was breathing his last. Uffra was awake the whole night taking care of my dad along with my Bhabhi and mom.

My dad saw me once and closed his eyes forever. I lost the second person in my life; who was always there for me. Three months later, Uffra's dad died of a heart attack. This left us alone again.

After my dad's death, we tried our best to convince my mom to come and stay with us. But she refused, hence we moved to Satara and I used to travel to and fro, 240 kilometres every day for four months. Every day we got up at four in the morning. She cooked breakfast and packed my tiffin and bags. Once I left, she used to clean the house, store water, took care of the garden and wait for me till twelve in the night. Though she had a nap during the afternoon, but think about the loads of work that she did throughout the day. During that period, she had a miscarriage and the doctor said that it would be difficult for her to bear another child.

My mom had not changed and some where I felt the same story repeating itself.. Finally one day the mother-son relationship came to an end. But that's a different story. We came back to Pune and started a new life again. After two years, Uffra got pregnant. However, during her fifth month, she developed complications in pregnancy. Though this was difficult for us I saw this as a chance to serve Uffra.

I thought this was my turn to pay off Uffra's debt. I discussed with my manager and took up a work option with half my salary. Though losing half of my salary was not a very good option; I agreed as at that point of time Uffra and my unborn baby was of utmost importance.

Many of us see a girl or a woman as a means to satisfy our physical needs. But put yourselves into a woman's shoes. It's not easy being a woman. I suggest to each male in this world, for a week's time try doing everything that a wife does and you will feel her pain.

I can confidently say that whatever Uffra has done for me in seven years; is something that I will never be able to repay. She gave birth to a wonderful princess. Now, my family is complete and I am a complete man, with a wonderful wife, a smart and a handsome son and a beautiful daughter. Because of my Wonderful wife I am here writing this story.

All the best to those who are searching for a wonderful wife…

Take care of your wife and your life will be taken care of …for those who are already lucky enough to have a WONDERFUL WIFE!!!

On the way home I asked Nazu 'Why did you hug me? You could have left me to die. I was cruel to you. You had got a chance to get away from me.' She kissed me on my forehead and said smiling with tears in her eyes 'Because, I love you. I can't afford to lose you.' the tears flowed from my eyes. I thought to myself,'Are we made for each other? We can't stay happily with each other nor can we leave each other. What kind of love is this?'

WHEN WE MET

Piyush Kaloni

She is very good at making ordinary things special and keeping special things intact, I am very simple and ordinary in a way.

Our drive through the plains seemed to be wonderful until our car started to hop and jump a little on the rocky mountain terrain of Tanakpur (starting point of Uttarakhand). The pleasant look of tall, cedar trees was extremely calming, reminding me of my childhood. I went back to my lovely old days of childhood where only adults had to bear responsibilities. I was about to nod off when I heard someone sobbing softly. I could not see the eyes as they were shying away from me. The cheeks were bloated with tears trickling down them. Her hidden sobbing brought me out of my reverie and I realised I was sitting with my wife. Yes! I was 'JUST MARRIED'. The responsibility of adulthood was on my shoulders. She was moving away from her homeland leaving her childhood, her friends and family behind to the unknown land and people where she was to be welcomed as the daughter-in-law of the mountains *(pahadi bahu)*. The only person she could trust was her husband. I had a very big responsibility ahead of me now. And here begins the story of my not yet wonderful wife.

My Wife

Well!! Troublesome (No! I am not talking about my wife yet but the topic). It reminds me of my school days when one was asked to write about My cow, My home, My parents and so on. I must confess that was easy. So coming back to the topic, I would like to start at the beginning. A man's mind is very clear with his thinking, work family and expectations. Now there is a reason for keeping the word 'Expectations' at the end for a very simple reason that expectations are born out of relationships and some are made because of bonds like 'marriage'. It is the only social bond that propels you to sow the seeds of maximum expectations whose benefits are only reaped by your soulmate. My stress is on the word 'Expectations' majorly because this the word I am still fighting with. In fact, we (both) are still fighting with.

She is very good at making ordinary things special and keeping special things intact, I am very simple and ordinary in a way.

When we met

A small family friendship turned out to be a lifetime upheaval for me. We met each other as family friends but followed each other secretly 'online'. We were also victims of the most practical and easy, technologically addictive method of finding love and probably getting married too, that is ie 'DATING ONLINE'. Through the keyboard you can easily 'ENTER' anyone's life which is not an open book anymore but an open 'Profile'. To show what you are. You need to edit your social media profile monthly. Your personality, character and identity is judged by these websites and so was the case with us. We were continuously 'orkuting' each other. Since, I am a guy and according to tradition, I had to take the first step in asking her out. So I dared to ask her out. To my disbelief she agreed (unfortunately) and we met at the South campus (Delhi university) canteen for the cheapest coffee date ever. It didn't take us long to consummate our coffee meet to marriage as our caste, creed and all the other parameters set according to the society were well-matched.

Marriage – The Mirage

In India, marriage means two families being bound together in a relationship. It is the responsibility of both the man and woman to maintain a perfect balance between both the families. Yet again the burden is more on the woman to beat all odds. She has to smile in the most difficult situations. She has to be the best daughter in law, the best sister in law, the best mother (in future) and the best wife (optional).

Not for nothing have elders maintained all these centuries that a marriage leads to the beginning of another life for any girl. For Amrita, this cliché has only been of proverbial significance. The truth of this statement came into being when she entered her new marital home with me. She was not at all prepared for the change. Having led a fiercely independent and over pampered life, made things more difficult for her and definitely added to our problems.

Despite the initial hiccups, resistance and reservations from some family quarters, our marriage took place smoothly. Relatives on both the sides had accepted the marriage with tight lipped skepticism. My wife was truly aware of the suppressed criticism on account of differences in our cultures and backgrounds. There were seeds of discontent and dissatisfaction which were visible in the Chinese whispers between the elderly women present at our reception. They made sure that their whispers were audible so that the bride got demoralised. Society has a very simple criterion to decide the beauty of the bride and that is that she should be fair and beautiful. From one end it was very clearly heard 'Ladki ka rang toh kala hai'. To that the response, 'Haan pata nai kya dekh ke shaadi ki?'. Well! The public glare, the excitement of the occasion, the emotional turmoil on leaving one's own past and family behind, the fatigue of travelling and the uncertainty of future had taken a toll on the bridal radiance and she could barely manage a smile. My situation did not merit a response. Though I badly wanted to tell the guests that personality should not be judged by complexion. However, we had to finish with the so called 'muh dikhai' ceremony and reception and move on towards our new life together.

For us the joy of being together and married, surpassed all these things. The cool air, the onset of dusk, the sense of beauty around and the proximity of each other perked up great spirits and we looked forward to the moments of harmony and intimacy. The moment had come when we were together in a relationship that bore the seal of social approval. Left alone we did not know what to say to each other and we just looked at each other and burst into laughter. We found it hard to accept each other as husband and wife as we still thought of each other as friends. This moment of togetherness after a so much conflict, took away all the tiredness and awkwardness. Then we lost count of time and almost came to a standstill

Days passed and Amrita's skills were put to test every now and then. From the colour of her sari to her hairstyle to the way she would make a simple cup of tea, everything was under scrutiny. Amrita was not aware of the criticism as she was a newcomer. I kept on telling her 'just make an effort to adjust. Take care not to hurt anybody with your words and actions. Even if anybody says anything that you do not like, just keep quiet and sport a smile. I am sure there won't be any problem then. And yes, another thing, Always keep your head covered with a *dupatta* in front of the elders and your eyes low while talking to them. This is a part of expected behaviour to show respect to elders.'

Amrita was at a loss for words and just dumbstruck. This was a different me who was talking to her, sermonising about the dos and don'ts. Further communication seemed impossible in such a tone now. She was definitely rethinking about her future as a wife with me. That's where I was wrong as a husband to make my wife a little away from being wonderful.

From Honeymoon to a Moonwalk

As per the trend we went on our honeymoon to the blue waters of Phuket which was very relaxing for both of us. After the portrayal of best behaviour in front of everyone we were away from the cobweb of traditions and ceremonies, it was a real break for us. It gave us a chance to discover each other. The happiness and glow of newly-weds was on our faces. The fun of married life had begun. For us, last fifteen days had been full of ceremonies rather than the meeting of two souls. A honeymoon was a break from this monotony. It had the beauty of togetherness, timeless wisdom and sharing of joy and sorrows. Marriage starts with the search for 'the perfect match' where nothing matters more than the act of balance and sense of maturity. We were actually now enjoying marital bliss, far away from everyone, together in each other's arms. When we sat on the beach, we both kept looking at the long stretch of water and sky. We didn't have to say a word to each other and so many things were expressed on their own. The expectations I had from her as a bride and the way I had tried to be a traditional groom disappeared suddenly. I just wanted to hold her hand for life and look at the horizon endlessly.

Our love for each other grew and we were prepared to start our lives as Mrs and Mr Kaloni. We promised to live our married life on our terms without any interference from others.

The Second Smooth Gear

We kickstarted our married life in the beautiful city of Pune. I used to go to office, proudly carrying the hot tiffin lovingly prepared by my wife. Everyone congratulated us and teased me about the three course meal I carried to office every day. At the beginning it was fun for Amrita as well, but it was pure love for her and not her profession. She was not made to make only good food for her husband every day. She knew that her husband would also soon get habituated to her food and the routine and everything that seemed special then would soon start looking very ordinary.

She realised that she had two options in order to avoid boredom. First was that of having a child which is a sure road to security. Second, she could have a career to increase her own productivity. She could also add value to her time and her marriage. Bringing a new life into this world would definitely be a wonderful experience but it was too early for us. The second choice was a better alternative as Amrita was educated and independent. She had impressed me with her wisdom and dedication for her career. She was talented and qualified and managed to find a great job at a prestigious institution. This helped her establish her own identity and not only busy herself with my lunch.

Both of us were doing very well at our respective workplaces and like any other married couple we spent our spare time and holidays watching a movie, meeting friends and dining out.

We had small quarrels which started in the day and ended by evening while having a cup of tea together. This was the usual routine until entered the famous villain of every family **'MOTHER IN LAW'**.

Mother-in-law

In the Indian culture, the groom's mother goes through the entire hassle of inspecting and rejecting scores of matches for him before she finds that perfect match who is not only a culinary expert, but also a beauty and equally docile. In my case I had taken this hassle away from her by choosing my own bride. This act of independence had definitely sowed the seeds of discontent in some corner of her heart. My wife was strong-willed, not a docile mouse (the desire of every mother-in-law), quite good looking and a good cook and dancer to boot. There was no reason for her to be disapproved.

She came to stay with us for a month. And like any other son I was very happy. My wife was equally happy as it was a change from our usual monotonous existence. The day started with a brief chat between my mother and my wife over the menu for breakfast.

They then hurriedly made it as both of us had to rush to office. Both of them loved tea, which gave them reason to sit together and chat. The common topic of discussion between the two was about the marriage and guests, the family members and gifts. My mother used to tell her about our culture and she expected her to know it by heart within a day. She felt that her son was being taken away from his culture and his favourite kind of food. No matter what; the fight in any house begins in the kitchen and ends in the bedroom. In my case as well it was the same. Introduction of bread and butter, cornflakes and muesli had disheartened my mother who looked down upon it as *angrezon ka nashta*. My wife making *rajma* was an act of Delhi culture intruding upon our traditional *pahadi* culture. Both the things were not liked by my mother. She wanted her to learn our type of food rather than introducing and experimenting with her culinary skills. Of course as a son I also wanted to have what I had relished the most since my childhood, yet at the same time I was open to anything new and tasty. From here began the tug of war between choices and expectations. Amrita was struggling hard to meet her mother-in-law's expectations. Since ours was a love marriage there was a lot of pressure on us to be one's best with each other's parents. We had to prove that we did not make a wrong choice by marrying each other. So both of us kept trying really hard to keep my mother-in-law happy. Amrita tried to learn new recipes and make them exactly the way she wanted. I behaved as the most well mannered son who loved his mother the most. While trying to be a well-behaved son I forgot that I had a wife who was somebody's daughter as well. She was also equally pampered and loved as I was. She also had an equal right to exercise her choice of food and drinks, her preferences also held importance. I had forgotten all these things. All this started distancing us. It was not that Amrita wanted to rule over the kitchen or the house. She hardly had time for it. The only thing she wanted was her dignity. My mother liked her for her will but not for her way of doing things especially in the kitchen. This interference brought about a lot of dissatisfaction in both of them

Finally entered the saviour of all households, the 'bai' or maid. She was like a god in disguise for me. I could actually see a halo behind her. Lord had heard me and why not.After all he is also a man in same kind of distress!! In Kalyug, God could not step on earth so he sent 'bais' (maids). The work would be done on time. Both of them could take a break now. We had everything now from hot food to a clean house and no tension. But nothing is as perfect as it looks. The moment I thought that things would go smoothly, I heard a cry coming from the corner of the kitchen, 'khane main tel daalti hai ya tel main khana'....and that was enough to bring us back to square one. It was not difficult to guess who could pass a statement like that. And so in order to avoid any more quarrels I retreated to my office, my wife went with a red face to her college. My mother watched her favourite television soap to feel sorry for all the daughters-in-law in the *saas bahu* serials.

The days passed with the same humdrum routine and the day soon came for my mother to leave. So, my work to maintain a balance between wife and mother had come to an end.

Min Fru-Din andra sidan

Pa Svenska, I mean in Swedish 'fru' means wife. My talking Swedish now could look strange but that's the most important part of my life till now.

The IT industry has made it a lot easier for idiots like me to go around the world to fix the smallest and easiest things inside wires. An idiot like me got a similar chance to go for a lazy holiday to a country like Sweden where things are so laid back that a day seems to have forty eight hours. The snow-clad landscape where temperatures drop to as low as -30 degrees at times, gave me a good freezing time to think about my marriage. We were two years married by then and my wife was supposed to join me six months later. This time gap was enough for Indian society to raise questions like, 'I think there is some problem between the two!!!!, Divorce toh nai ho gaya inka, do saal ho gaye shaadi ko, koi bachha vaccha bhi nahi hai....pakka koi problem hi hai.'

In India a woman has to live with her family till she is married, then with her husband after marriage and then with her sons in her old age. Any diversion from the so-called style of living raises eyebrows, opens foul mouths. You can never stop a raging bull (the aunties standing at the corner of societies talking endlessly about everyone). I bet if any news channel wants to know about any incident they must visit these aunties before the actual site. They would have to toil less for their work. So, my wife had to deal with certain questions like as I was away to a foreign land, when would she join me.

While my wife was struggling with such bulls I was far away in the North Pole. We always say that 'auraton ko mardo se kandhe se kandha mila ke chalna chahiye' but how much we practise this is quite doubtful. In Sweden I actually saw women on par with men. The independent lives are beautifully balanced when a man and a woman in Sweden live together. Living together is more common there than marriage, for a very simple reason that a bond could be pure and eternal and not necessarily forced in order to keep two individuals together. Again, this is debatable but for me that was not important.

The calmness around me was mesmerising. It was full of a quietitude which always let Indians like us feel that we have reached Nirvana. No meaningless honking, silent and eco-friendly vehicles, people busy with their own work honestly. The apartments were well-structured which gave one a feeling of Hollywood. I saluted the dedication and honesty of people who followed the rules in public so wisely. Looking at so much grace and organised work amidst nature, I couldn't feel the weight of my heavy baggage. I was enjoying the cool air and amazing scenery gripped my eyes throughout. The fragrance of greenery made me forget myself and I was lost in a fairy tale of my own. Swedes prefer walking to work and this boosted my adrenalin too for a long walk.

The transition is not easy especially alone. One thing I've learned is that it's much easier to move somewhere new when you have a structure to step into and a partner to support you whether it's work or school or some sort of project. I was all alone in Sweden except for a few known Indians and many unknown, yet warm and friendly Swedish colleagues. Sweden is driven by rules and regulations that are effectively followed only if you understand Swedish.

As we Indians start our mornings with a cup of tea Swedes drink coffee. But we drink it as a part of our breakfast to start our morning; Swedes take coffee as an experience. It is not just another beverage for them. I was obviously missing my bed tea with the morning newspaper, at which my wife shouts at me till date (yet she makes a point to provide the same to me at the right time as well). Another fact which surprises me is why women (who are wives) fight at every small thing that we demand and at the same time take responsibility to meet that demand too. My wife excels in the same. She knows what I want, when I want and how I want it, yet she will always fight or crib about my obnoxious (in her perception) demands. She will make it a point that my demands are met but always with a pinch of salt.

Truly, when I was all alone in Sweden admiring the beauty of nature, people and culture, I was missing my wife badly. Sweden is one country where living alone is not advised (it leads to depression), even the dogs bark after they have got the permission to do so in a restricted area with well-taught sophistication. People are more than just well-mannered. There is something very unique about them. They could remain silent for several hours, including Swedish women.

Particular aspects of Swedish culture have made me aware of how *inherently Indian* we are. We are never satisfied by what we are or what we have in life. We are always looking to do more or find methods to take shortcuts. Here Swedish mentality towards work and life could be learnt through the simple way they drink their coffee.

Swedes rarely rush or keep an agendum behind their coffee drinking. A coffee is taken (as they say) after every meal and is often included in the price of the meal. Most Swedes drink their coffee black, or with a touch of milk and/or sugar. It is not topped with cream, excessive sweetener or flavouring. As an Indian, I had been accustomed to getting coffee only at south Indian homes or restaurants. We mostly plan to meet over coffee to discuss business or catch up with friends in India (which the latest joints like CCD and the likes coming up). In Sweden, I've come to relish the art of what is called *fika*. 'Fika' as a noun refers to the combination of coffee and cake or sweet snack. But fika, as a verb, is the act of contribution in their culture. The usual office culture was to meet with colleagues every Friday for Fika after work, where wives and children were also a part. This helped them in building social bonds within the professional bonds of a very scarcely populated country. I participated in fifteen such fika meets alone. I was without my wife at a place where she was needed the most. It is true that distance brings partners closer to one another and we were really experiencing it.

Finally, I was glad as I was about to participate in my sixteenth fika with Amrita. She had finally arrived in Sweden. Now we had to experience the journey together. She was suffering a similar plight without me back home.

Inception and Conception

Being married for more than two years now, we had already been dismissed as impotent according to Indian society for not being able to have a child. But nothing was more important to us than to first achieve physical and mental maturity required to become parents. When we saw the health services, environment and people around us, we felt fortunate to be at a place where we are assured of the best services. So time, social pressure, economic feasibility and the environment, all of them were encouraging us to be parents. We made up our minds and before long we realized that we were about to become parents.

One doesn't realise the importance of parents till the time you actually become a parent. My wife had conceived and she was being a good would-be mother. She was careful of her diet, sleep and exercise. For me it was still a long way to go. This was another challenge for me. She expected me to behave like a good father way right from the day of conception but I was not even sure of how things would be. Again she used to feel bound by her physical inability to have fun or feel free as I was (being a man). But for God's sake was it my fault that I was a man? It was a daily routine and challenge for me to make that extra effort to make her feel like a princess. Not that I didn't understand her plight. The journey of pregnancy to delivery is very difficult for every woman. You call it a headstart or the beginning of the countdown, the journey is endless. The baby who grows inside the womb is as small as a poppy seed. It is well settled inside (unsettling us outside). There were many fears and insecurities in our minds especially with my wife, for instance, how would I look with a big bump? Will I always be like this, how will the baby, as large as a pumpkin, come out? For me the fears were, 'Will I ever be able to get out of this? What is this situation called? Does every man on his way to fatherhood feel like this? On one hand where I was dealing with my fears, I was missing my wife's attention too. Where once she was always dedicated towards me, thinking about my likes and dislikes, she now was involved in her own world. Counting her weeks of pregnancy, listening to the foetus' heartbeat, catering to her unusual cravings and so on. In a nutshell, I was missing my priority, my wife. In this experience what I had learnt was that we usually repent at what we have lost, we never see the new brighter picture. If on one hand I was losing my wife, on the other I was gaining a mother. This phase of her life would have suited us better. So I decided to stop thinking and start living in the present. I realised that each one has his own way of living his life and playing his role. I was at that point a husband, soon to be father and a weekend son? I used to call my mother every week. I had decided to live the moment practically. My wife and my yet-to-be born needed me the most, I decided to be a friend in need.

Our Europe tour coincided with Amrita's pregnancy. This helped us to enjoy the pregnancy better. We had found what we had lost (or probably we had lost nothing, only time changed our priorities). We were boating through the Venetian lakes, driving through Croatian mountains, sailing in cruises and climbing the Paris Tower. This adventurous tour brought us very close. Our lives were never so smooth. I was understanding pregnancy better. But the first actual experience of mine as a father was when I heard his first heartbeat and kick. We were five months into parenthood, and my wife was due for another sonography. In Sweden, The fathers are always a part of each and everything, right from the first blood test to the delivery. The sonography was an amazing experience for us. We could see the baby as a complete set of bones and muscles, having fun inside the womb, kicking and playing, gulping and snoring. It was a mesmerizing experience for us. We could hear his heartbeat and with each beat, my heart was pounding as well (with both thrill and fear).

Agnipareeksha – (My stay with my Mother-in-law)

As time was flying rather as the delivery date neared, the weather was getting better day by day. Our movements were now getting restricted because of two reasons, the snowfall setting in and the 'tummy ball' inflating in my wife. Again the frustration and depression was coming in. So we decided to call my mother-in-law to stay with my wife till her delivery. Now, that's one part of my life which I can never forget. My mother-in-law (I respect her a lot), considers herself to be a perfectionist. There is no doubt about it, as could be seen in her way of working and management of the household. But at times she forgets the thin line between a perfectionist and a dictator.

When she arrived at the airport, the temperature in Sweden was -15 degrees. She was already clad in woollens, the best and most protective as per Indian weather. But these proved to be inadequate and she had to quilt herself over to save her life. She was half dead by the time she reached home but when she saw her daughter, the warmth of love thawed her veins. Inside our home it was pretty warm. We started our conversation with a simple cup of *masala chai*.

The joy of becoming a first-time grandparent was reflected on my mother-in law's face. She was glowing all over and adoring her daughter whom she had met after a long time. She brought all kinds of pickles and dry fruits for my wife. For some time, the mother and daughter did not realise about my existence at home. They were chatting about various things, eating and enjoying, gossiping and laughing. I liked watching them so, so I decided to be an admiring spectator.

It was now my time to face what the usual daughters-in-law face, the harassment of ego adjustments (not ego clashes). What I used to do as an adjustment was never admired and what I was always expected to do was never done by me. So the valence always existed. But I realised that I really had an edge over my wife. I was equally pampered when I gave my mother-in-law an ego massage. See, it is very easy to calm a lion by caressing his mane (not true with lionesses), therefore, manipulating the ego can really help survival in such situations.

The D-Day

It was 03:00 a m on 21 December 2012, I was fast asleep. I had been away from hot and sultry weather for so long that I was dreaming of beautiful beaches and being carried away by the waves. Water, water all around, splashing and hitting me on the shores when suddenly I was woken up by my wife yelling, 'my water bag has burst Peeyush, call 112 immediately.' For a second I thought this was part of the dream, but soon I came face-to-face with reality. The bed was flooded with amniotic fluid. The baby was ready to flow out, but it was not as easy as I thought. We rushed to the hospital. My perfectionist mother-in-law had kept the bags packed for the same a fortnight before and till the last moment she was grabbing a few paper napkins and sanitisers.

The cervix had started to respond to the baby's arrival. My wife had started with labour pangs. From a stretcher she was immediately taken to the labour room which was as beautiful as a fairy tale. It was arranged in order to calm the pregnant woman in pain (but I think it hardly helps). My wife was trying to keep up with the increasing pain because whenever she yelled, the nurse said, 'this is just the beginning, you are going to experience more'. She was trying to keep her patience. I was being guided by the doctors to keep an eye on the monitor which was linked to the cervix and stomach, which was measuring the baby's heartbeat every second. It was important to monitor it, as any fluctuation would cause an emergency. My mother-in-law was waiting outside anxiously. I was also wearing the hospital gown and allowed to be there till the delivery. This was one thing I wanted to avoid because frankly I could not bear to see my wife in such pain. The sight of scissors, knives and blood all around made me sick.

On D-day you expect things to go as per plan, except marriages and child birth. Because both are absolutely unpredictable. The bride and the groom may act awkwardly or may some relative. In my case, my baby was acting lazy. He had decided to fail gravity too. The more my wife pushed the less he moved. The increasing contraction was unbearable for her, so our gynecologist suggested an epidural to ease the procedure.

The clock struck 2:00. It was a bright day. The sun was soon about to set in Sweden. The December chill was setting in. My wife was feeling exhausted and I was getting anxious. She was about to doze off. The moment she lost her patience and requested the doctor for a caesarean section, eureka, the baby's head started coming out.

My wife was revived with energy again. She started to push with all her might and voila, the entire labour room heard a big thud. No, it was not related to the baby at all. I had fainted. I don't know what happened next. At 4:00pm, I found myself on a big bed with a drip inserted in my vein beside my wife who was holding a small baby in her arms.

I was astonished and anxious because I had missed all the action and the precise moment of my baby's birth. I asked my wife about her and the baby's health. She looked at me and could not stop laughing. It was obvious. I felt embarrassed too. So, my mother-in-law decided to narrate the story of the delivery that I had missed. (mother-in-law's version). I was shifted to another room. My mother-in-law was asked to come inside. She caressed my wife and she stayed with her till my baby cried out to this world and took his first breath after the umbilical cord was cut.

So, when my wife handed over the little one to me, I asked her, 'what is it? A boy or a girl?' To which she replied, 'it's a boy'. So I felt happy to be the father of a son. I wish my son good luck as he is born into a clan where you have to keep big ears and tight lips. Welcome to the world of men (ruled by women) my son.

Our love for each other grew and we were prepared to start our lives as Mrs. and Mr. Kaloni all over again. We promised to live our married life on our terms and values with least interference of anyone in our lives.

LIFE WITH A WIFE TO RECKON WITH

Gautam Sen

What also remains hidden is the fact that she was one of the youngest to be awarded the PhD degree at the age of twenty two and whose thesis examiner was A L Basham.

Statisticians will most probably record that Cultural Historian Madhu Sen (nee Narang), born 1 April, 1946 at 72, Model Town, Lahore, Pakistan, did her PhD in 1968, Benaras Hindu University, in Sanskrit and Ancient Indian History Culture and Archaeology and married in 1968. She served Jammu University, Department of History from 1968–1990 and Gujarat Vidyapith as Professor and Head of Buddhist Studies from 1990–1996. She died on 14 May, 1996, at the age of 50 due to cancer survived by her husband and twenty four-year-old daughter. Her husband, a retired academic and her daughter, a corporate lawyer. However, not many would have the privilege to write about one's partner and wife who was a scholar, teacher and a researcher and shared not only a life but also lived as two independent professionals who kept two homes all through the twenty-eight years of married life. Statistically, we managed to live together for three years and seven months of the twenty eight years. We may have even been able to achieve another record when for nearly two years, three of us were in three countries – I in the US, Madhu in Canada and our daughter, Arpita in India. The family remained closely bonded and has become even more bonded after we lost Madhu in 1996. Curiously, we have not given up our old habit – I live in Pune while the daughter lives in Bangalore and catch up once in a month ever since she got married in 1997. Before that also, our daughter created another record for being in boarding schools for nearly seventeen years at a stretch from her sixth birthday. So we were used to having her home only during vacations. Therefore, between the three of us we lived in three different cities in India. Were we satisfied with such a life style? I can dare to say that none of us at that period of time and circumstances had the time to think because of our preoccupations. However, I suspect that our daughter may have accepted the situation then but must have decided not to follow such a lifestyle if she ever had to exercise her options. I am happy for Arpita because she has never been away from her family after getting married in 1997.

What incidentally does not meet the eye is the seamless brilliant career of a linguist, historian and an exponent of Indian cultural studies deeply rooted in the effort to rejuvenate the ancient Indian tradition of recording the oral history of ancient India as a modern historian applying the methodology of temporal history. What also remains hidden is the fact that she was one of the youngest to be awarded a PhD degree at the age of twenty two and whose thesis examiner was acclaimed historian, A L Basham. This made her the third generation of traditional Indologists spawned by Basham himself beginning with Romila Thapar, A K Narain and Devahuti at the School of Oriental and African Studies (SOAS), London, ending with the classical study authored by Madhu Sen (A cultural Study of Nishitha Curni). Recognised internationally, she emerged as a leading Indologist, with proficiency in Sanskrit, Prakrit and Pali languages. She was trained in linguistics from McGill University, Montreal, Canada. She became the epitome of Indian cultural history by the time she was forty years of age. Therefore, the caption 'Life With A Wife to Reckon With' rather than merely 'A wonderful Wife.' The loss is not personal but institutional to the entire academic community in India and the field of Indology.

I had known my wife from 1959, when she was thirteen years old. This is contrary to the common perception in her immediate family, which dates it two years later in 1961, when Piyush, her cousin and I joined the Indian Military Academy (IMA). This proximity was basically due to the fact that I was brought up in Punjab and she at Dehradun and often visited her relatives in Jalandhar, in Punjab. The families came to know each other especially because her elder sister got married in Amritsar and settled down there. My mother and my sister-in-law became close being in Amritsar and both often went on shopping sprees together while Madhu and I would run the other way as we both detested shopping. Piyush, her cousin brother, was my course mate at the IMA. I vividly remember, when both of us had returned back after the SSB interview in February 1961, she met us as we entered the house. She looked at me and in a matter of fact way said, 'Now that both of you have decided to join the Army, what do you want me to do?' 'Well', I said, ' you finish your studies which will take another six to seven years and then I will marry you'. 'That settles the issue', she said without a smile on her face, and then looking at her cousin squarely told him 'Piyush bhaiya, good that you have heard what Gautam said, now, not a word to anyone else'. Piyush merely nodded. Both of them were deeply attached to each other right from childhood and yet Piyush asked me, 'That was quite a decision. When did you both get the time to decide such a matter?' I said 'We never had time to talk or discuss since we hardly met but I had to tell her once she asked and what could be better than it happening before you'. Such was the culmination of the most important decision-making in my life.

Piyush and I joined the IMA, got our Commission in 1962 – Piyush in 3rd Jammu and Kashmir Rifles and I in 2nd Battalion of the 3rd Gorkha Rifles. We even did an Army course together and then the unpredictable happened. Piyush was killed in 1964, while on an operational patrol at the Line of Control in the Jammu & Kashmir sector. His body was never recovered and the family was shattered and it deeply affected Madhu and remained as an open wound all her life. She finished her studies in 1967 and we got married in 1968 while I was posted as an officer Instructor in the Indian Military Academy. Our house in IMA was 150 yards from the room in Kingsley Block where I lived as a cadet – a place she used to visit on weekends. She did not attend our Passing Out parade so Piyush and I pipped each other at midnight of 11/12 December 1962. We held our marriage reception on the lawns of the IMA Club. I introduced her to Maj Gen D K Palit, VrC, Commandant, IMA. She never lost her sense of humour and said, 'General, my husband has taken five years to cover the distance of 150 yards from where he stayed as a cadet to where the Academy has given the house for us to live. Do you think at this rate of progress this husband of mine has a future in the Army?' Gen Palit was sharp like a razor and I still remember he saying to my wife, ' Madhu, if he remains in the Army and doesn't get killed, he will reach the very top, if he leaves he will be an asset to the academic community recognised internationally, but he will never settle abroad since his sense of nationalism will take precedence over everything else.'

My mother-in-law and my mother were always worried about our attitudes in life which, according to them, were not only devoid of normal emotions but also our puritan attitude towards professional commitments – she with her studies and I towards my interest in the profession of arms. We would often hear the two mothers talking to each other to formulate a plan to get us married much to the amusement of my father who would often tell both of them to mind their own business and leave the two of us alone to do what we thought was best. It would be correct to state that they were not very sure if we would ever get married. While I was in the regiment, I created further confusion amongst the regimental officers by keeping a picture of my beautiful sister on my desk. None could ask me any question but were deeply intrigued. While on short vacations I would visit Dehradun and her family would, rarely, but sometime go out for lunch with me in tow.

Since my wife attended the local college in Dehradun for post-graduate studies till 1965, I was always with the extended family and her cousins and brother's children. Most of them were toddlers and had seen me from the very beginning of their life. I was no stranger to any of them including their family members and elders. It is odd to say that despite I being a Bengali and they being Hindu Punjabis from Lahore, they never saw anything strange in seeing us together as she would often accompany me when I went to visit the extended family members. As a matter of fact, they were too fond of me and all the children just loved me, numbering five sons and four daughters. Madhu's elder sister also became a teacher in Amritsar and became a lifelong academic. Equally interesting was the fact that my wife had a permanent place in my family, with my three sisters though most of my other family members in Calcutta had never seen her till we got married in 1968. My younger sister joined the Sharada Math, the women's wing of the Ramakrishna Mission and Order in 1972. Both were particularly fond of each other. In due course of time, this sister of mine raised the Sharada Math in Almora and today is one of the senior most in the order and is in Belur, Calcutta engaged in the renovation of the Sister Nivedita Memorial.

The most amusing thing that happened was when the news about our impending marriage was made public, the wife of the Commandant of my Regimental Centre (39 GTC) at Dehradun, accompanied by two other senior ladies from the IMA decided to visit the house of my mother-in-law to ascertain if I was truly getting married. In their perception, I was not the marrying type at all! I believe that my wife's research supervisor was greatly relieved when he came to know that she had decided to get married. Years later, Professor A K Narain told me that he never believed that she would ever get married even though she was such an eye-catcher!!

I have therefore four distinct images and perceptions of my wife. First, the scholar in the making, second, an abiding association with society and friends, third, as a cultural historian and fourth, as a homemaker.

The Scholar-In-Making

With her at the Banaras Hindu University (BHU), pursuing her doctoral programme and I serving in the forward areas, and then at Almora, I got the opportunity to study Ancient Indian History in particular and Indian History in general. I think the development of my intelligence quotient was during this period as I saw at first hand as to how a research supervisor guided research. Towards the last two years of her programme, Professor A K Narain would often ask me to look at the drafts of the thesis and that was the period I learnt historical methodology and brushed up my Sanskrit as the texts that were being analyzed were in Sanskrit, Prakrit and Pali. Years later, when I went back to graduate schools in Canada and the USA, this training proved to be invaluable.

At BHU, I saw her emerging as a classical researcher. There was no internet or electronic typewriters or computers. I learnt from her how to create reference cards in three-inch by five-inch cards. I learnt from her the three 'Rs' of research methods and research methodology. What surprised me was that from a near-perfect Hindi language scholar, she transformed into a pure English language scholar with a written expression well above the normal average. Her vocabulary was extensive and her capacity to translate from Sanskirt, Prakrit and Pali became phenomenal. Years later, while in Canada, I saw the way she acted as an interpreter to cover the lectures of Swami Satyamitranand, one of the four Shankaracharyas, when his holiness toured Canada. He spoke not in English but in a combination of Sanskrit and Hindi in a series of six lectures attended by over five hundred people every time in Montreal alone. Towards the end it became impossible to manage the crowd as every hall engaged by the organisers proved to be too small to accommodate the swelling crowd. The spontaneous translation and interpretation in English was almost near perfect to open a window for the Canadian audience to understand Indian philosophy, history and the cultural heritage of India.

She became close to Babu Sriprakasha, our first ambassador to Pakistan and a former member of the Constituent Assembly and later the Governor of Bombay. From him she picked up the nuances that had gone in the making of the Constitution of India. Her stay at BHU as a research scholar while pursuing her Ph.D was deeply influenced by some of the foremost Jain scholars and Jain monks. Muni Punyavijaiji initiated her into the reading of the Jain canonical texts from the original manuscripts kept under the close custody of the Jain religious orders. As a matter of fact, the thesis, based on the original text called 'Nishitha Curni' was not even permitted to be seen or read by junior monks till 1942, and never by any woman. The Cultural Study of India as depicted in this ancient text has become a window to the understanding of India, her history, culture and sociology covering the period between the eighth century AD and eleventh century AD. It was a period between the reign of King Harshavardhan and the advent of the Muslims in India in the eleventh century AD. Her study therefore became an extension of the part of trilogy initiated by Professor A L Basham with Romila Thapar writing on Ashoka, A K Narain on Numismatics in Ancient India and Devahuti completing the work on Harshavardhan. Madhu's work on Nishita Curni bridged the gap (from the end of the period of Ancient Indian History) between the Medieval History of India and contemporary Modern Indian History beginning with the gaining of independence by India. Her work therefore records the cultural and civilisational preconditions that prevailed in Ancient India, causes of the loss of the same and the beginning of the transformation and transgression of Indian History in the Medieval period and the impact of the British rule on India.

In the years to come, when Indian historians will examine the renaissance of the Indian culture and civilisational praxes in post-independent India, then Madhu's seminal work will be of great importance to bridge the gap of tradition and culture pursued in Ancient India and the present modern Indian Nation State, which got lost in the time warp of Medieval history of India when the Mughals followed by the British ruled for nearly eight hundred years. 'The Discovery of India' by Nehru written during the freedom struggle recorded the temporal history of India from ancient times till the end of British rule. Nehru's sensitivity as a historian led to the display of an emotional speech to record his anguish at midnight of the declaration of Independence through a speech entitled the 'Tryst with Destiny' in the Central Hall of Parliament. The decimation of the rich cultural heritage of India, bound in the moorings of tradition and oral history during the Medieval period of Indian History must have had a tremendous impact on the mind of this young historian endowed with the skills of language and who did not need to rely on any translations done by any historians of the Modern period of Indian history. I witnessed the turmoil and the passion in the behaviour, writings and research undertaken by her as a doctoral student to unveil the culture of India, who was not even twenty years of age. From then on it became a lifelong quest for her to unearth and rediscover the richness of life, tradition, moral, ethical and civilisational preconditions that were lost in the tumultuous history of Medieval India and which she considered to have shattered the very foundation of peace and tranquillity in India.

An Abiding Association with Society and Friends

Madhu's career as an academic, started in Jammu University. She spent twenty two years in the Department of History, teaching Ancient Indian History and Culture where the first set of her students in the MA classes were older than her. It will be essential to record her association with the Army and the love and care that she received from the doctors and others when she fell terminally ill with cancer. Hence, before expounding on Madhu's intellectual and academic aspects as a cultural historian, it will be well in order to record how she became an integral part of the Armed Forces as a Service wife too. Jammu became our permanent home while I served in the North-East briefly before being posted to a formation, which saw action in the 1971 Bangladesh War. One of the amusing incidents that happened while I was still in service, indicates the character and the spirit of nationalism ingrained in her as a service officer's wife. My formation was within seventy km from Jammu and faced the famous Shakargarh sector in Pakistan, where some of the severest fighting in the Western Sector took place from 3 December to 17 December, 1971. We had been inducted in the month of September, 1971. Since the Chief Signal Officer of the Jammu formation was our next-door neighbour in Jammu, I could talk to her almost every day over the phone. However, she was always uneasy anytime I mentioned that I might drop in at home in Jammu. She considered that my duty in an operational role must come first and there was no reason for me to visit home. After Prime Minister Indira Gandhi visited my formation on 30 November, 1971, my GOC called me on the evening of 3 December, 1971, and suggested that I should visit Jammu and see my family since my wife was expecting our first child. It was not too enthusiastically that I drove off, buying milk cake from Pathankot Bazar around 7 pm when the Pakistani started the pre-emptive air attack on the Pathankot airfield. Another officer who accompanied me who was also from Jammu, interpreted the bomb sound and the anti-aircraft gun firing as a mere exercise being conducted by our forces.

We thus carried on to Jammu with radio sets on silent mode for the next two hours. My landlord, a retired colonel, thought he had seen a ghost when he saw me. More amusing was when Madhu appeared on the gate and thought that both of us had deserted our posts in the field and run away from there. She decided to become the on-the-spot commander and ordered both of us to immediately return. I had a hard time in convincing her that we were unaware that the war had started and that going back now would be fatal because the entire Indian armored formation, led by late General Arun Kumar Vaidya, then a Brigadier, would be moving on the Jammu Pathankot axis and anything unknown like a jeep would just be shot and blown off. The time was 9 pm and we could not start before 2 am till the national highway was clear. Nonetheless, Madhu stuck to her guns, fed me reluctantly, and literally threw my driver and me out of the house at 2 am. On reaching back to the formation at 5 am, I found the GOC standing outside the Operation Room and did not stop laughing at both of us. My resourceful wife had, in collusion with the Chief of Signals at Jammu staying next door, rung up my GOC to enquire how he had permitted his two staff officers to come home when the country was at war. The GOC told both of us that but for our stupidity, he would not have been scolded by her.

The story became known quite extensively when I went to serve in the Army Headquarters and even the Field Marshal Manekshaw came to know who promptly dubbed me to be a 'deserter'. The net result was that she became more known in the Army and by many of the senior generals. Her association with Major General D K Palit, while writing the history of Artillery of the Indian Army, became another reference point. Service Chiefs like Gen T S Raina,

General G G Bewoor, General Arun Vaidya, Gen Bipin Joshi, and Gen V P Malik, were known to her personally. With Lt General M L Chibber, the Northern Army Commander, she initiated the process of establishing the course on National Integration. It was established in the campus of the College of Military Engineering at Pune in the late 1980s and is a permanent feature of the effort by the Indian Army to train military personnel to achieve communal harmony. Such became her reputation that when I let it be known that I intended to leave the Army, the Field Marshal wanted to ascertain directly from her by going and seeing her at our Delhi home.

Even after I left the Armed Forces and joined the academia, Madhu's association with the services remained intact. Our daughter, Arpita grew up knowing celebrated Vice Chancellors, academics, the service chiefs and Army Commanders. As Madhu's terminal illness was diagnosed and slowly sapped her life, she was visited more by the service officer's families with the last visit by Gen V P Malik and his wife at our University home, just a day before she went into a coma. So her last memory remained embedded in her association with the Indian Army. She was a regimental wife and till the last day remained so. On the other hand, her illness made the team of doctors become family friends. Dr. S M S Mody, Director, N M Wadia Institute of Cardiology remained her personal physician and Dr. Nautej Singh, Dr Dayanad Shetty, Dr. Shivram Bonagary, Dr (Mrs) Swapna Bonagari and Dr C S Sharma, formed part of the team. My friend, late Dr. M J Joshi, former Dean of Medical Sciences, Pune University, assisted by his son, Dr Mukund Joshi operated in one of the most complex operations lasting for eleven hours and she walked out of the hospital sixteen days later and resumed work at Gujarat Vidyapith in six weeks after she was operated. I am told that it was a record of some sort. Even today, nearly eighteen years after she has passed away, the doctors and academic colleagues have continued to remain in contact with our daughter, Arpita and several of them have gone to visit her at Bangalore to see our granddaughter Tara, after she was born in 2009. While the loss of her very special cousin Piyush remained an open wound, yet Madhu never showed her grief at any stage nor did she share that grief ever with anyone.

As a Cultural Historian (1968–1996)

It is interesting to record how I saw Madhu developing into an Indian cultural historian. Assisted by her in-depth training in Sanskrit and later in Prakrit and Pali, she began examining the roots of Indian history through the conceptual lens of culture, tradition and oral history tradition. She started initiating a new dimension of subaltern history of India. She realised that most Indologists of her time were less historians and more students of Sanskrit language and hence lacked the methodological training in historical research. It must have come as an intellectual shock to her when she found how ungrounded the medieval and modern historians were in terms of relating their historical enquiries and recording without the moorings of culture and traditions, religion and practices and lastly without the temporal aspects which gives dynamics to any form of history. She became extremely critical of even the work of her celebrated historian uncle, Jaichand Vidyalankar. As a cultural historian, she could not find the root cause of conflict between different communities, the socio-cultural differences between various traditions and the near absence of any authentic record of oral history of a country that had so many forms of practicing religions.

It was this feeling of rootlessness which made her equally adamant and persuasive to understand the main currents of Indian history as a whole and the role of Ancient Indian History having a rich legacy of tradition, culture and practicing religions to make Hinduism a way of life and not a dogma. Though her doctoral work was based on a Jain text, which reflected the cultural, socio-political and religious practices of the period from the eighth to the eleventh century AD, Madhu had never, for the first twelve years of her professional career, dipped deep into Jainism or Buddhism. She, I suspect, remained confined to understanding the main currents of chronological history as available to create an empirical architecture of Ancient Indian History and Culture supported by hard facts of archaeology and numismatics. However, it is important to note that she initiated nearly a dozen M.Phil and selective Ph.D. researches to understand the larger context of cultural study of the region of Jammu and Kashmir, where apart from Islam, there existed a strong base of Shaivism in Jammu region and Buddhism in the Ladakh region. She began mapping the physical route that each of the religions took to reach the state of Jammu and Kashmir, which included the Ladakh region too.

Once this primary research was completed, she focused on the exact geographical expanse of operation of the culture and religion in that area. Very systematically, she started enquiring into the oral history of these regions to corroborate with the empirical evidence on ground. She realised that Jammu and Kashmir being a region of tourist attraction, it would be necessary to develop each iconic religious place as a tourist attraction and hence contribute towards the process of national integration and communal harmony. She went to great lengths to learn from me the theoretical aspects of Peace Research and Conflict Resolution of Western origin. Not being trained in political science did not pose any serious questions while inter phasing with culture and tradition. By 1976, when she joined me in Montreal, she wanted to study linguistics to use as a tool to explain culture and tradition. Her three years as a graduate student in the Department of Linguistics at McGill University gave her the worldview in cultural understanding and incorporate inter-disciplinary methodology for the rest of her academic career, which lasted till 1997.

After she was back in Jammu University in 1979, she began by focusing on Shaivism in Kashmir and exploring the possibilities of establishing the Centre for Buddhist Studies. Her focus was on the Ladakh region and she got the initial support from the state as well as from Governor Jagmohan. She even realised the possible turf war to occur with the Department of Sanskrit but nonetheless she incubated the whole process for nearly three years before returning back to the Department of History. She, in a light-hearted manner, once remarked to me that after having learnt Conflict Resolution theoretically she could not implement it operationally on the ground! However, she did manage to provide an operational model to convert iconic historical sites of ancient heritage into tourist attractions in and around Jammu with State Government patronage. By the late eighties, she had emerged as quite an authority on Jainism and Buddhism and it became an incentive to move away from the State of Jammu and Kashmir to the hub of Jain and Buddhist studies.

She moved to Gujarat Vidyapith in Ahmedabad as a Chair Professor of History in the early 1990s. She began developing the Department of History and laying the foundation of Buddhist studies apart from Jain studies. Ahmedabad provided both the academic and intellectual stimulus in the Gandhian institute. I think that in the surroundings of Gujarat Vidyapith, which was founded by Gandhiji, she first became wedded to Gandhian philosophy and way of life. It is in the association of Gandhian scholars like Professor Ram Lal Parikh, who was the Vice-Chancellor of Gujarat Vidyapith, and other Gandhian Scholars from around the country that she started to develop and give a new direction to the study of Ancient Indian History by incorporating and integrating the two mainstream religious philosophies prevalent in Ancient India, that is Buddhism and Jainism. Like she started mapping the route of Shaivism in Jammu and Kashmir, she started mapping the routes of Buddhism and Jainism in India to understand the roots of the cultural history of India. She even initiated an empirical study, which remained incomplete due to her untimely passing away, to ascertain the dating of Jainism in India as compared to Buddhism being established in India.

Since Gujarat Vidyapith had a Centre of Peace Studies and Peace Research, Madhu's next endeavour was the examination of the framework of Gandhian Peace Studies and integrating it with the traditions enunciated in Jainism and Buddhism. It took me a while to understand what she was upto since she started questioning me about the theoretical dimensions of 'power' contained in the Western political theory. She was, to my utter surprise, trying to integrate the sociology of the power of non-violence and peace contained in the main philosophy of Jainism and Buddhism with the modern concept of non-alignment propounded by Nehru. The powerful essay authored by K C Bhattacharya in 1931, entitled 'Swaraj in Ideas' influenced her. She started critically examining the work of Indian scholars on non-alignment and argued continuously as to how ancient Indian philosophy contained in the texts of Jainism and Buddhism, had not been studied well by the scholars of modern India to enrich the Nehruvian strategy of non-alignment. For her, non-alignment was not to initiate the process of isolationism to be practiced by the Indian nation state, but to spread the influence contained in the philosophy of Jainism and Buddhism to propagate universal peace by ensuring total disarmament of nuclear weapons in the twenty first century. In her perception, modern India had to resort to the spread of the philosophy of the ancient past for influencing the global worldview; regeneration of ethics and values to safeguard the dignity of life in an inclusive way where the East-West rivalry of domination and the North-South divide would vanish. I warned her of the utopian nature of her thinking, to which her stock answer was, 'One needs to incubate a great idea for the people and wait a couple of centuries to develop that idea to become culture nursed by tradition. One life is hardly enough to see the fruition'. She even had worked out the Ph.D. research topics that she intended to make her research students to take up for the next twenty years.

How then is one to assess the dormant as well as potential credibility of Madhu the cultural historian? In the abstract sense, it looked very plausible. Had she lived her full life for another three decades she definitely would have influenced the course of history by creating a school of thought important enough to be taken note of. However, Nature works in mysterious ways to incorporate natural actions needed for the survival of those checks and balances which have been observed in the complex mosaic of evolution and regeneration from the very beginning of time. Madhu remains, like all intellectuals, a minuscule part of the symphony of ideas in the concert of Nature. She definitely was well ahead of her time and perhaps one day some of her writings will find the way to generate influence to shape the minds of young and restless Indian scholars.

As a homemaker

As we got married in 1968, while I served in the IMA, including the most interesting part was that when I started distributing the wedding cards, in which the RSVP was the Commandant of IMA, the wives of my Regimental Centre and some of the senior officers' wives from the IMA decided to pay a visit to my would-be mother-in-law's home to ascertain if I was really getting married! None of them believed that I was the marrying type. However, our first home was in the Indian Military Academy where I was posted from 1967 to 1970. She joined me after she finished her Ph.D. from Banaras Hindu University in 1968. By the end of 1968, she joined the Jammu University and that was the end of our first combined home which lasted less than a year. At the IMA, she was looked upon with awe, being so educated and most of the service wives could not believe that she knew how to cook.

There were no LPG gas stoves then and hence were quite surprised to see her making a 'Chullah' out of a steel bucket with mud. It became a talking point in the ladies' club and the Commandant's wife came down to physically see what she had made. She became particularly close to General D K Palit, VrC, the Commandant and his wife. Gen Palit was a scholar soldier and had the right intellectual rapport with her. She helped him immensely while he was writing the History of the Artillery in the Indian Army. The associations that she curved out with the senior service officers during her stay at Dehradun and later while I served at the Army Head Quarters from 1972 to 1974 were phenomenal. Our permanent home became Jammu and Jammu University campus from 1968 to 1990. It gave her the chance not only to bloom as an academic, teacher and a researcher but also develop her love for growing roses. Her ground-level flat had a beautiful rose garden, which she maintained for nearly twenty two years. It exists in the Jammu University campus even today. Our daughter, Arpita was born in 1972.

By 1974, I took premature retirement from the Indian Army to go back to graduate studies at McGill and Carleton Universities in Canada followed by going over to University of Illinois at Urbana Champaign, Harvard and the Massachusetts Institute of Technology. She took a study leave from 1976 to 1979 and joined me while I was at McGill University. She joined and pursued a postgraduate degree programme in linguistics. These were the only three years of our twenty eight years of married life when we stayed together, along with our daughter in Montreal. As I moved to the US, she stayed with our daughter in Montreal till we decided to admit our daughter to the Whelms Girls High School at Dehradun in 1978 and till 1979, the three of us were in three different countries – Madhu in Montreal, Arpita in India and I in the US.

As a mother, she took the extremely hard decision put our daughter in the boarding school when she was only six years old. Madhu was still in Montreal when Arpita joined Welhams Girls School at Dehradun in 1978. She did not see her mother for a whole year and I did not see her till 1980. In my absence, Madhu would travel nearly every month to Dehradun to see her and literally helped her to continue remaining in the boarding school despite her frequent rebellions against it. But for her, Arpita would not have had the ability to stomach the life as a boarder and the accompanying loneliness. Even when she went to study law at the National Law School, Bangalore, Madhu was a constant source of courage for Arpita to put up with the pressures of being in a boarding school. She naturally created another record of some sort by being in boarding schools for seventeen continuous years from the age of five. She, I must admit, has grown up with the values of her mother, organised and with an eye for detail. She chose to marry her Law School class fellow and has become a better Kannadiga, with proficiency in the language as good as I am proficient in reading, writing and speaking in Punjabi despite being a Bengali. She is a good professional and represents quite a success story. Of course, she is eternally worried about her headstrong father who has preferred to live alone for the past nineteen years.

Our two homes first between two countries, then between two cities in India flourished well. There was adequate space for two of us pursuing two different academic careers. We sometime met quite by surprise in the same committees of the Government of India apart from conferences and seminars much to the amusement of our common academic colleagues, who saw us disagreeing with each other, sometimes quite vociferously. However, Madhu never allowed any professional disagreement to percolate to her home. I will end by saying that separation of all the years of our married life created better bonding and respect for each other. It was never a normal lifestyle, no matter how hard both of us tried to make it look. Her strong personality, passion for perfection, loyalty to the profession, and uncompromising attitudes towards values and ethics, made Madhu more than a traditional Indian wife or homemaker.

She was educated beyond doubt and faced life as an intellectual. You had to respect her because of the grace and aplomb with which she carried herself and invoked a total sense of loyalty in the hearts of those under her. Asha, barely twenty years old, joined our home as a housekeeper just a month before Madhu passed away and has looked after our home for the past twenty years with total dedication. Madhu's commitment towards the social mobilisation of the marginalised sections of society was total. Even at the last stage of her life, she clearly told me that she desired that Asha should become a part of our home and that I must take on the responsibility to look after her son and his education. Today, in Asha's family, her son has become the first graduate degree holder from Pune University but not without the quota of an amusing incident associated with the parenting of this young teenager, who thought that his mother, being uneducated could be taken for granted. Once when I was officiating as Vice-Chancellor of Pune University, this teenaged son ran away from school making me, the President of Spicer Memorial College, the Dean and the Spicer Memorial School Principal go hunting for him to find him playing cricket! However, I am satisfied that I have been able to keep my promise to Madhu and that at least this family, from the most downtrodden section of our society, has been uplifted to a decent status and own a home for themselves rather than living in slums.

What was amazing was the way her doctors conversed with her. Dr M J Joshi told her that despite all the skills that he had, being a world famous surgeon, he could not guarantee her survival. Her reaction was, 'Dr Joshi, you do not have to play God. Tell me whether your skill can give me a year and a half to finish my work.' Dr Joshi said, 'I promise you that.' And the good surgeon lived up to his promise. No one could say that she was unwell or had so little time to live after she underwent the massive surgery. All through the post-operative period, she worked as a workaholic. Travelling across the country, developing her Department at

Gujarat Vidyapith as a Centre of Excellence and bringing in huge grants from national funding agencies. She desired her body to be donated to the Medical college and did not desire even a traditional funeral. Swami Ranganathanandan, President of Ramakrishna Mission in Balur wrote, 'Madhu now becomes a member of a very elite class of human beings with a very modern mind.'

In Conclusion

It was a privilege to share a part of my life with her, an honour to know the multitude of people who respected and loved her and continue to do so even today. The intellectual legacy she leaves behind has the incorporation of the ancient Indian tradition of an anonymous author whose intellectual property can be used by every individual of society and whose mortal remains donated for furthering the growth of knowledge in the field of medicine, does not leave any ashes to immerse or preserve for posterity. I can dare to say that Madhu was a 'Wife to Reckon With' in every sense of the term.

She considered that my duty in an operational role must come first and there was no reason for me to visit home. After Prime Minister Indira Gandhi visited my formation on 30 November, 1971, my GOC called me on the evening of 3 December, 1971, and suggested that I should visit Jammu and see my family since my wife was expecting our first child.

A Wonderful Wife and My Dream Girl

Commander Arun Jjoti

Aparna understood the value of each penny and our responsibilities towards my widowed mother and sister. Our elder son, Akshay was born whilst I was sailing on the high seas somewhere in the Arabian Sea. She went through a painful surgery and the complications were severe. I reached ten days after Akshay was born and I found her composed, smiling and brave as ever. Not even for a moment did she complain of her hardships and the difficulties of undergoing a difficult pregnancy at my home and sans the comfort of her own mother's home.

The rickety Military Ambulance started moving slowly from the Military Hospital at National Defence Academy, Khadakwasla, Pune on a sultry July afternoon in 1989. The military driver and his buddy were carefully instructed by the Army doctor just after the patient had been carried into the ambulance. They were told not to drive fast and ensure that the ambulance did not shake and jump. The journey from the National Defence Academy to the Military Hospital, Kirkee, Pune took almost two hours. Lying still on a stretcher in the hot and humid cabin of the ambulance, I wondered about the events that had happened over the last fifteen months. The future did not worry me as I was too engrossed in the thoughts of the past.

I was a medical stream student in my school days at Rohtak. Like any other medical stream student, I too dreamt of becoming a doctor. My small town of those years boasted of a medical college and its students were my role models. My father, however, had another dream with me as the chief protagonist. He kept on challenging me to join the Indian Armed Forces and especially the prestigious National Defence Academy (NDA). To insinuate my focus, he allowed me to watch Shashi Kapoor's "*Vijeta*" (which depicted life at NDA) and even rented a VCR at home to showcase the Hollywood Navy classic '*An Officer and a Gentlema*'. The persistent nudges and cudgels led to my joining the NDA in the autumn term of 1988, leaving my passion, the medical college, behind. Soon, time started to fly and I was reaching the end of the second term when the news of my father's untimely demise arrived at NDA. It shook my entire world. Amidst all the twists and turns of life, the shaky start to the third term was an ominous sign. My legs felt weak each day and my personal pressures and emotions left me high and dry. It was on one such July morning that I got waylaid by some senior cadets into an ambush of ragging and the result of the encounter were multiple fractures in my neck and lower back.

I was taken to the Military Hospital, Khadakwasla by my mates and soon the wet film of the X-ray revealed my grievous injury. My right hand and right leg were operating sluggishly and the Military Hospital, Khadakwasla decided to evacuate me to the Military Hospital, Kirkee, Pune (MH, Kirkee). The ambulance arrived at MH, Kirkee and the attendants from NDA soon wheeled me into the paraplegic ward. As I lay forlorn on the iron bed with a plaster from my head to my waist, I wondered and debated about the happenings in the past. Destiny had another choice left for me.

The recovery from the injury was a long-drawn process and I lived it in the company of IPKF Officers who were also admitted with me due to their war casualties from war-torn Sri Lanka. Captain Jerry was on my neighbouring bed in the ward and every morning he would move his stumped right arm and exclaim, 'Tomorrow shall be better.' Tomorrow indeed turned out to be better. As days and months passed, I lay on the same bed and prayed hard for recovery to fulfil my father's dream.

The miraculous recovery was followed by my experimental return to the NDA, albeit with many restrictions to my movements. Inspiration from my mates at the Foxtrot Squadron, NDA, saw me regaining my full strength and vigour. Soon, the time came when I passed out of the penultimate term of NDA and reached Rohtak for the term break. I kept on thinking hard as to why I faced those hardships and why had I left my lucrative seat at medical college to join the NDA? The answers were not coming forth and destiny was not giving me a clue either.

Finally, the time came for me to board the NDA Special Train to join the final term of the course. However, a plan by some of my mates saw us enjoying an extra day at home and we missed the NDA Special train to board the Goa Express from New Delhi to Pune. My mother was in tears as she bid me farewell at the Hazrat Nizamuddin Station. I was also getting emotional, as finally I was going to fulfil my late father's dream of passing out of the NDA, against all odds and the life-threatening injury and physical constraints.

Just before the train moved, a pretty damsel came and took a seat opposite mine. I did notice her but I was too deep in thought to think of striking a conversation with her. She was Aparna Sengupta, who was moving to Pune to join the Spicer Memorial College for the first time. Aparna was accompanied by her mother and maternal uncle. I gave a passing look to the family which was being seen off at the station by a Sikh family. The train moved and soon the family was engaged by the chirpy NDA Cadets. Aparna's mother was from the Sailo clan of Mizoram ruling tribe and a magnanimous personality. I was too engrossed in my thoughts and did not engage with the family till the train moved into the Jhansi station.

At Jhansi, I had my first hard glimpse of Aparna and I was struck by her shy demeanour and calmness. Now I knew that my delay at the NDA was for her. Soon, I entered into a light conversation with the family and we exchanged notes about our respective lives. The journey spanned to the next day and the train entered Pune station. As we departed, I told Aparna's mother that in case of any problems I would be around to help her. I looked back as I moved towards the NDA truck to take me back to the Academy, but, for sure, a part of me was left behind.

Two days went by and we had just got back from a cross-country run when I got the message that I had some guests at the NDA main gate. The main gate is located about two km away from the Foxtrot Squadron. I cycled to the NDA gate and to my surprise, I found Aparna and her mother waiting for me. My happiness knew no bounds as I escorted them to my Squadron and showed them around the NDA. Her mother was leaving the next day and she had come to thank me for making their journey from Delhi to Pune comfortable. I reiterated my promise to take care of her well within my limited capacities as a NDA cadet but I was firmly convinced that I had found the answer to life's tosses and turns which had catapulted me from a medical college to the NDA.

Ten days later, at the first available opportunity, I requested my Divisional Officer for a liberty visit to Pune. In the NDA parlance, as any other Military Academy, a day off is known as 'Liberty'. He was an affable officer and jokingly asked me my requirement, as prior to that I had hardly gone out of the Academy on liberties. I told him the truth. He shook his head, smiled and told me to follow my instincts. On a rainy day, I reached Aparna's college and met her and her classmates. We spent a couple of hours together and it was time for me to go back. I did go back to NDA but I knew that I had a confession to make and it had to be done fast. My gut feeling was that I had found my answers and I had to do the right things. The next opportunity to visit Aparna's college arose after almost a month of joining the final term at NDA.

I reached her college and met her at the hostel. She looked absolutely graceful as monsoon clouds built overhead. As we walked and sat in an open cafeteria, I told her that I wanted to tell her something. The words were not coming but somehow I mustered enough courage and asked her to wait for me for the next four years. She asked for what? Finally, the words flew out of my heart and I said that I wanted to get married to her. We were both smiling as she nodded in the affirmative. She was seventeen and I was touching twenty one. Thus began a wonderful journey of togetherness, happiness, sharing and caring.

Time flew past as we both departed. I passed out of NDA and moved for my further training with the Indian Navy. Those were the days when the most robust way of communicating was handwritten letters. Telephone connections were, costly and rare. We kept in touch with each other through letters and rare phone calls. After my naval training, I joined the Naval College of Engineering at Lonavala for my degree course. We had known each other for almost a year now and it seemed like yesterday. Aparna's mother came to meet me and I expressed my wish to her. This was the day when I took another decision. I knew that it would be difficult for me to complete my engineering course if Aparna stayed at Pune. So I requested her to go back to Manipur and wait for me to finish my degree. This was the time when she willingly made the first of the sacrifices for me and our future.

The sixty-km distance between Lonavala and Pune soon multiplied into a 2,500 km distance between Lonavala and Moreh, Manipur. The long-distance separation also meant slower communication as letters took almost two to three weeks to get exchanged and phones were non-existent. There is a popular adage in the Navy which says that time and tide does not wait for anyone. Sometimes, this works in one's favour too. Time soon flew by and I reached the final year of my engineering course and time was now ripe for me to fulfil my promise.

The events prior to our marriage on 25 May 1995, were dramatic and exciting. Hailing from diverse backgrounds, we both had nothing in common. Despite the odds, our respective families came around the 'two-states' barrier to bless our union and soon we scaled the biggest tide of our life and were united in soul and spirit. Thus began our journey of marital life. Aparna was left behind in my hometown, Rohtak as I moved onto my first ship, the mighty Aircraft Carrier Viraat for the sea training phase, two weeks after our wedding. Coming from a different culture and background, Aparna found herself alone in my rustic hometown. She had to adjust to the new environment, new people, new culture and even to new food habits. She began a journey that many would dare not undertake.

Our acquaintance was more through letters than regular meetings. We knew each other through our respective imaginations and now we were coming around to know each other thoroughly. I found her to be absolutely calm, pleasant, shy, always smiling and with a big heart. I just had a Bajaj Chetak scooter, a music system, ten pairs of jeans and three suitcases of belongings to call my own. The 'two-states' wedding meant that we both were on our own in this big, bad world. On finishing my training on board the Aircraft Carrier, I moved for my Specialisation Training at Jamnagar. Upon reaching Jamnagar, I informed my Assistant Course Officer about my wedding. He readily permitted me to make her join the Naval Base and promised to arrange accommodation for us. I immediately booked Aparna on a train bound for Jamnagar from New Delhi.

As she reached the New Delhi railway station, the AC Coach in which she was supposed to travel was found to be malfunctioning. The journey till Jamnagar was completed by her in a general compartment and I found her smiling and happy as I picked her up from the station along with another course mate. She was amused when she saw that the Ambassador taxi that I had hired to bring her back to the base was standing on top of a small hillock. The car needed a push start and as the driver saw us, he rolled the rickety Ambassador down the hillock and her engine fired. The firing of the engine also fired our lives as we moved in to the Base. We both were welcomed by my course mates and friends and thus began our journey of action and high drama.

Effective communication is an art and I got my first lesson in clear communication to clear all doubts at this stage. A couple of days later, my venerable Assistant Course Officer took me to the Executive Officer (Second-In-Charge) of the Base, to get an accommodation granted to me. On explaining the situation, the Executive Officer had a hard look at me and asked me who had granted me the permission to get married? I explained that I had informed my previous base and the issues in insurgency-prone Manipur, where Aparna's family was facing trouble as an ethnic battle had started raging. He then asked me how I could get married as a Sub-Lieutenant when the minimum rank at which an officer could get married was that of a Lieutenant. He lost his temper and blasted the Course Officer and sought written explanations from both of us. He even granted me ten days' leave to drop Aparna back home and I was told to leave the Base by evening. Confused and worried, both my Course Officer and I came out of the Executive Officer's chamber and did not know what had hit us. The PA was listening to the episode inside and he came out of his chamber and told us that in the previous Course, a foreign Officer had brought in an Indian girl and declared her as his wife. At the end of the Course, he dumped the girl inside the Base and flew back. The Executive Officer had faced a lot of flak for the issue and the Base which had a long tradition of helping young Officers to marry, had suddenly reverted its policies. The PA exclaimed that I was the first victim, as in my case, I looked different from Aparna.

The news spread inside the Base and my Course Officer and I were struggling to find a solution. Aparna said that she had no hassles in going back to Rohtak and wait till we were granted permission. We both prepared for our departure to Delhi as missing the Course could lead to more issues of qualification. My course mates ran around to find a seat in the first available train and Aparna and I sat with bated breath as we had to vacate the Mess premises latest by 10pm. The collective wisdom of my course mates came up with various solutions. A stay in town in a rented accommodation or a hotel check-in were all discussed, but the flip-side was the limited economic ability to meet such a challenge.

All through this passing phase, I could see Aparna continuing with her silent prayer and composure. At 6 pm, a senior under training Officer knocked on our room door. He said that he had made a room ready in his house for our stay. He had gone to the Executive Officer and told him that Aparna was his sister and she would be staying with his family. The Executive Officer, though very upset, permitted the stay but only till we got a confirmed train travel to New Delhi. We shifted to Lieutenant Harpal Sandher's small accommodation, which their family willingly shared with us. Soon, we both were on a train to New Delhi. Aparna held my hand and requested me to complete my training at the earliest. I looked into her eyes and saluted her positive approach towards life. She had started mellowing me down from my fire brand Aries image and she was silently teaching me to widen my perspective.

We reached Rohtak and all my relatives and neighbours were happy to see Aparna back because in her limited stay at Rohtak, she had built bonds of love and respect with each of my family members and neighbours. We stay in a Punjabi neighbourhood and every one would tell me, 'Teri votti vaddi changi hai. Sabnu vaddi izzat daindi hai. Saanu vhi ais vargi nooh chaidi hai.' (*Your wife is very nice. She respects everyone. We also want a daughter-in-law like her*). Aparna willingly sacrificed her comforts and was gelling around with everyone. In my three-day stay at Rohtak, I saw her cooking food as per requirements of my Brahmin family, cleaning and setting the house in order. She would always be up and about and her energy levels were tremendous. A big smile always shone on her face and she welcomed each and every chore that my folks asked her to do. I was to leave back for Jamnagar on the fourth day and the monsoons were in full swing. Suddenly, a devastating flood hit Rohtak. The city got submerged in a deluge and soon the water entered our house too. The training curriculum did not permit me to stay back. I evacuated my mother, sister and Aparna to my relative's house at Delhi and shaped course for Jamnagar. As the train moved out of the station, Aparna's charming face faded away into the sea of humanity and once again we got back to our letter-writing days.

I joined back the training and kept the sunny side up. Finally, the time came for my promotion to the rank of a Lieutenant. As I marched into the Commanding Officer's chamber, the Executive Officer was also present. The Navy's tradition is to receive the Rank Stripe from the Commanding Officer, go out, wear the new Rank and then come back to salute the Commanding Officer. As I came back and smartly saluted the Commanding Officer, he wished me good luck in my next rank and enquired about my family's well-being. The Executive Officer explained my unique 'Two States' situation, including the floods in my hometown and simmering Manipur and requested the Commanding Officer to permit me a married accommodation. The Commanding Officer gave his approval but due to some reason, no houses were available inside the Base. A Sri Lankan Naval Officer was moving out for a five-month sea phase on a ship at Kochi and he offered me a stay in his vacant house. Soon, Aparna was back and we both opened the house to realise that it was just a house with bare minimum furniture and a gas stove. All the other items had been given by the Sri Lankan Officer to one of his country mates who had also moved into the Base for his training. Aparna looked at my financial status which had almost nil reserves. She requested me to take her to the Jamnagar town where she bought two aluminium utensils and two spoons along with two plates. She got the names '*ARUN-APARNA*' inscribed on them and thus we started building up our assets.

We were the first couple amongst the Under-Trainee officers and soon our house was being raided at all odd hours by batch mates in the true tradition of the Indian Armed Forces. Aparna would willingly and happily cook for the raiders and she remained ever popular amongst my batch mates. She continued to manage brilliantly within our limited kitchen assets and was a wonderful cook. One day, two of my ex-NDA batch mates realised that we both never ate with them and they saw our limited kitchen. They both went away and the next day they raided our house again but with a full dinner set and pressure cooker as gifts for Aparna's bravery. Our assets became bigger and we now needed a steel trunk to keep our growing household.

The five months of Base Training soon came to an end and it was time for me to move to other bases for joint trainings and then join a ship for the sea qualifying phase. I had to again leave Aparna at Rohtak as Manipur continued to simmer. We were expecting our first child and Aparna had to be left behind at Rohtak. The tight training schedule does not permit leave and the tight finances do not permit frequent travel either. Aparna understood the value of each penny and our responsibilities towards my widowed mother and sister. She managed at Rohtak and our elder son, Akshay was born whilst I was sailing on the high seas somewhere in the Arabian Sea. She painstakingly went through a painful surgery and the complications were severe. I reached ten days after Akshay was born and I found her composed, smiling and brave as ever. Not even for a moment did she complain of her hardships and difficulties of undergoing a difficult pregnancy at my home and sans the comfort of her own mother's home.

Soon, we both joined back at Jamnagar for the last six months of training, but this time around we had a young child with us. I went through the grind and rigmarole of training and Aparna single-handedly took care of little Akshay. She would never wake me up as my studies and trysts with activities of the base kept me engaged. Slowly, she was building up our home with my limited salary. Our house kept on getting raided and Aparna was always cherubic and happy to welcome the raiders. The Navy was bent on testing me and posted me to Mumbai after my base training. Mumbai was a difficult station vis-a-vis the accommodation. Hence to get an accommodation and to augment my finances, I joined the Submarines. This meant a move to Visakhapatnam which offered an affordable house and also a chance to get the Submarine salary which was almost twenty five per cent of my overall salary.

The Submarines are 'Iron Coffins' and the Submarines call themselves 'Bubble Heads'. My Submarine was breaking out of a long repair programme and the routine was difficult. Visakhapatnam was still a simple, Andhra town and the new city was breaking out. Aparna was left behind in an unknown town with an unknown language as my Submarine became operational and clocked maximum days at sea. I became a bearded Submariner, would enter our home all sweaty and smelling of diesel, for a short rejuvenation, before setting out again. Little Akshay and Aparna managed their lives on their own in my absence. Aparna kept on adding to our household inventory and the nest became warmer and warmer as hay kept on adding slowly. Submarines and Navy kept us engaged and after fourteen months of stay we shifted to our first Naval Accommodation in Visakhapatnam. Aparna was by now grappling with an acute migraine problem but silently bore the painful attacks.

In 2004, we were expecting our second child and I was posted at the Naval Shipyard in Visakhapatnam. The Command desired to sail all the premier warships based at the Eastern Naval Command.

My department was in the middle of hectic schedules and I was managing many ships as they prepared to meet the targets. The repairs were being expedited and my shop floors and test beds were full of machines as my workers rejuvenated them to meet the operational targets. The situation so emerged that there was only one more officer other than me in my big 400-plus workers' department. I managed the shop floor affairs and he was running from ship to ship to get the equipment going on board. Finally, the day came when the ships had to cast off and I had gone home for only a few hours since the last week.

Five of the premier warships were being buttoned up and my mobile rang. Aparna was not feeling well and my neighbour was moving her to the Navy hospital. I promised that I would be with her soon. The fire fighting of the service continued and I got a call after two hours and the neighbour wanted me to reach hospital at the earliest as she had developed complications. The last of the two big warships cast away and I swung my jeep towards the Navy Hospital. Aparna was inside the operation theatre and I was told to sign the mandatory papers. Five months into the pregnancy and she had a miscarriage. As she was wheeled out, I held her hand and the brave fighter told me not to worry. We were both distraught and I was cursing myself for not being able to avoid the situation. Aparna consoled me and took this major setback as a decision of the Almighty. She fought well and took charge of her life again.

Our second child, Agastaya was born in 2005 and this time around, I was standing in my Naval Uniform to welcome her and the little one to our world. Aparna had bound my family together and our two little boys became our best assets. Surviving on our own, Aparna had built up our full house and she decorated our house and lives with her vivid imagination and creative abilities. Dignified in her mannerisms and binding in her outlook, Aparna kept pace with my professional life. With each day, she kept on strengthening the bond between our families. She became a pillar of strength for my family.

A few years later, I was selected to join the prestigious Defence Services Staff College at Wellington, Nilgiris. Aparna's mother was battling a rare cancer and she had to keep one toe at Manipur and another at Wellington. Catching late noon flights out of Imphal with three-year-old Agastaya, she would change airports at New Delhi and then reach Wellington in late at night. The next day, she would be up and about early, to take care of the house and meet social commitments. We were a socially and academically active couple at Wellington and performed to our best as per the requirements of the magnificent Joint Services Institution. Aparna's cheerful gait and well-polished mannerisms earned us lifelong friends in the entire course and across the Services spectrum. During one of the NDA Squadron get-togethers, we felt the need to connect to my Squadron types. On 22 Mar 2008, we formed a web-based Fox Group of the alumni of the Foxtrot Squadron, NDA. The group started from a humble twenty three members and today it has crossed 1,350 members.

The last six years made me see the rare side of Aparna. She put all her requirements and desires on the backburner as I toiled in my tenures and also my passion for building the Fox Group. We organised large Fox Jams at various locations within India and abroad. The culminating social of each year happens in New Delhi wherein ex-Foxies converge from diverse locations worldwide. These get-togethers bring back nostalgic times and memories as many alumni touch base with each other after decades. The beauty of these socials is the ever-widening generation gap. The members are spread six decades apart as of now. It is a great feeling when a twenty-two-year old, young Army Lieutenant shakes hands with an eighty-three-year old retired Lt General. I could not have been able to capture these mesmerising events had Aparna not stood solidly behind me and helped in my efforts to build up the Fox Group.

Our bonding has been a unique experience of humanity and its beauty. It started from a glance, moved on to a commitment and then we united against all odds. We began from two utensils, two plates, and two spoons and today we have built a house of our own at Gurgaon. The icing on the cake is the vast and ever-nostalgic Fox Network, which brings many people together and spreads the bonhomie and *joie de vivre* across the world's spectrum. Aparna has been right beside me in all my endeavours and a pillar of strength, youth and vigour for me. Her careful and watchful nudges ensure that I still run and play actively to maintain a healthy lifestyle. We leave our impact on many lives that we touch and we connect to make lives happy. Each and every person coming to our house is treated like a part of us and I have learnt to respect and honour humanity from the warmth that Aparna leaves in each heart she meets.

One life is not enough to savour this journey of togetherness, happiness and bliss. Each morning, as I see her lovely face, I get the feeling that this is just the beginning. We have a long way to go and I will keep holding Aparna's hand in this beautiful journey where challenges are surmountable with happiness and blessings from the Almighty. I met Aparna on that fateful train journey in 1991. She struck me as my answer to all my questions to my fate till then. She began a journey of togetherness with me and held my hand with her faith in the most trying times. Those moments of sadness and happiness are etched in my memory forever. It has been like a song and I wish that I still have miles to go with Aparna. Kahlil Gibran had said, 'To be able to look back upon one's life with satisfaction, is to live twice.' I could not agree more with these wonderful words. I would love to live this life over and over again with Aparna-My Wonderful Wife.

Our bonding has been a unique experience of humanity and its beauty. It started from a glance, moved on to a commitment and then we united against all odds. We began from two utensils, two plates, and two spoons and today we have built a house of our own at Gurgaon.

THE STORY OF MY WIFE

Vineet Mathur

'We had been married for just about two months and a cousin of mine arranged for a one-room house on rent. We moved into the house with half a dozen cardboard boxes, wooden packing cases and a couple of steel trunks. Soon enough, using her ingenuity, Charu had converted each of them into tables, settee, and side board. With the purchase of a few more pieces of furniture, she managed to convert the house into our first home. She had brought along a lot of her paintings and embroidery, and when she had finished setting up everything, our home did not look bad at all!'

The year was 1984. I had passed out from the Delhi College of Engineering in 1983, cleared the Combined Engineering Services exam conducted by UPSC, and was working with Uptron during the interim period till I got a posting in the Department of Telecommunications. For an Electronics and Telecom Engineer, the opportunity to work in DOT was manna from heaven, not only because we got an opportunity to work in the core telecom sector, but also because it was a prestigious job in the public sector, with no private telecom companies on the horizon yet.

Born in an upper-middle class family, I was the only offspring of my father, who was working in the Home Ministry and my mother was a homemaker. Happy in the knowledge that their son had become an engineer and would soon join DOT, the next logical step for them was to find a suitable match for me and get me married. I am pretty sure this subject would have occupied a large part of any conversation they would have had with their friends and family, since in our community, people consider it their right and privilege to seek or suggest suitable matches for their sons and daughters.

I entered the scene quite at the end of the exercise, when I had to make the final choice from the shortlisted, shall we say, 'candidates'. I was quite uncomfortable with the idea of choosing somebody from a list to be my wife. Moreover, my parents would have certainly put in a great deal of thought before suggesting somebody to me, so who was I to question their wisdom?

Charu's name was suggested by somebody very close to both our families. Charu's father was a renowned ENT surgeon, settled in Dehradun. Her mother was a homemaker. She had completed M.Sc in Home Science, a gold medalist from Agra University, and was teaching Home Science in the prestigious Oak Grove School in Mussoorie.

Things started moving at a fast pace. To cut a long story short, Charu visited us in Delhi along with her parents, the alliance was fixed, with the engagement in December 1984. The wedding was fixed for November of the following year. While our parents chatted with each other, I took Charu out for lunch. I was nervous as hell, and I am sure she was too! We went to a restaurant in Connaught Place, and started talking to get to know each other. The first thing that we discovered about each other was that we were not great talkers, even after discounting the fact that the occasion was quite unsettling for both of us. And then a minor disaster followed – when the bill came, I realised that I had forgotten to bring my wallet! Keeping a straight face, I had to ask Charu to pay the bill, and this was only the first meal we had together. She would have a great story to tell to her parents when she got back! What a huge embarrassment. To this day, I do not have the heart to ask her about the reaction of her family!

Dehradun used to be a quaint little town in the eighties. A typical hill station, where life went on at a leisurely pace, night fell early and the primary mode of entertainment was either watching TV or visiting friends and relatives. Charu's father had set up his clinic, and was quite well known in the city. So well known, in fact, that it became a source of amusement for all of us, when I visited them in the later part of 1984, after we had got engaged.

Charu's parents told me that there was a wildlife park just on the outskirts of the city, and suggested why don't I take Charu out for a drive. An alternative suggested was to go see a movie. We chose the former, and I borrowed his scooter and left for the park. When we returned, there were knowing smiles from her parents and her brother, and I realised that they knew the exact route that we had taken! It transpired that the moment we had left home, her father started getting calls from his friends as well as his patients, who wanted to know who this person was, driving his scooter with his daughter riding pillion!

Charu's mother was a down-to-earth, modest, friendly, fun-loving person and an excellent cook. She, as well as Dr. Kumar, Charu's father, were very easy going people and they both had the ability to connect with people. Above all, they were extremely humble. They could talk about their accomplishments in a matter of fact manner, without a hint of pride, or about their shortcomings without being embarrassed. I can recall that there was only one phrase which Charu's mother used for her when we first met, and it was that Charu is a person who was a resolute individual, *'apni dhun ki pakki'*, as we say in hindi.

Both her parents carried a lot of positive energy and sunshine with them, and I am fortunate that Charu had imbibed all their goodness and brought it into our lives.

Charu has inherited her sensitive nature, keen aesthetic sense and a responsible nature from her parents. But above all, it is her inherent nature to make everyone around her feel comfortable and at ease that makes, her an adorable person.

I had to undergo eight months of probation after joining the Department of Telecom, and we arrived in Pune in January, 1986. We had been married for just about two months and a cousin of mine arranged for a one room house on rent. We moved into the house with half a dozen cardboard boxes, wooden packing cases and a couple of steel trunks, and soon enough, using her ingenuity, Charu had converted each of them into tables, settee, and side board.

With the purchase of a few more pieces of furniture, she managed to convert the house into our first home. She had brought along a lot of her paintings and embroidery, and when she had finished setting up everything, our home did not look so bad after all.

Charu had worked as a science teacher in prestigious schools in Mussoorie and Dehradun, had been financially independent, and was living a comfortable life till now. And now she was in a totally new city without her job and friends, a small house with not many comforts, made livable by her own creativity. But she did not complain. Not even when we had guests at home, and we had to sleep in the kitchen. Her parents came to visit us, and stayed for a few days. I am sure they would have liked to see us enjoying a more comfortable life, but I could discern that such material trappings did not bother them a bit, and all that they cared for was that we were happy.

It was the first time that both of us were living far away from our home of so many years, and had to manage our lives ourselves. My mother, being relatively more conservative, believed that it was the duty of the womenfolk to do all the housework, and, as Charu would sometimes tease me – would not allow even me to get even a glass of water for myself. Honestly, I also found that quite illogical, but since it was to my advantage, was not against such theories!

Charu's parents had encouraged her to be independent, and at the same time, shoulder responsibilities which came her way. Charu found it quite amusing that my mother would always be at the beck and call of both my father and me, and happily too. This was a big change from how her parents led their lives, caring for each other, and at the same time, not being excessively obtrusive. She would joke about all such misdemeanors of mine, but did not ever make a big issue out of it. Slowly but confidently, she went about the task of putting together our home, as only the lady of the house can.

We have been fortunate to straddle a tectonic shift in technology, culture, values, and most importantly, relationships – from Vespa to SUV's, telegrams to SMS, Beatles to Lady Gaga, friendships to live-in relationships. Every generation carries its own baggage, and is loathe to discard any of it. Your real test is what do you pass on to the next generation.

Ankur, our son, was born five years later and on the same date as our marriage. Since then, we have been pestered by everybody for going to such extremes to save on a party. Ankur was extremely naughty and quite a handful during his childhood. Charu had minored in Child Development during her post-graduation and the standing joke between us was that her University had designed a tailor-made practical exam in the form of Ankur, which she had to undergo for the next five to six years. Ankur's favourite pastime was to throw things out of the window, and he was not partial to any particular type of object, nor to any type of relationship we had with those whom those things belonged to. People used to take advance action when they knew that we were to visit them, and the action was similar to what they would do in case of floods – leave things which are heavy enough not to be washed away on the floor, everything else should be either tied to the floor, or moved to a higher level so that it cannot be reached.

Bringing up Ankur was one of the most gratifying periods of our lives. It was also one of the most grueling ones. He was very attached to my mother, who was staying with us after my father expired. With his antics and typical childish gibberish, Ankur had easily wrapped his grandmother around his little finger. But his mother he could not. She pampered him like any mother would, but that never came in the way of discipline, and Ankur understood that. Of course, he had his own tricks of the trade to disarm her, and would not hesitate to use his charm when things got rough. The scene would play out like this – Charu would be carrying Ankur in her arms and doing window shopping, while he scanned the space within his range to launch his attack. He notices a girl of his age with long tresses, comfortable in her mother's arms, grabs her hair and starts to pull. The law of physics kicks in, the action invites instant reaction from both the mothers. After dealing with a crying infant and a furious mother, Charu glares at Ankur, and without uttering a word, conveys her anger. Ankur would simply widen his eyes, look down and hold her even more tightly – case dismissed. As Ankur grew up and realised the power of words, after such an incident, he would look at Charu and ask her 'tum mujhse naraaz ho kya?', 'Are you angry with me?'

Ankur holds a special place in her heart. Even at times when he is away, her instincts know exactly what is going on in his mind. There is a sort of telepathy going on between them, and many a times, she would call up Ankur and talk to him, only to be told by him that he was about to call up and discuss the same matter.

True teachers are those who teach not just a subject, but expand the horizon of their students and develop in them a passion for acquiring, assimilating and using that knowledge gainfully. Charu seems to have what it takes to be a good teacher, which is why she could easily switch roles from being a home science teacher to a science teacher and then to teaching Hindi to American students, and finally teaching 21st century skills to children.

Charu's role as a teacher did not end when she came back from school. She would spend innumerable hours making Ankur learn the subjects, complete his homework and generally help him in completing whatever the school required him to do. Of course, given the exuberant nature and attention span of Ankur, there would be short periods of teacher – student interaction, followed by long spans of extra-curricular activities comprising of pleadings, threats and running around. Akin to *Guru Dakshina*, after each such session, Ankur would have given his mom, the power of patience and endurance.

In March 2005, I was transferred to Assam. Being a hardship area, it was a tenure posting of two years. It was a crucial time for Ankur, since he would be taking his board exams for 10th Std. After a few months. he would have to apply for admission in another school for 11th Std. since this school was only upto 10th Std. It is a done thing for people in situations like this to apply for postponing their transfer, however ridiculous it may sound. Many of my colleagues and friends suggested doing so. Charu and me thought about it for a few days, and finally decided that I should take up the new posting. While I was away, Ankur gave his exams, while Charu took care of all the paperwork running around to see that he got admission in a good college for completing his high school. She would feel mighty stressed at times, but at no point in time did she ask me to take leave and help her during this period.

Charu used to drive to her school on her fifty cc moped, which was quite a popular vehicle in Pune during the late eighties. It was gifted to her by my father when she joined as a science teacher in a school. The school worked in two shifts, and when she joined school a few months after Ankur was born, she opted for the morning shift, so that she could be at home with Ankur for the rest of the day. Before leaving for school early in the morning, she made sure that most of the chores were done, so that my mother did not have to bother too much about the daily household routine, and could keep an eye on the immensely likeable, but naughty brat.

For Charu, running the household, looking after her family and her responsibility towards her students were never a question of either this – or that option. In her mind, each had its own importance and value, and the wisdom lay in carrying out all of these duties without compromise. It also followed that since it was her decision to lead her life in a particular way, the entire responsibility lay with her, and she never took the recourse of choosing or prioritising one over the other. She has always given attention to things that really matter in her life – her home, family, her kith and kin and her friends.

It was Sunday, 23 November, 2008. As was our routine for the past twenty years, Dr. Pravin Joshi, Mr. Mishra and I were playing a round of tennis. I had known Pravin, a doctor by profession, but more like a brother to me, for quite some time, and Mr. Mishra had joined us sometime back. Suddenly, I felt a severe pain in my chest. Assuming it to be a bout of cramps, I rested for a while and went back to play. The pain increased, and I told Dr. Joshi that there was something seriously wrong. He immediately bundled me into his car, gave me medicines and rushed me to the hospital. I had enough energy left to call up, not home, but my neighbor telling him to inform Charu that I was getting admitted to the hospital and in all probability, had suffered a heart attack. I do not know why, but I knew that I would pull through this. However, I was more concerned about what Charu would go through when she heard about this. I cannot describe the relief that I felt on seeing her and my son Ankur by my side.

Dr. Shirish Hiremath put me through the required tests and declared that there were multiple blockages in the arteries and I would have to undergo angioplasty immediately. Putting up a brave front, and facing the situation with a balanced frame of mind, she went about doing all that was required to be done for the surgery. She did not let even an iota of emotion show up on her face, as she went about getting everything organised. Even with all the turmoil within her, I did not, for a moment, see her flustered. She has this ability to be able to see the big picture, and then zoom in to focus on the minute details. While I was still in the hospital recuperating from my surgery, she would not only be juggling her responsibilities at home and by my bedside, but also keep a very close watch on things which could disturb me and get my heart rate up. She conspired with all those who were visiting me not to utter a word about the terrorist attack in Mumbai, which had started on 26 November, and somehow avoided putting on the news channels for those couple of days. However, she arranged to celebrate our wedding anniversary on 27 November, and that certainly worked in lifting the mood of everybody.

During the next few months, while I was recuperating, she would keep a close on me, manage her job, our son's routine, the household chores and social commitments. She kept an eagle's eye on what I was eating, and developed expertise on extolling the virtues of extremely healthy but unpalatable and insipid stuff. Armed with her home science degree, she would always win an argument about the advantages of green vegetables and broth over a meal of fried 'poories' and tandoori chicken. But it was because of all that that my arteries are as clear as new and my heart can withstand a vigorous jog every morning.

Very often, Charu used to mention that she was awestruck by lady doctors, and dreamt of becoming one herself, but God saw that she could not stand the pain of others and therefore did not destine it to be. Seeing me undergo a major life-saving surgery was frightening enough, but I can realise the agony she was undergoing beneath her cool façade every day, till I was able to return to my normal routine.

I believe that destiny, the supreme force, or whatever one calls it, plays a major part in what one does with one's life. We only assume that we know our strengths and weaknesses, and that we can shape our future as we want it to be. Somebody up there knows exactly what we are capable of, and when he sees that we have been in our comfort zone for too long, he picks us up and throws us in the deep end, with the belief that we have the capability to survive.

It was the summer of 2011, and Charu had just returned after completing a six-month long 'International Leaders in Education Program' at Kentucky University. This Fulbright-Foundation-funded programme recognises that teachers not only prepare future leaders, but they are leaders in their own right. It provides them the domain knowledge of the latest advances in pedagogy, the necessary motivation and confidence to go back to their countries and bring about a quantum change in their education system and align it with the requirements of the world of tomorrow.

Within a few days of her return, she was informed that she had been selected for the Advanced Space Academy@ NASA Program at Kennedy Space Center, Florida. She had already completed the Basic course of NASA Space Academy for Educators' Program In 2008, and now she was raring to go and use the newly acquired skills to invigorate and enthuse her young students to learn science, not from chapters in a book, but by relating it to space science and technology. Upon her return from NASA, she applied for, and got funding from the U.S. government to conduct a workshop on 'Developing Critical Thinking skills in Students', conduct a professional development workshop for teachers and start 'International Space Science Clubs' in eight schools, including the one where she was teaching. With a great deal of meticulous planning, coordinating with experts from ISRO, designing the activities, the workshop got on to a great start, with the teachers and students enthusiastically engaging in the various sessions. Charu was quite keen to use the tools that she had acquired to engage and excite her students in the field of science. Though eager to start on this journey, a few thoughts continued to bother her. The goal of ILE Program was not about the latest advances in pedagogy, but also to go back to their countries and overcoming challenges in the education system, leading the teaching community to bring about a change. A crucial part of the programme was to prepare the teachers to be change agents, and they had been briefed about the difficulties they would face, the overt and covert resistance that they might have to bear, and how to overcome these challenges.

With a lot of enthusiasm and a strong urge to enliven the classroom, she started motivating her colleagues to change the staid and ineffective lecture method to a system where both the teacher and the student are equally involved in the learning process. She would often quote a line which very aptly described the paradigm shift in the education arena – 'The role of a teacher is no more that of a sage on a stage, but a guide by the side'. She discussed her ideas with the school management and the changes that she wanted to bring about in the teaching methods.

With much fanfare, the first workshop funded by the Bureau of Education and Cultural Affairs (ECA) US Department of State and International Research and Exchanges Board (IREX) was inaugurated in the last week of June 2012. It was such a proud moment for her – luminaries from the field of education and Indian Space Research Organization (ISRO) were present and promised to help and guide her in this venture. The workshop commenced with students from eight schools, including the one where she was teaching for the past so many years, enthusiastically participating in the sessions and it was a dream come true for her. I had never seen her happier than she was then, and with childlike enthusiasm, went about the task of ensuring that everything went off well.

It came as a shocker to her, when she sensed that the school administration was not so gung-ho about her initiative to bring the best practices in pedagogy to her school. There were subtle hints and resistance to her methods. She was at a loss to understand the reason or the genesis of this change in attitude, but it disturbed her. Things came to a head some days later, and it was clear that she would have to choose between continuing to teach in her school without being able to put to practice all that she had learnt in the ILE Program, or quit. She was flabbergasted. People in whom she had reposed a lot of faith did not back her. She was aware of the cold reality that personality clashes and a feeling of insecurity was the reason for this change in attitude, but her heart still felt that she was blaming them wrongly. Her doubts were confirmed when she came to know that students from her own school had stopped coming for the workshop. She had to now make a choice between continuing in her school and teach using the same method as all others were doing, or break out on her own.

The decision to quit was not at all an easy one for her, and the final act of crossing the line was almost forced on her by all those who believed in her dreams. She had only two options – continue to teach in the school or give up the comfortable but unfulfilling job and do something for children which was much more than mere classroom teaching. She was unwilling to take a decision, since her mind was telling her that her proficiencies were not being utilised efficiently, but her heart would not allow her to leave her students in the lurch.

Matters came to a head, and finally a day came that she could take it no more. I drove her to school, and she handed over her resignation letter.

Her association with this school was for about twenty five years, but God gave her the emotional courage to break free and move on. She had decided to devote all her time and energy to what was her passion, and that is how the 'not – for – profit' organisation 'Socrates Foundation for Enhanced Learning' was born.

I still recall the words of Charu's mother about her – 'Apni dhun ki pakki' every time Charu takes up something new. She has seen so many changes – from teaching home science to secondary school children to teaching science and mathematics to primary classes and then to secondary classes, travelling alone to USA to attend a course at NASA and then going to study for a semester at Northern Kentucky University, learning to use technology in education as extensively as the western world. The common factor which runs through all these changes is how she persevered to learn what was new to her. Unlike the education system in India, most of the western countries have realised the importance of integrating technology into education, and have incorporated the available technology tools to assist teachers and students. Many of the participants in Charu's group at NKU were already quite adept in the use of computers. Though Charu did use a computer for her work while in India, the proficiency level required during her course was quite a few notches higher. The situation was similar to a person, who knew enough of English language to write a brief essay, being asked to write poetry. Charu kept her nose to the grindstone, working long hours after classes, discussing technology issues with her faculty as well as with us, and finally making a project which was very well-appreciated. Her anthem always is 'Lage Raho Munnabhai', and you will succeed!

Concluding Part

Charu has been my soul mate for the last twenty eight years. During these years, we have indulged in slanging matches and stepped on each other's toes, and I have had more than my share in it, but she has held her cool, argued in favor of her views when she was convinced, changed her opinion when she concluded that she had erred, and moved on. She believes in 'fighting and getting over it' rather than not confronting a situation and sulking for days.

She believes that, conventional, 'so called' traditional values like respect for others, being humble, empathy, god-fearing, loving, caring for others even if it means discomfort to self, are never out of fashion, and are even more valid in today's materialistic world. She has a strong sense of what is right and what is wrong, and will not hesitate to convey it to even her closest family members or friends. Many would take offence to such a gesture, and I have seen her agonise, when people attribute all the wrong reasons for her plain speak, but her innate sense of wishing well for others, helps her maintain relationships, even if they are imbalanced for a while.

A person's true nature is known by the way he or she reacts to situations, and more so how he behaves in times of difficulty. There have been some extremely difficult times, which have drained us emotionally, mentally as well as physically, and there have been times when our joy knew no bounds. Even in situations where she had to undergo hardships due to others, she would still give the benefit of doubt and leave the matter there. In instances of great personal achievements again, she would be the one to give credit to others. She would, of course, talk about what she had accomplished in her life, but in the most matter-of-fact manner. Nevertheless, if anyone talks about her achievements to her face or in front of people, she still gets terribly embarrassed.

Charu is a mix of a modern outlook with traditional values. She is fiercely independent, and at the same time, respects the opinion of others. She has never been judgmental, and evaluates others on exactly the same value-based scale on which she measures herself. Unlike many of our generation, who feel that the modern age has made people materialistic, self-centred and obsessed with the western culture, she feels that our outlook is shaped, not by these extraneous influences, but by the choices that we make, and it is quite possible to hold on to our value system even in this age.

It is not in her nature to sit back and watch the world go by. I am more laid back, preferring to watch, read and listen, while she prefers to be in the thick of things, more of an 'action' person. She has always been excited by anything new which jogs the mind.

Epilogue

The very process of writing this account has been a therapeutic exercise for me. Written over a period of a few months, recalling and reliving certain moments of our lives has given me an occasion to go back in time, savour the happy moments again, thank god that the not-so-happy one's were very few and far between, and did not influence our lives at all.

I do not know if I have been able to do justice to the central theme of this book. My intention is certainly not to portray my wife as some unique specimen of the human species, endowed with supernatural qualities which would be hard to come by in mere mortals. Mine is also not a unique story about my wife, there would be many others whose narrative about their spouses would be much more inspiring and stirring. In fact, my contention is just the opposite – it is that one need not possess extraordinary virtues to become a good person. All that one requires is a certain amount of kindness and humility, coupled with a value system which does not change over time and the capacity to hold differing points of view without judging them. Marriage is a partnership where both the partners bring in as much capital as they can. They invest not only in themselves but pride in each other's growth and well-being. Problems arise when one or both the partners become too preoccupied with self to invest time and energy on his or her partner. Sometimes, having a modern outlook and being focused sometimes leads to a situation where we get wrapped up in our own self, to the extent of being obsessively self–centred. Charu understands the pressure that the young generation faces in modern times, but she believes that it does not preclude couples from making room for each other in one's life, ignoring the rough edges of each other, and helping each other fulfil their own dreams. However, it is also true that given our quest for gender equality, men and women are wired differently mentally, physiologically as well as emotionally. Both of us love Ankur, but I cannot connect to him in the same way as Charu does, nor does it happen vice versa. Given a choice, I can have my 'dal roti' every day, while Charu cannot endure this for more than a couple of days and would long to have a soup and salad, albeit homemade. It would be futile to search for a life partner, who would have the same likes and dislikes as one's own. Rather, we should see ourselves as one half of a jigsaw puzzle, and seek the other half which, when joined, presents a complete and beautiful picture.

There is no doubt in my mind that only the lady of the house can convert it into a home. This means not just beautifying the house with physical objects, but to fill it with love, laughter and joy.

They have their own little box of skills to do just that, and God bless them for that!

'Independence' has become a much-maligned word today. Most of today's generation uses it to convey that they want to be left alone or with people who have a similar worldview. Virtues like patience, accommodation, dependence on others have lost their value and are considered retrograde. Like the blind leading the blind, they prefer to seek support from their own peers rather than from those who have gone through the grind and spent more time on earth.

But is this generation to be blamed? I do not think so. This is the way we have brought them up, conditioned them. Extended families have changed to nuclear families, thus robbing our children of the feelings of sharing, not only of material things, but also our emotions. Like a broad spectrum antibiotic, our interaction with family members, outside of our parents and immediate siblings, helps children to develop not only sensitivity, but also sensibility towards others. Yes, each generation is a lot smarter than the previous one, more focused, better at networking and multi-tasking with the ability to take decisions independently, and they should get due credit for that. But the process of growing up too fast has not only robbed them of their childhood, but also made a majority of them more selfish and self-centred without them realising it. It is like two persons, one embodying values and emotions, and the other comprising the material self, growing up inside the same body. A fine balance has to exist between the two, but alarmingly, as we are progressing, the material self is growing up faster, leading to a situation where the person's values and emotions have not matured enough to rein in his or her selfish needs. The problems aggravate when people marry, and this selfishness is then masqueraded as convenience, leading to each one having his own credit card, bank account, car, favourite show on TV, favourite holiday destination, in short, one's own life where no one can enter, not even the life partner.

As the parents get busier, they spend less time with their children and sometimes overcompensate by providing them with material things. I am not sure about the concept of spending 'quality time' with somebody. I think this is just wordplay to justify lack of time and priority for things which are more important than money and career.

It is very difficult to define the thin line between advice and interference. It all depends on the subject, the manner, the time and the forcefulness of the advice.

Charu's parents made sure that they proffered advice only when asked for, though there were occasions where, I am sure, they would have been concerned enough to take charge and made sure we heeded them. The typical issues of conflict between parents and newly-wed spouses relate to whether the girl can continue her job after marriage, whether they can still stay in the same house as the groom's parents and the like.

My parents were extremely fond of Charu, and my father would take enormous amount of pride in her culinary expertise. They were used to having their 'dal-roti-vegetables' routine every day, never getting tired of it for days on end; cakes were meant to be bought on birthdays and dessert was 'kheer' prepared at home. Charu enamoured them by bringing in a whiff of continental into the house. My father was particularly fond of the cakes she baked at home, and would make sure that all the ingredients and tools she required were always at hand. Both of them loved her very much, but their nature of being overly protective now extended to Charu too, and sometimes this used to give us a feeling of not able to be on our own. In the pre-cellphone era, there was no way they could keep track of us and we would find my father furiously angry if we returned home late. I could understand where the anger was coming from, but not Charu, and my mother would subsequently explain that to her. Despite their possessive nature, they let us take major decisions in life on our own.

I reckon that both Charu's parents and mine had tremendous faith in each other as well as in us, and knew our capabilities to take decisions. They left us on our own, but watched over us very carefully, and like a typical fine leg glance by Gavaskar, would nudge us in the right direction without using any force, if they found us losing direction.

In a few years from now, Ankur will be ready for marriage, and I hope we have been able to instill in him the right values, which will make him a warm and caring person who has both respect and a sense of responsibility for his family.

A fine balance has to exist between the two, but alarmingly, as we are progressing, the material self is growing up faster, leading to a situation where the person's values and emotions are not mature enough to rein in his or her selfish needs. The problems aggravate when people marry, and this selfishness is then masqueraded as convenience, leading to each one having his own credit card, bank account, car, favourite show on TV, favourite holiday destination, in short, one's own life where no one can enter, not even the life partner.

My Love Story

Suresh Taneja

A day in my life without my wife is a day wasted in my life.

Ours was a typical arranged marriage. It was through a common reference. I was in the Army and had come home on leave in Chandigarh. My would-be wife's parents came with one of their close friends, Mr Singla, to our house. They first wanted to approve of the boy before they let him meet their daughter. My parents had not even informed me that someone was coming lest I leave the house on some excuse as they knew my escapist attitude in such matters. I still remember it was around 11.30 am and I had just about woken up, when my mother came to my room and told me to get ready and come to the drawing room, as some guests had come. I immediately guessed something was fishy but could do nothing about it as the exit from my room was through the drawing room. So with no other option, I dressed up casually and went to the drawing room to meet the guests.

One look at them and I understood what the whole fuss was about. I looked at my father, who too was an army officer and I could see the triumphant look in his eyes saying that he had got me this time. Just to make conversation they asked me a few basic questions like where I was posted, how much leave I had left and so on. After some time my mother brought tea and snacks and I took the opportunity to slip out of the room and went outside. As I was standing in the lawn and wondering what to do next, my would-be father-in-law, along with Mr Singla, came with their teacups in their hands. This time they started asking more personal questions which I found very awkward. They asked me whether I smoked or drank. I replied in the negative. As they both liked to drink, they found it hard to believe that an army officer did not do so. Actually, this turned the tide in my favour. After sometime Mr Singla asked me what type of girl I liked. By this time I was beginning to lose my cool but still with a straight face I blurted out, 'When I meet the girl I would know whether she is the type of girl I like or not'. Boy! This was the jackpot answer. I heard Mr Singla tell my would-be father-in-law, '*munde di gal bilkul theek hai* (the boy is absolutely right). And lo and behold, that was the end of my interview.

They went inside and fixed 3 March 1985, which was two days later, as the date for my parents and me to come to their house in Patiala, so that we could meet the girl.

On 3 March 1985, my parents and I went to Patiala. My would-be father-in-law had a huge bungalow with a big drawing room but even that looked small as it was filled chock-a-bloc with people. Besides her parents and two brothers, there were her uncles, aunts and cousins. I was wondering what I had got into. We sat for about twenty minutes with our parents doing most of the talking and I realised what it felt like being caged in a zoo with everyone staring at you.

After sometime her mother and other relatives took me to the dining table. Then she appeared, escorted by her cousins. She was made to sit opposite me and tea and snacks started appearing one after the other.

I do not know whether it was love at first sight or not but I do know that within a few minutes, I had the gut feeling that this was the girl I would love to share my entire life with. If you ask me what it was that made me feel that way, the answer is, I do not know. From then on the crowded room did not matter, nor the gaping eyes, they were all blurred. It was only her....

I was fascinated by her obvious nervousness. The way she kept the cup back into the saucer after taking a sip, I was expecting the tea to spill over any minute. I do not know what we spoke or what we didn't but I loved her '*adaa*' (style), the way she put her hair back in place, the way she smiled, her shyness, the way she met my eyes while speaking to me.

After sometime we were made to sit alone in another room which was just next to the drawing room, so that we could speak in privacy. I could see her aunts and cousins straining their neck and ears to hear our conversation through the open door. By now I had come to know that her name was Anita. Just to start the conversation, I told her, 'You have got a very nice family.' She just smiled. Our conversation must have lasted for about ten minutes or so. Before getting up I told her that I was going to say 'yes' to my parents and if she had any apprehensions she could let me know. She said that she had seen me through the curtains as I was entering the gate and she had liked me from that moment itself. I was on top of the world. I went to the drawing room and gave a 'thumbs up' sign to my dad. My parents had already made up their minds in the affirmative and were only waiting for my opinion. Having got that, my father announced this to the girl's parents. By this time Anita's mother had gone and got her OK and she also conveyed it to everyone. There was cheer all around and everyone was hugging each other, offering sweets and saying 'Mubarkan' (Congrats).

The parents started discussing about the marriage date. My dad told them that my leave was up to 11 March, so either we have the wedding before that if it was convenient to them or later when I come on leave as I was posted in Nasik Road. He said we would like to have a small and simple marriage. In the meantime, I went to meet Anita's grandmother in her room and took her blessings. After that I met her dogs, rabbits and cow. I could learn that her father was very fond of keeping animals. Her brother showed me his makeshift gym.

After some discussion, it was decided that we would get married on 8 March 1985, so that on 9 March when I was scheduled to leave for Nasik Road, I could take Anita with me. At this point there was another round of hugging and offering sweets. I heard her parents and relatives say '*Army walon key yeh baat bahut acchi hai, phat se decision le lete hain* (the good thing about Army people is that they take quick decisions).

On our way back home, my mother said that she was very happy and that she found Anita to be very sweet and nice. This meant the world to me as in our family we have the utmost regard for my mother's opinion.

The very next day I sent a telegram (there were no e-mails those days) to my unit asking for ten days extension of leave.

5 March 1985 was the Holi festival. So it was a good excuse to go to Patiala and meet Anita. This was going to be our second meeting. I reached her house around noon. I met her younger brother and mother who were at home. They told me that Anita was having a bath and would join us soon. In a few minutes Anita walked in with her hair all wet and uncombed with a towel around her shoulders as she was not aware I had come. The surprised look on her face when she saw me made my day, 'Ohhh! You have come', she said. Her mother brought color in a plate and we all applied colour on each other. This time we could talk more freely. I found her even more beautiful without a trace of make-up. She was shy, but frank and honest in whatever she said and it was as if she spoke from her heart. This has been an endearing quality of hers which has not died even with the passage of so many years.

She took me to meet her grandmother and I could see that she was very attached to her. After lunch we went to her bedroom with her brother and we played 'paploo' (a game of cards). There was a cupboard behind me which had a mirror and after sometime I noticed that both brother and sister were giving mischievous smiles to each other. It was then that I realized that they were trying to see my cards through the mirror. When I pointed this out, we all had a good laugh. The day just flew by and after evening tea it was time to say goodbye.

We both did not want to part and I could see it in the look of her eyes. It is amazing how in two meetings one can get so attached to each other.

The telegram informing me of my extension of leave having been granted reached on 7 March, a day before our marriage. This was the best gift my unit could have given.

The next time I met her was on 8 March 1985 at our wedding during 'Jay mala'. We got married in a hotel, so there were no hassles.

As my leave was extended, I could now have the luxury of going on a honeymoon. We decided to go to Shimla. Our honeymoon was, well, what a honeymoon is meant to be, total bliss. By the time we returned, it was as if we had known each other all our lives.

Our stay in Nasik was like an extension of our honeymoon. The grape season was nearing its end, so we used to sit in the balcony daily and have grapes. Every weekend, we used to plan to shop for household stuff.

She would see me off every day when I used to leave for office. She would have the door half open and from there see me, till I was out of sight. A ritual which she still performs. Incidentally, later I noticed that her mother used to also do the same thing when her father used to leave for office. How, some things daughters imbibe from their mothers without even realizing it.

I soon learnt so many good things about her. One, that she was a very organised person and the other that she was very quick on the uptake. It comes naturally to her. Maybe being a university volleyball player and athlete helped, as they say that sportspersons are well organised and quick on the uptake. It was evident in the way she would keep the house, organise her day's work and plan the monthly budget.

At that time I had a Yezdi Bike and we used to go for long drives on it. She asked me to teach her how to drive it and within few days she became an expert driver. She loved to go driving in the rain and at times when it used to rain very heavily she would be all excited and happy to stand under a tree thoroughly wet. Years later, when I bought my first car she learnt to drive it and now my children prefer her driving to mine.

Every other day I would come home from office to find that she had rearranged the furniture and other stuff in the house to give it a different look. She would hide when I came and the first thing I had to do was find her. Later my kids too used to hide and the first thing I had to do was search for all of them.

I found her to be an excellent cook and it was a lovely coincidence that we both had exactly the same taste when it came to food. Even while cooking one could see how well-organised she was, a fact which even my mother noticed when she came to visit us for the first time.

After a couple of months, we came to know that she was carrying our baby. Our joy knew no bounds. We informed our parents who too were very happy. After some time, my parents decided to pay us a visit. I still remember the arrival time of the train at Nasik Road station was around 1:30 am. As I was a junior officer I had got a one-ton (a small truck) to go to the station to get my parents.

I told Anita that that I would prefer going alone to get my parents as the timing was odd and in her condition she should avoid travelling in a one-ton vehicle. She would have nothing of that, she said that it was the first time that mummy and papa were coming to meet us so she would come. Sure enough, the first thing my mom said on seeing her at the station, 'Beta you should be resting. Why did you take the trouble to come?' My parents stayed for a fortnight or so and we had a great time together. We used go for walks together and play cards almost daily as my dad was very fond of it.

Later, I took a week's leave and just for a change of scene, we went and shacked up in a hotel in Nasik which was just about ten kilometres from our home. On our bike we visited all the places of interest in and around Nasik, saw movies and ate in different hotels. It was a carefree and fun-filled life.

I remember the first 'Karva Chauth' festival after our marriage. Incidentally, this is a festival which is mainly celebrated in the northern parts of India wherein married women fast for the longevity of their husbands. This is a one-day fast from sunrise to moonrise. While I was still sleeping, Anita had got up and after taking a bath had something to eat before sunrise. During the day, she and some other women had gathered in one house and watched movies on the VCR and singing songs. In the evening, she was dressed in her finest sari and jewellery. We went out of the house in the open so that we could see the moon. There were many other couples like us. The whole area had a festive air about it as all the ladies were in their best traditional clothes. There was a huge roar from everyone as soon as the moon was spotted. Anita first offered water to the moon and said a silent prayer (I guess she was asking God's blessing for my long life) and then I gave her some sweet which Anita had brought with her which symbolised the breaking of her fast. After going home Anita had a complete meal.

In subsequent years, I have tried my best to dissuade Anita from observing this fast because somehow I do not feel comfortable that she should fast for my sake. However, this is one instance where she does not listen to me and observes the fast regardless.

A month before the due date I took one month's leave. We used to go for long walks in the mornings and evenings. At home we used to play indoor games like Ludo, Chess and Cards etc. How the month went past by we just did not come to know. My mother-in-law came for the delivery.

My son was born in Military Hospital Devlali (near Nasik Road) and the day she was discharged from hospital was also her birthday. In the evening we had a celebration at home which left my mother-in-law very touched as she could not imagine how I managed to make all the arrangements in such a short span of time.

The arrival of my son, Amit started a new phase in our lives. If Anita was a very good wife she was even a better mother. Her whole day revolved around the child. She would do everything on her own and not depend on a maid. Even while cooking she would keep Amit in a pram near the kitchen door and keep talking to him even though he was too small to understand. Later, she would do the same thing with my daughter. Every day, before sleeping she spends some time with each child, listens to their day's activities and puts them to sleep. A habit she maintains till today. It makes me immensely happy to see her excellent bonding with both the children. I think amongst others, this was one of the main reasons why we did not have any problem or generation gap with both our children when they were growing up and even when they were teenagers.

In a year's time I was transferred to Assam. We were staying in a remote place where there was only the Army. I had a hectic schedule and I used to be out of station most of the time on practice camps, exercises etc. Every time I used to come back, my child would call me uncle and by the time he would got used to calling me Papa, I would be again out on some duty. I remember I had gone for a practice camp for a month and everyday my wife would show Amit my photo and he would say 'Papa'. But when I came back his first response was again 'Uncle', as the child could not relate the photo to the actual person.

During this time, due to the Chinese incursion we were ordered to be deployed in Arunachal Pradesh. My sub-unit was deployed in a remote area near a village. By this time, my wife was carrying our daughter. I was out there for seven months with fourteen days leave after four months. The day would pass by as one was busy but nights were really lonely as I was the only officer in the sub-unit. The popular song of the film 'Guide', summed up my plight ' *Din Dhal Jaaye par Raat na Jai, Tu to Na Aayi teri yaad sataae.*' Every evening I used to see all the photographs of Anita and Amit that I had brought with me. After that once again read all the letters which I had received. Then slowly without realising it I started writing poems to her sending them with every letter of mine. To my surprise, she too wrote a few poems. She has preserved them till today.

Our mail used to come once in a week or ten days and that day used to be a special day. I used to get seven to ten letters together as she used to write to me daily. I used to first open all the envelopes and put them date-wise and then read them. The same used to happen at the other end. Once out of the blue, I got a call from her and could not believe my luck. Later, I learnt that in order to speak with me she used to go to some Signal (communications)

Officer's house and wait for hours at a stretch for the call to get through and many a times return home without the call having got through as the lines of communication were very poor those days.

We planned to have my daughter's delivery in Patiala at my parents-in-law's place. I left Anita and Amit in Patiala and came again on leave well before the due date as I wanted to be present when my daughter was be born.

Early morning on Sunday, 8 November 1987, Anita started getting labour pains. I remember that day vividly, the Reliance World Cup Cricket Final was being played in Kolkata and was scheduled to start by 9 am, so the serial Ramayana which used to start at 9 am on Sundays was rescheduled that day to 8 am. Around this time, when we all were getting ready to go to the hospital, Anita noticed that her parents were watching the serial Ramayana which was on TV at that time. Seeing this Anita suggested we watch a bit of the serial Ramayana and then go.

We reached the hospital by 9 am and in an hour or so, my daughter Sonali was born. Our joy knew no bounds, it was a very special moment for us, as our family was complete. My son Amit was also very excited and happy when he cuddled his sister for the first time. As we had got a private room, we all stayed together in the hospital till Anita was discharged.

After my stay in Assam and Arunachal Pradesh, I moved with my unit to the J&K Valley, another area where families were not permitted. During this time, I was nominated at a very short notice for a course in Devlali which was of a ten-week duration. I decided to go with my family as we were staying separately for such a long time. I took a few days leave and reached Devlali about five days before the commencement of the course. My aim of going early was to find a place on rent and settle down before the course started. My unit officer who was from Nasik, had told me to take his scooter from his house in Nasik. So I was mobile on the first day.

The next day I went to the Quarter Master (Officer who is in charge of allotting accommodation and Transport)) to find out if there was a possibility of getting government accommodation. For short courses the chances of getting it were very less. I explained my situation to him and I was pleasantly surprised when he said that for my course they were giving 100% family accommodation as they were putting us in the newly constructed Delta Mess. I could not believe my luck. He told me that I could shift immediately even though four days were left for the course to start. Normally officers are expected to start arriving two days before commencement of the course. He was even kind enough (God Bless him) to give me a vehicle to shift my family and luggage.

In the Delta Mess, as I was the first to arrive, I could pick the room I wanted. So here I was, with family, accommodation and a scooter, it was like I had everything in the world. Such joy over such mundane things one can experience only in the army.

We had a ball during the course and used to go out every weekend on picnics, watching movies, going to the club and meeting friends. Amit used to stand in front on the scooter and Sonali used to be in Anita's lap on the pillion. We visited all the places where we had gone when we had come for the first time after our marriage; our old house, the hotels where we used to go out to eat, the tree where we stood while getting wet in the rain, the hotel where we shacked up in Nasik and so on. I still remember that my daughter, Sonali first started crawling while we were there. It was evening time and we were in our room when we saw she had started crawling. Seeing her Amit was so excited that he started crawling in front of her, so that she would follow him.

The ten weeks just flew by and I was back in my unit after leaving Anita and the children in Chandigarh with my parents. After two to three months, I was transferred to a Brigade Headquarters in J&K itself, but on the other side of the Valley. So my wife and children continued to stay in Chandigarh. The only good thing was that there the families were permitted to come for a short duration so combining this with leave one did not feel the separation so much.

Once when I was staying alone in the month of December, one eye of mine started watering badly and after a couple of days I went to the local Army Hospital. There, the doctor told me that

that my left eye was not blinking and so I was admitted to hospital immediately.

After about ten days, when my eye started becoming all right, I informed Anita that I was in hospital. I told her that I was now fine and would be discharged in a few days, so that she did not worry. The very next evening, when I was in my room in the hospital, the nursing orderly told me 'Saab, your family has come'. And then my wife entered with two tiny tots holding them in each hand. The kids looked so cute wearing monkey caps and woollens. She also had her luggage as she had come straight from the bus stand. I learnt that immediately after my call she took the next flight from Chandigarh to Jammu. From Jammu, she came by bus which was a good six-hour-drive to my location. I was very touched to see how she managed the whole thing with two small kids, that too in such cold weather. But I was not really surprised as by now I knew that in an emergency she could achieve anything in the world.

After a few months, while I was still in J & K, I got the news of the sad demise of my father. At that time Anita and the children had come to meet me. My boss gave me his jeep since it had the permit to go to Jammu and within no time we left for Jammu. We reached Jammu in the evening and at that time I had two options, either to go by bus that night itself or stay the night in Jammu and go early next morning. Travelling by night by bus through Punjab those days was not considered safe. My wife understood my predicament and told me 'Don't worry, we will go tonight itself no matter what'. We managed to get the last bus and it was going to Ambala.

By dawn, we got down at the Rajpura by-pass as that would save us time to go to Chandigarh. We waited for some time and did not get any bus, so we took a lift in a truck. We reached Chandigarh by truck and we were at home as early as it was possible for us. By now many of our relatives had come and I saw Anita take charge of the house. She not only consoled my mother but also looked after all the relatives and guests who had come. Her organised manner once again came to the fore, she took stock of the supplies at home, made out a list and got all the rations that were required and took charge of the cooking. After all the guests had gone, Anita told me to go back alone because she needed to stay with mummy.

Next I was posted to Nasirabad in Rajasthan. This was my first proper peace posting after four and a half years. Sonali started to go to school at this place and simultaneously Anita also picked up a teacher's job in her school. She used to say that she would start working only when both the children start going to school. Thereafter, she continued to teach in whichever station I was posted in.

During this period, we decided to buy a flat in Pune. We had gone there and finalised a flat. However, after taking into account all my savings and the loan that I could get, I was still short by Rs 80,000. I was thinking of dropping the whole idea as in the early nineties that was a huge amount. But Anita was not the one to give up so easily. She told me that we could sell her jewellery. I was reluctant but she convinced me that it was just lying at home and later we could always buy it, but we may not get the same flat again. I told her once our loan EMI started we would not have much saving for us to buy back the jewellery. She said never mind and so we sold almost all her jewellery. As it turned out, this was one of the best investment decisions I have ever made. My first rent was more than my EMI. So in effect, my monthly income increased because of this investment and in a few years I could buy jewellery for Anita.

Later, when my children were doing their graduation, whenever I used to be short of money to pay for their fees, Anita would make it up from the kitty money she used to save.

After two years I was transferred to Ferozepur. Here too, Anita got a teacher's job in the same school where both my children got admission. They used to go together in the Army bus and come back in it. My wife joined a dramatics club and once when I had come back after a month from some exercise I was pleasantly surprised to know that she was participating in a three-act play which was about one and a half hours long. It was held in the local Army Club and was attended by all officers and ladies of the station. I was surprised to see that she had one of the main characters in the play and as usual she had come out with flying colours. I felt mighty proud when everyone was praising her performance. After the play there was a party and the senior-most officer who was the GOC (General-Officer-Commanding),in a lighter vein told Anita 'I can understand what he saw in you but I wonder what you saw in him'. I was at a loss for words but without batting an eyelid Anita answered,' I am glad that what I saw in him no one else saw before me and I was lucky enough to marry him.' I was amused to see the General stumped for a change.

During this phase, my mother had two cataract operations in a span of six months. Both times we went to Chandigarh and after getting her operation done, we got her to Ferozepur, so that Anita could look after her post-operation.

I too was once admitted to the hospital in Ferozepur and was operated upon for appendicitis. I was operated by noon or so and by late afternoon when I gained consciousness, I found that Anita, the children and my mother were not there in the hospital to see me. In fact, they came rather late in the evening. I was wondering as it was very unusual of her to be so late and that too on a day I had been operated upon. She came and said that the car was giving trouble and hence she got late. It is only later when I was OK that she told me that actually that day she was coming in the afternoon, when she met with an accident on the way. A boy, aged about twelve years, had suddenly come on a bicycle from the wrong side and hit the car. So she had taken the child to the hospital and got him checked by a doctor. She had also informed his parents who too had come to the hospital. There were very minor superficial injuries but they took a CT scan of the head to make sure. My wife left the child at home and gave her address to his parents and told them to contact her in case of any problem. Luckily there was no further problem in this regard. I really appreciated my wife's action in that she amicably solved the problem all by herself and took care of the boy and only then came to the hospital to meet me, even though I was operated that same day and she had not met me after the operation.

I was again posted back to J & K, this time in the Valley. Initially, I left my family in Ferozepur, so that my children could finish their academic session. Later, during the summer, we decided to go for Amarnath Yatra. I was a bit apprehensive about my mother being able to cope with the rigours of the Yatra. But Anita convinced me that we must take her. We were able to complete the Yatra safely and I remember my mother was so overwhelmed and happy that she kept blessing us. I too felt very nice that as a son I could do something for my mother which made her so happy.

The following year during my children's summer holidays, we all went to Leh for a week. We went by the Army bus. The route was via Kargil. In Leh, we visited all the sightseeing spots. On our way back, when we had just crossed Kargil, we were fired upon from Pakistani posts. As it had just become dark we could see the bullets coming towards us as they had tracers which illuminated the path of the bullets. They were narrowly missing our bus. The lights of the bus were immediately switched off and we were in total darkness. We were made to stop and no vehicles were being permitted to go ahead. In total darkness, the bus was slowly reversed, so that we were safe and out of the line of fire. We were halted there and it soon became apparent that we would not be permitted to go ahead for the rest of the night. Besides my family there was another officer in the bus who was also with his family.

I remember, seeing the firing and the commotion, Amit and Sonali, who were aged twelve and ten years respectively, were very excited, as one would expect from children at that age. My mother started her evening prayer repeatedly chanting the name of God, '*Hare Ram, Hare Krishna, Hare Hare.*' Anita was cool as a cucumber as we were out of the line of fire. Her only concern was, how would mummy spend the entire night in the bus.

After some time, two jeeps came from the Infantry battalion which was occupying the posts in this area. My family and the other officer and his family were taken to the Battalion's Officers Field Mess which was at the base of the posts. There we were greeted by the Second-in-Command of the Battalion. There was no other officer including the Commanding Officer, who we were told, were on the posts because of the firing. After dinner, the Second-in-Command excused himself and he said that he too was going to some post. We were given the Commanding Officer's and Second-in-Command's residence to sleep for the night.

I now understood why the Commanding Officer and Second-in-Command had gone to the posts for the whole night. They had done this so that we could stay in their respective residences since we were with our families.

Such hospitality where people who are total strangers, vacate their own premises for you for the entire night, can only happen in a wonderful organization like the Army.

After a year or so, I shifted my family to Pune, as we wanted our children to have a good schooling in a proper place. I had come on a short leave and after a great deal of effort, I could get both my children admitted in very good schools. I had also applied for an out-of-turn telephone connection as it was permitted for persons serving in the Valley. I was given assurance that it would be installed in a week's time. However, it never materialised in spite of my wife's best efforts.

After a few months, the Kargil conflict started and I was in the thick of it. For these three months, my only connection with my family was through my neighbour's telephone in Pune. The scene was such that only I could ring her up but she could not. I was extremely busy and I used to return late at night. It used to be too late to disturb my neighbours at that time. Everyday my wife used to keep the front door of the house open so that in case a call came my neighbour would not have to waste time ringing the bell. I knew she would be eagerly waiting for my call, but I couldn't help it. I could, on an average, manage to speak to her only once a week.

After the Kargil conflict, I was transferred to Nasik Road. However, my family could not join me as my son was in the 9th standard and we did not want to change schools at this juncture and that too from the good schools in which they had got admission with so much difficulty. After a lot of deliberation with Anita I decided to put in my papers as we both realised that for the next five to six years it was not possible for Anita to shift out of Pune, due to both our children's education.

Moreover, my mother was also staying with us and due to her old age we did not want to keep shifting her along with us.

I have now been staying in my own house in Pune for almost thirteen years. I got a job in the education sector. It is for the first time in my life that I have stayed so long in one place. Both my children are now working after completing their respective MBAs.

Initially, Anita worked as a teacher in Pune, but after a year or so, she left the job as she had to go to Patiala to look after her mother as she was serious. It was not possible for the school to give her long and indefinite leave. Thereafter, Anita started a beauty parlour which we opened at home in our servant's quarter, as I did not have the money to invest in a shop. Before starting the parlour she underwent a sixteen-week training programme from one of the best training institutes in this field in Pune. She has since taken a sabbatical from this work and is presently enjoying life and keeps herself busy with her friends and kitty parties.

My mother is now no more. She expired about two years ago at the age of eighty-five. Two years before she expired she had a paralytic attack and she was more or less bedridden after that. Anita devoted herself to looking after her. She got a 24x7 maid to help her and she used to personally supervise everything and made sure my mother was well taken care of. We had got my mother a wheelchair and Anita would make sure she took her out on the terrace. She would have meals with her and at times read the Ramayana to her as it made my mother feel good. There were times when the maid was not there and she used to do all the work like cleaning her bed, taking my mother to the toilet, giving her a sponge bath and combing her hair.

In those days Sonali was working in Mumbai and whenever she would come home on weekends she would spend lot of time with her grandma and listen with interest to all her stories. I remember when both Amit and Sonali bought anything new they would excitedly show it to their grandma. They would both talk about their respective jobs and what they did even though my mother did not understand most of it.

After my mother's cremation we were to go to Haridwar to immerse my mother's ashes in the Ganges. It was decided that Anita and I, my brother, my sister-in-law and my sister would go by air from Pune to Delhi and from there by road to Haridwar and back in a similar manner.

However, Anita told me that we should also take both our children as they were very attached to my mother and she wanted them to be part of all the rituals. Later, when I saw how much it meant to my children, I thanked God and Anita that I changed the decision and took my children to Haridwar as well.

My son got married a couple of years ago and we had another addition to our family, my daughter-in-law Smriti. I was very pleased with the way Anita welcomed Smriti to our fold. She personally got her room renovated with a lot of interest and enthusiasm. I remember her telling me that we would treat her like our daughter and will not differentiate between her and Sonali.

After the wedding, they stayed with us for a few months as both of them were working in Pune at that time. We all had a very good time celebrating each other's birthday, going to the club and for movies. They are now both in the US.

It has been a blissful journey of almost thirty years with Anita. We still feel as if we got married just yesterday. What makes us tick so well, I guess it is love, love and more love for each other. I live for her happiness and the same is true of her. My happiest moments are those when I see her happy. I remember in our early years she used to say' *tu toh main hi hoon*(you are me only) and whenever any of us commits any mistake or does or says something wrong, we remind each other of this phrase and everything is forgotten. My kids sometimes tell me 'Papa you should go out more often to meet your friends', and I proudly tell them 'I don't have the time, as your mama is my best friend.'

On her part, she treats me like a king. After coming back from office, I have no other work to do as she manages everything and that too very efficiently. Every day, when I am in office besides getting the house in order she will do all the jobs like paying bills, buying vegetables and groceries, any bank job, any work given by the kids, even getting the plumber/carpenter/electrician job done when required. When I am at home even my dinner is served to me in the bedroom as I am busy watching TV.

Whenever we have to take any major decision we discuss it threadbare with each other and only go ahead if we both agree on it.

If we have one issue of discord between us it is that she feels warm when I feel cold. When she wants the fan on, I want it off. So, I take on the blanket and she is without it and we have the fan on and enjoy.

I have hardly a year before I retire. We are really looking forward to it and we keep making plans of what all we will do. We would be back to our carefree and fun-filled life (not that it is not now) and as they say, *'Picture abhi baki he, mere dost.'*

She used to say that she would start working only when both the children start going to school. Thereafter, she continued to teach in whichever station I was posted to.

I LOVE YOU MORE

Siddharth Mishra

We observed each other's habits and lifestyle but never really did anything together as we were literally living in two different time zones. Slowly but surely both adjusted. I helped her break the 'early to bed and early to rise' regime and she gave my life some sense of discipline. We decided that in order to spend time together, we needed to modify our timing a little. For her morning started at 6:30 am and the day ended by 10:30 and I really struggled to wake up at 6:30 but then I managed to wake up by 7am and everything fell into place.

When we got married, my wife made a statement 'I love you' and waited for a response. None came her way. She became upset and asked me if I felt anything for her. I replied that the general response would have been 'I love you too' but that never felt right to me. The word 'too' spoilt everything. It was as if you were not sincere enough. Somehow, there should have been a better response. It did not do justice to what I felt. I have been looking for an answer since then.

Ours was not a traditional marriage, love or arranged, rather the internet had a big role to play in arranging our marriage. But it was love at first talk (not sight). We both had been trying to play the field in looking at prospective mates and had met quite a few interesting people (at least on paper) but every time the conversation would dry up in five minutes and the rest was all a very laborious experience where decency would make us try to keep the conversation alive. I had heard that when the right person came along, we would get to know instinctively and I would always treat such talk as rubbish.

Twenty minutes on the phone. That is all it took. We decided we were meant for each other. I know in today's world this is a bit too fast but then somehow it happened. It was not that we had not met others, taken our own sweet time with them, and then refused but there was a connection here. We just knew we were meant to be. I had decided that I would speak for five minutes just to see if we could even talk. Time flew and before I knew it, we had been talking for half an hour and I felt that the decent thing to do then was to end the conversation as one never knew if she found the conversation equally interesting. Of course, there was the ego. I did not want her to get the impression that I was really interested, which truthfully I was. Oh, we could have talked for a much longer time. This got us interested in meeting one another. We got engaged the next time we met, had a six-month courtship and then started life as we know it today.

Our courtship was defined by one contentious issue, which is generally the bane of all long-term relationships, phone bills. The telecom companies earned their profits from us and our parents got worried. In fact, there were many customs and rules invented so that we would spend less time on the phone but the best incident was a discussion between her and my dad. He asked her to find a solution to these phone bills telling her that she had to help him. Her solution left him stumped and the issue was laid to rest once and for all. She suggested that we get married on Diwali as it was an auspicious day and this would ensure that the phone bills would come down as we would be getting married almost two and a half months in advance.

We did have our secret meetings where once I travelled almost fourteen hours by bus to meet her for seven hours. There were the customary fights where she switched off her phone and became almost unreachable for short durations of time and I would always manage to reach her, either on a landline or through someone and I feel that went a long way in building her confidence that I would always be able to track her down and reach her. She would never be alone. I would always find a way to be right there with her.

I consider our marriage a rather interesting one given the fact that we feel we are newly-married even after all these years. Laugh all you may but that feeling does persist and we rather enjoy it. Everyone who gets to know us feels ours is a love marriage, which, in some way is rather enjoyable. This vindicates how we feel about each other and makes us feel closer.

The first few days we spent together were our honeymoon days. They were really exciting if you realise how we managed to sacrifice as well as try to ensure that the other did not really find out. The eating habits were the first to really clash. My wife was 100% vegetarian who did not even take any sweet products (healthy lifestyle), while I was a foodie. She would have six small meals a day and I would generally have a heavy breakfast and forget food till I became hungry around 4pm and then I would eat anything I could lay my hands on. I used to have a late dinner to round things off. Hence once we were out of the hotel, I would never look for any food as I assumed that she would have had her fill and we should concentrate on sightseeing rather than look for food till late afternoon. She kept quiet for four to five days and could not take it any more after that. She just burst into tears and would not say anything. It really got me mad that I had a crying wife and had no idea what it was all about. All my queries were in vain. We were on a fort and someone had gone to make some paranthas for her. I was mad as it was eating into our itinerary and I would not get to finish one item on my "Patel point" list. He turned up and said that he had run out of potatoes and then the gas was not working and he had no food, he had only fried snacks. She was very upset with this. My suggestion was that we move to the next destination, about two hours away, and look for food there. But she expected that I should be more worried about some food for her rather than going to the next destination. I was all about visiting places, taking guides along etc. And she could not understand why I did not want to spend any time getting to know each other. My logic was that we had our entire life to do that but how many people visit the same destination twice when there are so many places to visit so let's make the most of it. Anyway, we soon found an eatery and normalcy returned. Both of us realised what the other person wanted and we decided that we should plan the next day together taking all details into consideration. For her, the thing that really mattered was how we would get to know each other and become close and for me, the "Patel points" obviously. So we planned around both, I gave up two points and she planned the food-stops as well as other activities. Soon it became a really enjoyable time. But I must add that on our seventh Diwali together, we went back and I finally completed all my points and she did all her shopping but now it is really a very smooth affair where we both know what the other wants and anyone can plan for the other. Of course, now that holidays are with the parents and family, we work to accommodate what the other wants.

It was a real learning experience once we got back to our normal lives. We literally lived in different parts of the day. She would wake up by 5 am and fall asleep by 9 pm and I would be back from work by 8pm. So we really struggled to match our timings. Maybe that helped as we did not get in each other's way but learnt a lot about each other. We observed each other's habits and lifestyle but never really did anything together as we were literally living in two different time zones. Slowly but surely both adjusted. I helped her break the 'early to bed and early to rise' regime and she gave my life a sense of discipline. We decided that in order to spend time together, we needed to modify our timing a little. So then for her morning started at 6:30 am and the day ended by 10:30 and I really struggled to wake up at 6:30 but then I managed to wake up by 7am and everything fell into place.

When I started writing this, it was a free flow of words and thoughts that came to my mind. Slowly as the ideas, feelings and thoughts started taking shape, I realised that I could organise everything in a more meaningful manner and that's how the structure of this piece of writing came about.

Our marriage has been guided by the word 'caring'. We do care for each other but what caring stands for we realized when we took this journey together. It actually helped us set some rules by which we live. The only startling thing was that I never realised it till I started putting pen to paper in this case. The details are as follows:

C = CASH
A = ARRANGEMENT
R = RELATIVES
I = IRRITATION
N = NEWNESS
G = GROWTH

Cash

When it comes to money, traditionally in India, it's the man's domain. He keeps the purse strings to himself; he has the responsibility of providing for the family. The finances, in a typical family, are broken up into the man's finance, everything like rent, loans and investments fall into this category. The wife's finance, all household expenses, she generally saves from here too. There is a budget, expenses are apportioned, and there is an accountability or calculations of how the money was spent. This system brings in a lot of heartburn and small games. The husband will never admit that he does not earn enough to fulfil their dreams (I doubt if the earnings and dreams will ever match) and the wife is always short of money to run expenses. The very fact that most Indian wives have a secret stash and pride themselves on saving some money for themselves from the household budget must make one question the trust issue as well as the fact that there has to be some 'over billing' of household expenses done by the wife. Many husbands are aware of the same, in fact few secretly depend on it for luxury purchases, but the entire scheme of things is not smooth sailing. Needless to add, when egos and secret savings are in play, there will be discontent and there will be mind games and there will be some trust issues, this often boils over to the other aspects of the marriage and one of the basic pillars of trust is very severely compromised.

I had often been a spectator to many such skirmishes between married couples (often across three generations) but the theme was always the same. It always ended with challenges and defiance, 'You handle all the expenses for a month and you will understand how difficult it is', or 'You have no idea how I manage the household expenses within our limited means'. These are generally where the arguments end up or the best one, which women, generally, after a few years of marriage say, 'If you want me to run the house, do not ask me to explain myself, you have to trust me'. This often got me thinking that both of them support each other, do things with each other on all fronts but on the money front, there is always that battle on the face of it while both of them will stand united against the rest of the world. This would lead to some really big fights and often it was just a battle of egos and nothing more. So I had decided that I would never let this come in the way of marriage.

The very next day after our marriage, I promptly took my wife to the bank, made her my joint account holder, and asked her to take over our expenses. I had married a working professional who would be contributing to our household income and it was only right that she be a part of the spending. Another small point which worked hugely in my favour was that she had done her MBA in finance and well (very difficult for me to admit), she was the expert here. Having swallowed that humility pill, I must say that whenever I look back, it was the smartest thing I had ever done. She never had to ask me for any money and she knew exactly what was coming in and going out. Hence, there were no unrealistic dreams and wishes. This was one of the most transparent things that we had started our marriage with.

It made a huge statement of where I wanted this marriage to go. She was also aware of the money-game between couples, so she expected it to be that way. The very fact that I took this, adopted this went a long way in reassuring her that 'whatever is mine is yours and whatever is yours is mine'. This really put a strong foundation to our relationship and has worked so strongly for us that I have become the biggest advocate of this. Throughout the years, she has been so sensitive to our income status and when it comes to spending for us and our family, she comes up with a spending schedule that hugely favours me and we are often arguing about spending for each other rather than the traditional battles that I mentioned before. That leaves a lot of positive vibes. There is often a lot of planning, we sympathise with each other, try to find methods to augment our income together. The entire relationship started off on a strong footing and we have continued to build on the same.

There is this one incident that comes to my mind. My 'smart' tax planning had resulted that towards January, I had very little salary coming in as they were deducting all the tax in the last three months and I was down to almost fifty per cent of my salary. Needless to say, all my insurance payments also were due then. To top it all, my marriage anniversary and my sister's birthday was also in January and I had made big promises of how we would be celebrating the same to both my wife and my sister. All this really pushed me into a corner and I was left in an uncomfortable situation. But to her credit, she understood the situation really quick. I am sure she wanted our first anniversary to be special but she handled everything really well. She had some savings before marriage with which she promptly paid my insurance dues. She planned a great gift for my sister and together with my parents, planned a nice dinner for all. To my surprise and relief, she said that instead of a big celebration and gift, she wanted the first anniversary to be special and hence she would cook something special for me and we would share it with the family. I fully understood what was going on but to her credit, she made all the arrangements so well and made it seem so special that I felt really blessed. To this day, we have never discussed this but we both know what really happened and this really set the tone for the future.

Arrangement

Life is not always fair and the best thing is to accept the same. We all have our own compulsions and the best way is to acknowledge the same and have certain arrangements. The key here is to accept that we need support and be upfront about it. We are partners and should turn to each other first before others. We definitely have the right to expect a lot from each other and we decided that we would never question each other. We would accept the other person's line of reasoning as that was what they were comfortable with and we would definitely discuss it at a later date. The entire idea was not to try and drive home a point but rather be supportive in any which way possible.

Likewise, we could expect the moon and the other had to strive to that standard. It was very difficult at first. But the 'no complaint' agreement was what stood us in good stead. We never complained about each other's expectations. However unreasonable the demand, there would be no complaint. The basic premise was that we needed each other's help and we were not trying to complicate each other's life. Hence we would definitely do everything necessary. This helped build a sense of anticipation. Moving forward, we started realising the real interpretation of what the other wanted. Many times, we had decided that a certain request would be crazy but the problem lay in the interpretation of the request. Soon there came a time when we started anticipating each other's requirement and we realised that it was all in our head. When we decided to do it, we did. It soon became a thing where we both wanted to arrange for the other to become more comfortable.

The freedom issue came next. Many a time, bravado is often mixed up with freedom. Driving a two-wheeler is the most convenient mode of transport in our crowded cities but when you have a spate of accidents in the past, this is definitely not the way to travel. The first, big issue that we agreed to disagree upon was the mode of transport that my wife would typically be taking. She was adamant on a two-wheeler while everyone was against it. We had to reach a solution. So it was she who compromised. But that gave her a pass card, it was like a power she had that when it came to me doing something for her, she would get something in return for what she had sacrificed. I, in turn, decided it would be an ever-changing 'pass card', which she could use to get me to do different things all the time. As we progressed everything about the 'pass card' was forgotten. It had become an arrangement, wherein we would decide to help each other in whatever way we could.

A small thing had turned the way we would actually look at each other and the way we would make small arrangements so that each other's life became more comfortable.

She would wake me up with morning tea and I, in turn, would drop her at her place of work, or at least half the way, depending upon what our timings would permit. I would try and link picking her up on my way back and the very fact that she had to travel in a little more difficult manner was soon forgotten.

Then we agreed that we could have different takes on different issues and situations but we would respect each other's views and whether we agreed on it or not, we would not push the other to our way of thinking. This helped us tide over a lot many situations where we realised that romance did not mean having the same opinion on everything but rather letting the other keep her views and we keep ours. This eased up a lot of things. The beach was as much preferred as the mountains for a holiday. If we planned one holiday on the beach, the other would nearly always be in the mountains. Chinese meals would be followed up by Italian dinners. A masala blockbuster would follow a romantic movie. Old Hindi songs would be in the same playlist as Item numbers. The list could go on and on. If we did things together, we need not do all the things we both liked but rather we would give space and time to each other's preferences. This helped us appreciate each other, loosen up and appreciate the finer aspects of what the other liked. I know some of you may wonder about what the finer aspects of item numbers and masala movies are, but well, sometimes you just learn to enjoy what the other appreciates.

Relatives

A cranky relative or some distorted views from either side of the family has to be put up with. We are already under compulsion to fall in line with the discomforts of having funny relatives on each side. Imagine having to play a cat and mouse game with your spouse so that which family is more distinguished becomes a vital part. There is a basic fight as to which side of the family is more superior and that leads to an all-out ego battle.

We decided that there will be no negative back-biting, but we will protect each other or help each other deal with the 'lovely' relatives.

We would forewarn each other about them, lay some ground rules, never talk back to anyone and never try to pass off our personal issues with the relatives to each other. So whenever the cranky aunt said something unflattering, we would sit back with a smile, ask each other about the comment made, tell each other if that comment was important and move on. Each one fought his own battles with the relatives.

There were times when our parents put us in difficult situations where in we needed to decide our stand but we followed the path of non-interference. Our parents have made us and that really put us in a difficult place. There were times when we did not particularly agree with their views but more than agreement, the fact that these were our parents could not be ignored. So we devised a plan. We would never take a stand for our parents. It did not matter if they were right or wrong, we would not interfere and we would let things work themselves out amongst the concerned parties. We would deal with our parents-in-law ourselves. I would never talk to my wife about issues she had with my mother nor would she discuss them with me. They were issues between a mother-in-law and daughter-in-law and they would have to learn to sort them out amongst themselves without involving me or anyone else for that matter. That was the single biggest reason for things smoothening out as we realised that we never had many disagreements between ourselves. It was mostly standing up for my part or your part of the family that got us to fight. The same was quickly conveyed to our respective families of orientation that they needed to handle our spouses themselves. We had an arranged marriage so we turned the tables. Everything that was preached to prevent us from going in for a love marriage was used here. This marriage has happened as everyone has agreed so getting each relationship to work individually was everyone's responsibility. So no one ever had to take a stand. The pressure that was relieved was immense. No one was talking about another anymore. The other big factor that we decided upon was that when we found that people were complaining to us about each other, we would make it clear to them that we will take up this issue with each other and name the relatives who were complaining. We did this twice or so and then everyone suddenly stopped discussing the other with us.

The other thing that helped us with relatives was that we would always reassure each other that our relationships with each other's family members would have no bearing on our relationship. It could even be our parents, we could have had a difference of opinions but we would never let that come in our way. If my mother did not like something about my wife, I promised myself that I would not let that cloud my opinion nor would it reflect in my actions. It is easier said than done when your mother is almost in tears and hints (women and their art of subtle connotations) that your wife is the reason behind it. It may drive you into a fit of rage but it is always better to explain to your wife about the situation and let her sort it out. We often feel we should try and teach lessons to our better halves so that they can appreciate the situation better but letting it all out is much better. Both take a little more time to understand the same but with time they get used to it.

In my village, I am known as the city boy owing to my place of upbringing. I am continuously the butt of jokes where everybody does not miss the chance of pointing out how difficult it is for me to adjust to the village surroundings. Naturally, my wife was expected to be the city girl. When she entered our village after marriage, there were a lot of awkward comments and some downright warnings given to her on what would be tolerated from her and what was expected of her. The fact that she was more used to village life was unknown to all. To everyone's surprise she was more at home and knew her chores and other activities better than some of the women staying in villages. She knew several tricks that were used by people in the village and had no problem showcasing them. It did not take her long to be loved by one and all and very soon she became part of a few inner circles that I could never penetrate. I had expected to be protecting her and helping her in my village but to my surprise suddenly all those who had looked down on me or felt that I had too many issues with village life and living conditions, began to accept me because of her. This was indeed a surprise and things became more smooth, thanks to her. She became the darling of the elders and very soon people would give her example to me and others when it came to how we city dwellers should take to life in the village.

Irritation

Our culture teaches us to keep our irritation to ourselves and try and deal with it ourselves. Often, this results in a lot of bottled up emotions and the manifestation of the same results in us letting go in one instance and saying horrible and terrible things, half of which we do not even mean, and the situation just keeps getting worse and worse. It did not come easy but we decided that we would reach out and state in a matter-of-fact manner, the points that troubled us. The key was that there would be no response from the other side. There would be no explanations and justifications. We would state to each other what irritated us and what we understood and how we would have liked to be approached on the issue. It was very difficult not to explain our point of view but the fact that we decided that these were not discussions but monologues where we would just listen, helped a lot. This would help in a big way when the next situation arose. There were fewer debates as explanations were out of the way and we would just keep learning.

My wife, being the traditional Indian that she was, would often say yes to everything I suggested. I came from a family where my sister often made most of the decisions and seeing my wife as the submissive one made me wonder what was going on. I would ask her to voice her opinion and that would lead to a deafening silence almost always. This used to irritate me. I would choose the food, the menu, the movie, the holiday destination, household décor (though later we mutually agreed that I was more adept in the same). One fine day, I decided that I would no longer do these things. If we were to eat out, she would have to decide everything, if we watched a movie, she would have to choose it. This really got her to open up and express herself and has now reached a point where she plans and I implement. Very soon she had an opinion, more importantly, fought for it and expressed herself.

Then we came to a stage where there were plenty of times when we shouted at each other, argued like crazy but then one fine day we reached a pact that one of us had to keep quiet when we realised that the other was visibly upset. This worked both ways. It kept some arguments fairly civil but at times, the one who did the ranting would often be in the wrong and end up saying a lot of wrong things. What this did though was make the other person realise the line of thought in each other's mind and how to deal with it. Often the angry one would realise his/her folly and this would make us more careful in the future.

We were at Kruger National Park in South Africa and food became an issue. My wife was a vegetarian then (though she had had meat before) and all the food in the park was mostly meat. We managed to find one place that had one vegetarian dish and it was mashed pumpkin and spinach. We were to be there for five days and all she could get inside the park was the pumpkin and spinach mash. I had been trying to get her to eat meat and she had resisted. I felt that she would not be able to have this food more than a day and would soon consider meat. But I was wrong. Day one went, day two passed, day three, and she was still having mashed pumpkin and spinach. She did all these with remarkable cool and I was getting irritated as there was a part of me that was guilty that I had not done enough research before coming here, especially when I was fully aware of her eating habits. Then we decided to go out of the park and pick up some food from outside. She picked up what she liked and I did my shopping. I was glad to see that she had picked up some burgers. She had one and really liked it. They were mushroom burgers and she really loved them (I felt anything after mashed pumpkin would be a hit). Then she asked me to take a bite. Upon the first bite I realised that she was having some meat which she was mistaking as soya. (All our brethren who have had cheese burgers in McDonalds abroad can identify with this…the cheese burgers are actually beef cheese burgers but they are called cheese burgers and everyone enjoys them till they realise what they are). We were experiencing something similar. The so-called mushroom burgers were actually meat mushroom burgers. I was in a quandary. If I let her know she would go back to mashed pumpkin and if

I did not, it would be a huge, religious issue. So I informed her. She was distraught. Here is where I found my opportunity and I reasoned that now that she has had meat, she could eat meat for the rest of our stay and not torture herself with the same food for five days. To my relief she relented and the saga that started that day is still continuing. Whenever we eat out now, there is no need for a vegetarian and a non-vegetarian dish to be ordered. We order and eat the same food. Thank God for that.

Newness

We make habits when we become comfortable with something and they go on to consume our day slowly and slowly and before we realise it, our life is just a routine. Marriage often becomes a routine. The same things over and over and soon boredom sets in and before you realise it, we are looking for exciting avenues (you are free to interpret this).

It is not as if we realised this at the start but as time dawned, life did become a routine. Everything was not a problem as it helped us anticipate each other and we became subject matter experts when it came to one another. To be frank, manipulating one other became rather easy and we could often make each other do things we wanted. Then we realised that we were tired of each other's company as we were often repeating the same things again and again. Hence we felt that there must be something that we can do so that we can make things interesting once again. We decided that every three months we will try something new. The first attempt would be for something that she wanted, the second would be for something that I wanted and finally would come something that both wanted.

The idea here was not just doing something new but allowing the other a peep into our hidden wishes and interests so that we could participate in each other's world. These resulted in happiness, frustration, anger, fights and whatever emotion you could think of but what really mattered was that we were there with each other. There was a lot of support, a lot of encouragement and togetherness. There were few times when we made big fools of ourselves but the support never wavered.

When I tried to sing, my wife, a trained singer, would try to help but then there are times when God has decided that you shall not have the required skills and nothing us humans do can change that. I never moved beyond the basics and for her, the basics were conquered in her childhood, where they would never be covered for me. Whoever said that if you try hard enough nothing is impossible, should really come and spend some time with me especially when I am trying to learn to sing. This endeavour became a source of irritation for me as I could never understand that despite sincere efforts, I could not do anything while she was a nightingale. I never admitted it but my ego had taken a big beating, but the support that I received from her made me realise the lengths my wife would go to so that I was happy, felt I could accomplish anything. But this experience made me come crashing back to earth where I realised that I just could do everything I wanted. It was like trying to get a crow to preen like a swan, futile attempt, but she persevered. It took amazing patience, I gave up, but she continued. It was then that I realised that when people say it is all in your mind, they are not necessarily correct. When it is in the heart, the mind becomes irrelevant. The heart will try to make you go after the impossible even when the mind may not agree. I had heard that such things happen but I experienced it for the first time. This was the same phenomenon that would make us take this behaviour in a light-hearted manner and even make fun of others, but when you experience it, it is not at all funny. There is a certain sincerity to the foolhardiness that makes it very endearing. It makes you want to do more for your partner as we realise that the heart does win over the mind at times.

Growth

The person you married gets older, he/she changes, their habits change, their likes change and even what they like in you changes. This growth aspect can become very difficult to handle. Sometimes, the girl becomes a free and independent person for the first time after marriage. They love to live their independent life. There are so many things that their parents did not let them indulge in. Experiencing all that becomes their first priority. Simple things bring a lot of joy. Eating junk food, an ice cream or even not having a proper dinner but having a lot of snacks give so much excitement that life looks so simple.

But these things do not last. Slowly they lose their charm and then the house and the career come to the fore. There is no doubt that the Indian girl has to really juggle both. She has to be responsible for the house. The situation becomes a little more complicated if her financial contribution is not really necessary for the house. Then her working is not looked upon as a family necessity but rather something that she is doing for herself. It may not be entirely wrong but this puts a lot of pressure on her.

What most of us do not appreciate is that everyone looks for some meaning in their lives and the wife is entitled to do the same. The burden of the household chores has to be borne by her and after that if she is left with some time and energy, she can do something to fulfil her professional aspirations.

This was a source of despair for me. My parents were very supportive and my mother would really make her life easy but what when we were on our own. Her day would start at 6 am with household chores which went on till 8 am and then office from 9 am till 6 pm and then again the house. So I decided that we needed to split some of the work. Rather, the lazy thing that I am, I decided to sub-contract. The thing that took up most of her time was cooking. So I decided that we would not prepare food at home. This saved her time and my ordeal of having to accompany her shop. We decided to use tiffin services. This was a great help. The food was ready when we were back and we had no tensions about picking the right vegetables and meat, deciding what to cook and finally cooking or even supervising a maid. This did make our life comfortable as we could now spend more time doing whatever interested us and attending to our hobbies.

So when she grew from someone who wanted to just be at home to someone who wanted to go out and live her life, we could achieve that. Then again, I also grew (apart from the waist size growth), I wanted to do something constructive for society and here she was a big help. There were many times that we disagreed about what was constructive for society but she would support me in all my endeavours. She even took the trouble of joining in even though she had no interest just so that we could do things together. This included a lot of soccer camps and the like, which she felt was more of a way I wanted to pass time than anything really constructive.

Today we like really different things, have grown together to appreciate each other's likes and dislikes. There is still that something which churns in our stomach when we see each other, we get cranky if we do not spend time together, we have to watch a movie every week, we have to go to the classes where we teach every week, we buy board games and we shop for clothes together. We do a whole lot of things but the movies have changed over the years, the books are not the same genre, the music is radically different, our food is vastly different. The trick I feel is that we have done this together. Hence each thing we accepted or indulged in, the other understood and even participated in. This makes us comfortable in each other's settings and life, I guess.

I would like to conclude by bringing out a small secret about us. The person that each of us had portrayed to the other when we met for the first time after the talk, we are not that. There were a lot of half-truths, a lot of safe answers and a lot of things that were false. We built our foundation on that but we wanted to be with each other. As the years progressed, we gradually discovered each other and embraced what we were all about. The only thing that endeared us to each other was that we could speak to each other comfortably. I guess communication is the key and we talk to each other a lot (my wife a lot more than me). There is very little that we do not share. This has made us close and the attitude that 'come what may, we will always be together'. Three cheers to Ahuti Siddharth Mishra for making me finally say 'I love you more' each time I see her. I finally found the perfect answer for her.

I would never talk to my wife about issues she had with my mother nor would she discuss them with me. They were issues between a mother-in-law and daughter-in-law and they would have to learn to sort them out amongst themselves without involving me or anyone else for that matter. That was the single biggest reason for things smoothening out as we realised that we never had many disagreements between us.

My Wonderful Wife – Kirti

Aniruddha Harne

*Marriage, in my opinion, is another name for trust, love, respect
and mutual understanding. I feel marriage is like a three-legged
race (a sport where you and your partner's one leg each are tied
up with rope) in which individually one may be able to run
faster but after marriage every decision is a joint one and in
order to complete the race both the husband and wife need to
take all that together. Being together at every step is happiness in
itself, which is possible only in the institution of marriage.*

Precursor

In Sanskrit, one of the words to define wife is 'bharya', as a
leader and supporter she embodies creation and brings the
bliss of creativity and wealth. In hard times she supports and
nurses her husband.

That's true of Kirti, my wife, soulmate, best friend and 'ardhangini'
(my better half). She wears many hats at the same time especially
if you look from my eyes. She is represents the new generation of
Indian women who are equally able to manage the household and
a job at the same time. Be it performing 'puja' (Indian ritual) at
home on festive occasions or doing complex, financial calculations
for multinational banks, Kirti does it all with a smile on her face.

This is an attempt to share my story with readers especially the
young generation who are living in two worlds, India and the West,
thanks to new-age technology. The modern day technology enables

people living and working abroad to have links back home. Over the years, I have observed that our real, virtual and social life is quite interlinked and people-to-people ties among countries are manifold. People who are studying or working abroad have strong connections in India for various reasons. Be it keeping in touch with parents or relatives, chatting with friends, doing business with Indian companies or taking part in India's democratic reforms or even finding a life partner for themselves.

Your experiences in life make you the person you are. This is story of a simple, educated and courageous girl from a good family and good values being able to bring in happiness in our family and make my house a home.

There were too many surprises which happened in the last two-three years. You can term them as miracles or plain luck. These surprises are the manner in which we got to know each other, how we actually met and decided to marry. Considering the fact that we both were living 7,000 miles apart and had never met.

Family background and Upbringing

Before we continue further in our story, let's dive a bit into my brief background to understand my perspective about relationships and family values. Being born and brought up in an educated, middle-class Indian family from central India, I had always lived in a joint family culture. During my early childhood days, I grew up in a joint family which taught me family values and the importance of being a support pillar for your near and dear ones. Today, our relatives live and work miles apart, but we share a common bond, not just because of the common surname but because we share each other's happiness and sorrow as well.

After my engineering and management, I had started working for one of the IT MNC organisations. Further, my job took me to UK, where I have been living for almost a decade now. I had the opportunity, like many others of the IT era, to see India from outside. The more I observed India from outside, the more I believed in Indian cultural values, the importance of family life and living a life of balance. My view regarding my future wife was (at least I was expecting) a 'modern girl with a global outlook and Indian values.' Kirti too belonged to an educated, middle-class family from western India and had stayed in a joint family in her childhood. She completed her engineering and took up a career in an IT organisation.

So we had many similarities. Our parents strove their best to provide us with good education and imbibed values to guide us and empower us to take right decisions.

Courtship

As part of the marriage, there are various routes which leads to two individuals getting to know each other better. It may be through parents, common friends, relatives, colleagues, and nowadays may be social media, matrimony portals and places of common interests. In our case it happened to be the internet, that is, a matrimony site. Now onwards, I feel that new generation couples, will most likely meet in the virtual world first than in person. Even if they are in the same building or same college.

Coming back to my story, I feel I was quite lucky to meet Kirti.

Both being busy professionals, busy with our current jobs and working in two different continents, it is sheer luck which made us meet. Due to time zone differences, we had limited time on weekdays and we used to e-mail each other or send texts. It were weekends we both looked forward to for long and interesting discussions. We eventually got to know each other well. The topics of discussion, you name it and we had it. But it was an all-round discussion to understand the person, her family, and background, professional and personal likes and dislikes, hobbies, views on political, social, family-related matters and health. Kirti was interested to know, what my free time and weekend activities in London were, which social groups I followed or subscribed to and what views and opinions I held on various topics.

She wanted to know my view on India, freedom to select the choice of career for both of us, my future residence and work plans. I did that to the best of my abilities, the most important criterion for me, was be honest to myself and let the others think or decide, whether they appreciate your views or otherwise. In my case, I was lucky that not only did we both have the same views on a majority of life's major issues but we also shared the same wave length. However, I must admit, it doesn't mean we both agreed on everything but the best part was that we both listened to each other. This habit is proving to be a boon now, especially when I realise that after marriage, one has to make more complex decisions regarding career, work locations, buying a house, a car and key financial and heath issues. In such critical situations we always try to work out the 'best option for both' rather than 'You win sometimes and lose sometimes' situations. This means adjusting to the situation with responsibility and love than trying to convince your partner how best is your method/solution than her.

Our courtship period was fantastic and we both made use of every possible use of technology to call, chat, send messages and email each other regularly. More importantly, we were able to see each on a daily basis by using video calls and face time. Sounds interesting, but technology comes with own limitations and as they say, 'you finally marry a female and not an email'.

After a few months of virtual friendship, it was time for meeting in person. I have decided to fly to Mumbai and meet the girl of my dreams (and hopefully my future wife). The excitement was at its peak, and to be honest with some goose bumps, I landed in Mumbai. Kirti was more than happy to receive me at the airport, and from that point on, there was no looking back. We both have enjoyed each and every moment of our togetherness.

Though our first meeting was enjoyable, memorable and lovely, it resulted in all my annual leaves for that year being booked for travel to meet Kirti again. And to be honest, I used to count the days before my next visit.

The courtship period was fun-filled and exciting but at the same time this was the testing time for both of us, being new to each other. Before taking the major decision of marriage, we have to spend some time together. But all that was worth it to meet my best friend Kirti. By then she was my best friend with whom I could share all my inhibitions and fears and at the same time listen to her and give her friendly advice.

Ups and Downs

Life is not an easy ride and we both have our share of ups and downs. We took time to share, discuss and understand each other and more importantly able to measure what comfort level we had in the presence of each other. After a brief courtship period, we got engaged and decided to get married. Our parents were also supportive and gave us their blessings and support.

If we take birth once in life then marriage is another rebirth for a man. This is perhaps the single most important decision any human will make in his life, which will influence all his future decisions. One thing I can tell you for sure, it is not an easy decision of how to select your life partner and there are no formulae for this. Even if there is a formula, it is different for everyone!

Marriage, in my opinion is another name for trust, love, respect and mutual understanding. I feel, marriage is like a three legged race (a sport where you and your partner's legs are tied up with rope) which individually one may be able to run faster but after marriage every decision is a joint one and in order to complete the race both the husband and wife need to take all that together. Being together at every step is happiness in itself, which is possible only in the institution of marriage.' I am lucky to have Kirti as my wife, soulmate and best friend.

Marriage Ceremony

We both appreciate and value the Indian traditional marriage ceremonies and decided to plan our wedding ceremony accordingly. Needless to say, it was with all 'Band-Baaja and Baaraat' with our friends and relatives being a part of the celebration. The rituals were performed according to traditional Maharashtrian customs and we both were decked up in Indian traditional dresses with 'henna' (mehndi) on our hands.

Our wedding day is the most memorable day of our lives when we vowed to share with each other lifelong happiness, love and care and being with each other through thick and thin. We were able to enjoy the festivities and firecrackers with our friends and family in India before starting our journey to UK.

Choices to be made

Though as they say, some testing times do come in a relationship, when living together, there are certain decisions to be taken and sacrifices to be made to move forward. These situations would differ from person to person, but in essence, such a scenario would exist now and then, in which one of the partners will have to compromise. Marriage is not a zero sum game, it's a sport where both partners play and both win.

One of the important things for today's generation is their career as it not only provides financial status but also a social standing which largely defines the person in society.

When we first met, Kirti was working for an MNC as a financial analyst and was doing well. Through our discussions we realised that after marriage, one of us will need to relocate and possibly leave her/his career and be ready to cope up with the challenges and opportunities. Kirti proved to be more strong and ready to take the plunge with confidence; and she was one to suggest that she was ready to leave her current job and adjust to the new career post-marriage. Bravo!

This meant that she would have to prove herself again in a different country/economy (which is just on the verge of coming out of recession) with the hope that she would find a place for herself.

Kirti did mention to me that for the sake of our family, present and future; she was ready to make certain adjustments in her career graph, and decided to leave her established career role. It was not an easy decision to leave a career or take an unplanned break, but possibly that is the step of mature understanding my partner shared, which I respect.

A few months later in UK, she proved to be right. With her education, experience and skills, Kirti landed a job as an IT consultant in one of the leading UK banks. She enthusiastically started her role in new organisation in a different work environment with her new team of Liz, Martin and Dave. Kirti soon got adjusted to her new work environment and is currently enjoying her job.

New chapter in Life

For Kirti, life was opening up a new chapter every day after marriage, and soon she was in a foreign land where she knew only one person that is, her husband. It may sound silly but it's true that people take time to adjust if anything major changes in their life such as being married, getting a new job, living in a new country, different culture, different climate and surroundings and most importantly new people. But all this happened to Kirti at the same time! This was a new chapter for her and for both of us together, where we both need to support each other. Be it going for buying groceries or visiting the local doctor, or mundane things such as house cleaning and paying bills. We both are working as a team and enjoying every moment of it.

Life in London

From one metropolitan Mumbai, Kirti landed in another metropolitan, London, but I guess, the similarity ends there. And then she discovered, in fact I should say we both discovered the lovely city of London and UK together. For me, the London Bridge and walking through the alleys of Thames had never looked so romantic and beautiful. I read somewhere that there are more than 200 different spoken languages in London, so the city is truly multi-cultural with its pristine beauty still intact and maintained. It was a perfect place to start our new journey of togetherness.

On weekends, depending on our schedule, we usually visit some of the historic landmarks, be it the world-famous London Eye, London Bridge or walking through Greenwich Hill to see the world clock, taking a cruise in the river Thames, watching magnificent palaces – be it Windsor or Buckingham Palace, London has something to suit everybody's taste.

The place offers much more than picturesque locations and nice photographs. Basically, it gives individuals the freedom to live, explore and contribute to society as per their choice with a more open and honest approach.

The picturesque city encourages you to have nice long walks along the river Thames, especially if you are out on a romantic date. Weather permitting we are able to enjoy outdoors. Apart from that, we are always on the lookout for the Indian cricket team's England tour. This is definitely one of the highlights, which NRIs enjoy. The reason is very simple, you get to meet your favourite cricketers in person and get autographs and photos easily. We do plan to watch some cricketing event soon, when next time, India tours England. Though Kirti does not like cricket much, she is happy to give me company, just as I accompany her to her favourite Disney movies.

We enjoyed all those things which UK/London offers to the Indian diaspora, things which will make you feel at home, be it religious temples, gurudwaras or mosques, Indian restaurants, Bollywood movies, regional dramas and shops with Indian clothes and utility items.

Thanks to Kirti, I have developed some taste for arts and theatricals and we do watch some stage performances, ballet and English cultural shows in our free time. The latest I remember was 'Sleeping beauty on Ice', and I had seen people performing as part of the musical and at the same time skating on Ice! In fact, that was a pleasant surprise from my wife as she got the tickets in advance and told me just before the show, when we landed at the theatre. I look forward for such beautiful surprises from my wife. Now, when I reflect back on such instances, where my wife has given a gift or a surprise, I appreciate the thought and love behind that more than the event itself. It gives me joy and makes me happy to have such a nice partner.

Social Life

Life has varied aspects and we try to make the most of it by participating in social, cultural and religious events here. In UK, the growing South-Asian and Indian diaspora is able to make its presence felt in every walk of life. From NHS (British Health Services), transport, media and politics and the business sectors, there are enough examples to motivate us to do better in our careers. We are able to understand family structures and other society issues as well. Sometimes, it becomes difficult to really understand, whether east and west will meet, are they travelling towards each other or travelling round each other. Well, I leave that for the readers to decide but being able to experience various situations and places, definitely makes a person appreciate things better.

As part of our social gatherings, we take part in 'Satsang' (Devotional songs sung by Individuals in a group) and spend quality time with friends and like-minded people. Kirti likes to sing and she participates in such events. I knew that she sings well before our marriage, but was able to hear her mostly after marriage. Kirti did sing a romantic Marathi song on our engagement, and I felt like I was on cloud nine. Apart from social activities we take time out for strolling in the nearby garden, boating on City Lake or cycling around the town together.

Festivals

For a newly-married lady, there were so many new things to observe, understand and adapt to, including the way we celebrate all Indian festivals with fervour and zeal here in UK.

Before, marriage I told her that we had a huge Indian diaspora here, and all major festivals, be it Diwali, Holi, Eid or Baisakhi, Navratri or Janmashtami are celebrated enthusiastically like any other festival.

After our marriage, when Kirti saw all these festivals being celebrated here, she was surprised and said, 'I never imagined that festivals are celebrated with such zeal here in UK.' We both actively take part in the festivities and share our happiness with others. Here, we have more opportunities to mix with friends and people from other religions, countries and different languages which provide us with a wider perspective and understanding of people from various parts of the world. My view is that all these festivals are there for a reason and bring out the best in a person, with a message of love, care and brotherhood for all.

There are multiple places of worship; we usually offer our prayers in temples on auspicious occasions and visit Gurudwaras occasionally.

Honeymoon Phase

By the time of writing this essay, Kirti and I have completed more than three years of knowing each other and more than two golden years of marriage. For our first anniversary we travelled to Barcelona, Spain and to Channel Islands near France for the second one.

Wow what a nice and romantic place Barcelona is, especially when you are with your loved one. The travel together to a new country brought new facets to our relationship, be it jointly deciding the itinerary, agreeing and disagreeing on which place to visit first (and not) and where to eat and shop! Well, it seems simple, but most married people will agree with me, these simple things can sometimes become hotly-contested topics between husband and wife, more than our politicians' views about each other. We both like travelling and it was fun exploring new places together, working our way through complex maps and understanding and trying to make sense of new languages. Well, life seems on a roll when you have an understanding and caring partner, and sometimes correcting you for your not so good habits. This is all a part and parcel of the overall package called marriage and we are enjoying it, nurturing it and growing it!

Cooking made interesting

Someone rightly said, 'The way to reach man's heart is through his stomach.' Kirti adorns her apron and makes some delicious food. Strangely, sometimes technology comes to her rescue as she gets some really good tips from her mother on video call. Technology is touching the lives of every one of us and making relations possible in new ways, many of which would not have been possible five or ten years ago.

Recently she tried her hand at pasta, fish curry and Indian rice with pudding. She, in fact, has taught me a few new dishes which makes me a part time cook and support to her. We both enjoy variety of cuisine. As you know, cooking doesn't only mean eating, so one has to plan, buy, prepare, cook, serve and then wash the utensils as well. Why I am saying so is because there are no free lunches for new working age couples and we both share and segregate our responsibilities. We finish our chores on time and also have sufficient time for each other to discuss, hobnob and plan for the future.

English breakfast

Food-related things are always interesting and close to everyone's heart. As I have seen over the years, people who come from South Asia or India to western countries find it difficult to adjust to the bacon and cheese culture over here!

As for Kirti, I was really not sure, how she would adjust to the food, popular eateries and other easily available dishes here in UK. In the beginning, she took some time and we mostly used to cook what was known rather than unknown. But soon we started exploring. She enjoyed a wide variety of cuisine here, from English breakfast to Latin and Japanese food she also started cooking a few of those dishes at home. I was totally surprised, as first I used to like it and also because I was not able to do it myself over the years. It is really surprising that now Kirti prepares all the English breakfast, scrambled eggs, baked beans, toasted cheese sandwich with fried mushroom and of course, tea. So now, I feel really lucky to have a choice of Indian or English or Continental breakfast, though on a few Sundays it is my turn to prepare breakfast. And I am really good at making sandwiches.

Anyway, all these are pleasures of life in small chunks as I call it and more importantly, Kirti has managed to adapt with the culture here while maintaining her identity and inclusivity.

Finance management

When it comes to finances and managing savings, Kirti is leading our team of two! Strangely and surprisingly, though, I am not sure whether it is because of her financial background or Indian family background. Or is it the simple habit of small savings making a big difference. She is able to think through and plan far better finances than me. In fact, in the past we did try this multiple times, be it reducing credit card dues, making some joint loan application or savings for the future, she was able to calculate, explain and put across analytically to me, that why it makes sense for certain investments over others. I am glad I did listen to her and we both made the right decisions. At this stage, we are able to understand, comprehend each other's view points, plans and financial goals. Based on mutual discussions we go ahead in terms of financial planning, whether it is buying a new TV or a car.

Buying our first car

Recently, I passed my UK car driving test and it is definitely one of the tests people are proud of clearing. It is reasonably complex considering the pass rate is just thirty six per cent for the first time. After that, we obviously decided to buy our first car. This was altogether a new experience for me, as over the years, travelling mostly by public transport, which is reasonably reliable and effective, I did not feel the need to have my own vehicle. With marriage, comes additional responsibility and also your travel increases. Anyway, before one buys car, there are many things to be researched, including brands, make and model, car features, resale value, mileage and so on. It was great that my best friend, Kirti was there with me, giving her valuable inputs. Be it reading car reviews, reading dozens of articles on differences between duel fuel, hybrid and electric cars and what was best for us to discussing car finance with banks and so on. I felt very relieved that all these things could really become fun together, which otherwise would seem very mundane tasks. She has got the knack for organising and analysing things.

Moving House

Recently Kirti got a job in an adjoining town and we decided to move closer to Kirti's workplace. Well, that decision was the easy part but it was followed by a series of small things which one needed to do to complete the house move. I was able to handle the co-ordination with the landlord and other bits, but when it came to the core engineering stuff and packing furniture and other goods, Kirti was able to visualise that and she was the leader once again. We both worked as a team and it was really a daunting experience made easy.

We faced a similar situation regarding the household furniture. As a term 'DIY' Do It Yourself, sounds easy, and you would know, in western countries, usually human services being fairly costly, sometimes, you have to ' assemble ' your own furniture. This was a completely new thing for me, and I have never done this in my life. After marriage, when we moved to an apartment, we purchased some furniture from a website, and it arrived in wooden planks in boxes. I didn't have a clue how to put them all together, but Kirti downloaded the manual from the internet and figured out the three-D-fixture diagrams and the sequence of nuts. Phew! It was altogether a new experience for me, we started with the computer trolley and then went to assemble the bed! Sometimes, I wonder what if even she had not understood those bits.

Photography and Writing as Hobbies

Kirti is a budding photographer as well and she tries her hand at nature, people and event photography. Though she has to manage this with her demanding job and other household things, you can see her quite motivated when she handles the camera. Personally, I am happy, as my photos are getting clicked the most. Let us see what life has in store for us in the future in that aspect.

Kirti is also involved in supporting charitable organisations through her photography skills. Recently, she volunteered for the day-long event of a charitable trust on their annual day and she was clicking photos of all the events, right from the puja till the dances, and yoga classes and other fun events. The organisers appreciated her efforts and assigned her as their official photographer for future events. I am thinking that how one thing can lead to the other, you never know. At the moment she is happy to pursue photography as a hobby.

Also, there is a quarterly magazine published by the local community which includes regular features on health and safety, food, new technologies, holidays and visits. Kirti actively contributes to the community magazine and has written a few articles for them. It makes me quite proud to note how she manages such diverse things with such ease and still manage to do a full-time job at a multinational bank. Last but not the least, that inspires me to do more at my end, and one of the recent examples which I could think of is the Half Marathon.

Recently, the McMillan Cancer Research Group, a charitable trust in UK, organised a Half Marathon like every year. Till last year, I never thought of or should I say dreamt of running in a marathon. But this time, as I had enough motivation in the house itself, I prepared for the same. Though I took part in Phase 1, 5 km run, it helped me to boost my confidence level and I realised, pushing your limits is more of a mind thing than a body thing. Once I successfully completed my run, I shared my experiences with one and all and Kirti was very proud of me. This was achieving multiple things at the same time, personally I enjoyed running and participating and at the same time, it was good to contribute for a social cause.

Movies and Moving Together!

Coming to movies, I am sure this must be happening with all couples, the movie genre which one person likes is not necessarily liked by the spouse. Kirti likes all Disney movies, romantic comedies, science movies and my visual skills are adapted more towards action thrillers and suspense and we both don't like horror. So with this choice of cinema, initially, we both used to like completely different movies but now I have started watching Disney films and romantic comedies. Kirti joins me for the D-box, action-packed thrillers. It seems we have developed a taste for each other's likes as well. Now we are better equipped to handle a wide variety of cinema or digital content.

No two people will like the same things, at least not with the same intensity. The million dollar question is, how do you go forward, how you agree and travel the same path. My view is that marriage is a complete package for both partners and it is like a car, sometimes the front wheels dictate the direction and sometimes the back wheels, but as a whole the car moves in one particular direction. Similarly in marriage, a wife or husband can be the front wheel or the rear wheel, depending upon the scenario and circumstances, but as a whole they need to move together, they are one unit, and they are best performing as one unit, seen by others as one!

We are getting there, and our car (read likes and dislikes on various things) seems to be moving forward and backwards at times, but at least it is travelling in one direction. That's a good start and we have a long road to travel together which we are hoping to travel with love, peace and togetherness to make our life's journey a pleasant one.

Yoga

As they say, it is one of India's gift to the world, Yoga and we observed truly the impact of it here in UK. We both are reasonably fitness conscious and perform light exercise regularly to help maintain reduced stress levels, handle anxiety and feel healthy throughout the day. They say it needs two to tango, my wife and I act as motivators for each other, and sometimes when one person is not feeling like doing exercise, the other person is always ready with the yoga mat to encourage the other.

Doing yoga together may be a small thing in the overall scheme of things, but what it means is, it is telling your partner I like and appreciate what you do and I will do the same with you always, if you slow down, I will help you to move fast. This bond of togetherness is more important than anything else, which makes us feel valued, loved and taken care of.

At this stage in life, I feel quite blessed to have such a loving and caring wife. We both share each other's sorrow and joy together and enjoy every bit of togetherness in all the activities we do.

Life can be good. One needs to look beyond, look ahead and always keep hope alive. That keeps a man going!

I salute all married couples who overcome all challenges and face this world together, they are our true inspiration and I wish all the best for the new, hopeful couples who will take the plunge in this age-old yet meaningful institution called marriage and exchange vows of togetherness!

> *No two people will like the same things, at least not with the same intensity. The million-dollar question is, how do you go forward, how do you agree and travel the same path, so both can move forward together. My view is that marriage is a complete package for both partners and it is like a car, sometimes the front wheels dictate the direction and sometimes the rear wheels, but as a whole, the car moves in one particular direction. Similarly, in a marriage, a wife or husband can be the front wheel or the back wheel, depending upon the scenario and circumstances, but as a whole, they need to move together, they are one unit, and they are best performing as one unit, seen by others as one!*

A BOND FOR LIFE
AND BEYOND

B.S. Rao

*Getting into the mode of living together was a new experience
for both of us, my eating habits underwent a 360-degree
transformation; no more eating out, breakfast at home, my
wife's packed healthy lunch. I inculcated the habit of eating
home cooked food. The initial months of marriage taught us
both, sharing, caring and accommodating each other. After
three months of rigor, we found life running smoothly and it
continues till date. This apart, she is highly intuitive, she has
a sixth sense, quite often, as my son Aditya quotes, 'Whatever
mama says, quite often comes true, I do not know how?' At
times, we both are baffled but the reality is such, that both of
us have accepted the same with grace.*

We got married in the summer of May 1995 in Bangalore.
Ours was an arranged marriage, though I knew my wife
Padmashri very well before marriage. One evening, my would-be
father-in-law pulled out his car and we both drove towards one
of his friends, residence in Pune. During this journey he asked
me if I would like to be Padmashri's life partner, and my answer
was an instant 'yes'. I had known her as an intelligent, bright
and cultured person who was a product of Kendriya Vidyala
and completing her graduate studies. Subsequently, after our
conversation, a formal visit to my residence, and discussions

between my parents, my father-in-law and his parents resulted in the formalisation of our engagement.

Our engagement was solemnised at my fiancée's residence in the presence of my fiancée's friends, my parents, my two younger sisters, Bhavani and Shanti, my would-be in-laws including my young brother-in-law, Ashok. The camera did its assigned job click-by-click and we had captured all the moments. When we sent the film for development, to our horror, it drew a blank. Not to be disappointed, we did a re-shoot after a week and captured the moments as they occurred. Well, I must say our engagement was quite eventful and enjoyable. We were indeed privileged to have had two engagement photo shoots within a week. We enjoyed it thoroughly with no regrets and the only thing all of us had to was 'Say Cheese', well, our engagement was indeed an enlightening experience.

It is said that, an engagement is akin to putting a ring on a woman's finger, and two under the man's eyes. This didn't hold good in my case. Rather, I was extremely delighted to be engaged to her, the disciplined daughter of a soldier, well-travelled, exposed to varied cultures, balanced, open-minded and full of life – she brought in invaluable cheer and pace in my life. Padmashri and I would spend a lot of time, catching up with each other after my work, going for long drives or walks and sharing our thoughts and humorous jokes. We would also spend time during the weekends, walking on Pune's M.G.Road, having cold coffee and macaroons at Marz-O-Rin and at times the tasty Kachi-Dhabeli at the nearby eatery. After my work, I would often visit my fiancée's residence and invariably end up having dinner hosted by my father-in-law. He was both humble and caring, a wonderful host making us burst with laughter. He would pamper us with his hospitality. One instance of him serving me a meal, is very fresh in my mind – I would say, 'Uncle. I am done, no more "khana", please do not serve me anymore, but he would serve a chapatti or two more saying, 'Yeh khana nahi bhai chapatti hai'. That is how loving and caring he has been and continues to be. This was fine, until I moved to Hyderabad for my new assignment, a place that I wanted to return to since my childhood and spend some time both professionally and personally.

This separated us for almost a year. During this period, I would make several trips to Pune to catch up with my fiancée.

Our marriage was solemnised according to traditional south Indian custom in Bangalore in the year 1995. The wedding ceremony begins by invoking Lord Ganapati – the God of Initiation to remove all obstacles followed by Nandi Devata pooja by five 'sumangalis' (women whose husbands are living). Later the navagraha pooja is performed to appease the nine astral planets that rule over man's destiny. This is followed by 'vratham' performed separately by the bride and the groom where the bride, ties the holy thread on her wrist acting as a protective armour to ward off all evil spirits. The groom performs the 'vratham' appealing to the gods Indra, Soma, Chandra and Agni, thereby preparing for a new chapter as a householder or 'Grihasta' bringing an end to his 'brahmacharya' (bachelorhood).

The next activity is Kasi yatra – a journey towards Kasi in Varanasi, after a student life towards a life of a sanyas (asceticism) wearing a pair of plain slippers, holding an umbrella and fan. So as I held the umbrella and walked towards Kasi, my father-in-law intervened and advised me to let go off my thoughts on life of a 'sanyasi' and instead adopt the life of a married man. He offered Padmashri as a companion to face the challenges of life I nodded in an instant, lest he change his mind. To this day, the umbrella remains with me as a constant reminder of his piece of advice during the marriage and the responsibilities that come along. As I nodded the 'Yes', I recalled a classmate from my college (Nowrosjee Wadia College in Pune) make a mention that there were four rings involved in a marriage – the engagement ring, wedding ring, suffe-ring and endu-ring. But I was chee-ring all the way to the marriage. After the Kashi Yatra, several other rituals, a 'vara' pooja is performed followed by Kanya daanam where the bride is given away as gift by the bride's father, to the bridegroom – that's me. Later a ring made with 'kusa', sacred grass called 'darbha' is placed on the bride's head and over it, is placed a yoke. The 'mangal sutra' (Thaali) is placed right on the aperture of the yoke, and water is poured through the aperture. The mantras are then chanted for a happy married life. The bride then is given an auspicious ablution, and an exclusive new koorai saree is draped around her. This is done by the sister of the bridegroom. A belt made of reed-grass is tied around the waist of the bride, followed by mantras declaring her purity, healthy body, good mind and the intention for a lifelong companionship of her husband (Sumangali Bhagyam) and children. She vows to stand by her husband virtuously. After the thanksgiving vedic hymns to the celestial caretakers of her childhood, the deities soma, gandharva and agni are recited. Having attained nobility, the girl is now is at liberty to be given over to her man, the bridegroom, and hence, my father-in-law now offered Padmashri as my life partner. This was followed by 'mangalya dharanam', the tying of the 'mangala sutra' (Thaali) at the auspicious hour and time. Subsequently, we paid homage to the fire god, Agni by 'pradhana homam,' by circling around the fire, and feeding the same with ghee, and twigs of nine types of trees, as sacrificial fuel. The fumes that arise, are supposed to possess medicinal, curative and cleansing effects on our bodies. God Agni, the mightiest power in the cosmos, the sacred purifier, the all-round benefactor, is deemed as a witness to the marriage which means 'Agni Saakshi'. This was followed by treading on the grindstone, the bridegroom showing 'arundhati' star to the bride, Laaja homam followed by showering of 'aksadai' (akshantalu), rice grains coated with turmeric and saffron, were showered on us by elders and invitees as blessing. After which, Padmashri left her parental home and joined me and my family.

A few days after our marriage, we both left for Wellington, Nilgiris and visited Conoor and Ooty. We had planned Kodaikanal as a part of our itinerary. Kodiakanal is also called as the 'Switzerland of the East' or the 'Princess of Hill Stations'. The name Kodaikanal means the 'gift of the forest'.

We had booked a bus from Ooty, which would halt at Wellington for a pick-up. At the scheduled time morning 6:30 am, my wife and I reached the pick-up point and waited for the bus. A couple of buses passed by, and the appointed time was fast approaching. We saw the bus nearing the pick-up point but it showed no signs of slowing down. We waved frantically but the bus just sped past. My wife and I looked at each other in disbelief. We missed the bus! But as Providence would have it, we saw a military policeman driving across the road. We stopped him and requested for his help and like a god sent angel he agreed. He asked me to hop on to the Bike and he drove past the bus and we stopped him forcibly. I spoke to the bus conductor and he apologized for not stopping. My wife joined me in the next few minutes. Our honeymoon journey to Kodaikanal wouldn't have been complete without the help of the army man. We thanked him profusely as our bus left Wellington for Kodaikanal. To this day, me and my wife are thankful to the army man, Mr. Shaji. I must say our honeymoon was indeed very eventful and adventurous.

After having had a good time in Kodaikanal, we left for Hyderabad, where we set up our home. My wife helped me transform the 'house' into a 'home'. She played a key role in inculcating the discipline of reaching home straight after work and managing the work life balance. To this day, I am thankful to her. Our first few months went in setting up the kitchen, setting up the drawing room, the bedroom, adorning the walls with artifacts and experimenting with decorating the house. Shopping for vegetables, groceries, paying electricity bills, water bills and related things was altogether a new experience for both of us. We both would frequently recall how our parents were such fantastic managers, managing work, home, household chores and our continuous demands for education and other needs. We both tried implementing some of the learning from our parents in our new life.

Getting into the mode of living together was a new experience for both of us, my eating habits underwent a 360-degree transformation; no more eating out, breakfast at home, my wife's packed healthy lunch and inculcating the habit of eating home food. The initial months of marriage taught us both sharing, caring and accommodating each other. After three months of rigor, we found life running smoothly and it continues till date.

The first few months were also very adventurous, as me and my wife would take off on the weekends and drive to a nearby tourist destination and return by Monday morning to attend office. We discovered Hyderabad to the hilt. This included visiting some landmark locations, selecting outings for dining, including visiting popular highway 'dhabas' situated at the city's outskirts, watching movies, the best releases. On several occasions we dared to pick up tickets for a late night show and we would drive home by midnight. And yes, we always reached home safely, which perhaps in today's times would have been difficult. We also happened to visit Shirdi and take the blessings of Shirdi Sai Baba.

Life continued to be eventful, my wife later picked up a work assignment and we got busy with our work routine and home affairs until we visited the doctor. We received the good news that we were to be parents soon. October 1997 was a special month and year, as Aditya arrived into our life. He was special for both of us. He was born in Wellington. In fact, he was fortunate to have his grandfather (who is an army doctor) present while he was born, in the operation theatre and hold him as he arrived into this exciting world of humans. My wife quit her job and has since focused her attention completely on him. She is a daunting, caring and compassionate mother. Aditya's arrival ushered in a new transformation in our life, yet again. We stopped all adventures, weekend movies and focused on his upbringing, taking him to the paediatrician for vaccinations, regular checkups, stitching cloth diapers, waking up in the night to attend to his night feeds and changing his nappies. I would keep a continuous vigil so that Padmashri could rest in the night. At times Aditya would cry and at times I would be at loss to understand if he was asking for water or milk. First, I would pull out the water bottle, he would at times push it out forcibly. So I would help him with a milk bottle and lo and behold he would take to the bottle and acknowledge it with a twinkle in his eyes, a quick wave of arms and shake of legs. A lot of time has passed since and Aditya is now a teenager and it feels like just yesterday. However time has passed by rather quickly. We vividly remember his first day at school. I had requested my boss to shift our meeting with our technology vendors for our Internet Operations (I was spearheading an ISP and we were soon launching our services) till noon so that my wife and me could see him off to his school. We drove to his school, we dropped him at the entrance, and he started crying, 'Mamma, Mamma, Mamma. ' But we were advised to leave. We left him away from us for the first time. That experience is very fresh in our minds even today. My wife has played an instrumental role in grooming Aditya into a wonderful young boy. Though she is well-educated being a degree holder in sociology and an alumnus of IIM, Bangalore, she sacrificed her promising career, dedicated herself to him, looking after all his needs, his demands for toys, special choice of home food. She would also take him out to play with neighbouring kids while she allowed me to focus completely on my work. She is both a wonderful mother and a wonderful wife. Words cannot express my feelings and gratitude, she is beyond words. She is the best gift of my life.

One day, as I returned from work, Padmashri and my son Aditya were eagerly waiting for me to freshen up and as I sat on the sofa, my wife started narrating how they had come across a pup which was very cute and Aditya wished to get the small dog home. All three of us, have known the cute little pup, who would be fed milk and food by my wife every day. The pup was brought in by our neighbour and they planned to raise the little one to be a watchdog. My wife and Aditya both convinced me on the adoption, and said that I should speak to Mr. Gowda, our neighbour. The next day happened to be a Sunday. We called upon Mr. Gowda and conveyed our request. He sat in silence for a few seconds and said a 'Yes' much to our delight. We adopted Blackie in the year 2008, when Aditya was just eleven. Ever since, Blackie has been the cynosure of our eyes and an integral part of our lives. She has been a great teacher to all three of us. She taught us the true meaning of unconditional love, loyalty, compassion and selflessness. I thank my wife for being a thoughtful human being and for having a wonderful mind to care for Blackie. My wife has single-handedly toilet-trained Blackie, unraveled her eating needs, and now keeps a track of all vaccination needs and dates. She regularly escorts Blackie to our family vet, Dr. Pavan, who saved Blackie from near death, when she contracted tick fever. We are thankful to Dr. Pavan for saving Blackie. Blackie ensures we are around her while she spreads cheer all around. She is by far the best thing that could ever have happened to our family.

During the year 2010, I plunged into my entrepreneurship journey, which has been altogether a new experience. I discussed with my wife, and she consented and took the plunge. My journey of entrepreneurship has been nothing short of a sailing expedition, rough seas, dark nights, full of challenges, changing and redesigning business models and so on. Yes, all through this journey, my wife has been a solid pillar of strength, playing the role of a supportive wife, as I continued to battle the challenges of launching a new cloud concept in the next few months.

Like an ECG graph, life has its crests and troughs. What has kept us going through these phases is acceptance of truth, reality, patience and maturity, thanks to our culture, parents and the values imbibed by them. This apart, my wife has stood by me all through the best and most challenging phases of my life. She is also my strongest critic. My journey of entrepreneurship has been one of my most challenging phases of life, but for her moral support it wouldn't have been possible. My attempts at entrepreneurship were encouraged by her with words of caution, yet she stood by me and still stands by me. This has unraveled a new untold truth; behind every entrepreneur there is an extremely supportive spouse.

Trust has been the foundation of our happy marriage. Both my wife and I have unflinching faith in each other. We were engaged when she was just nineteen and we have grown up together. We believe each other with neither questioning the other's credentials. We are more friends than husband and wife. This perhaps has been the cementing factor of our married life. Another reason is that we both enjoy spending time with each other, we are happy being together, sharing lighter moments with no inhibitions, being frank, faithful, fun-loving and caring. Both of us have spent more life together than with our respective parents. This has built a strong emotional bond enabling the trust factor.

My wife and me have walked together from our early age of twenties, to thirties and now forties and we have crossed each stage of our life, bound by a strong, emotional bond. This very mind association has seen us through various phases of our life, the good, bad and the ugly.

Padmashri is very honest, ethical, practical, non-materialistic and highly spiritual. This apart she believes in optimisation of resources such as electricity, water and time. This apart, she is highly intuitive, she has a sixth sense. Quite often, as my son Aditya quotes, 'Whatever mama says, quite often comes true, I do not know how? At times, we both are baffled but the reality is such, that both of us have accepted the same with grace. We owe her ability to her yogic meditation, which she practices with great zeal. This apart, she has a practical approach to situations in life.

She is very conservative and adept at handling finance, while I am quite liberal. I do not mind handing over a ten-rupee note to a guy at the tyre filling station, for me it's a question of helping a fellow human being in my own way. My wife, Padmashri being highly practical, would say, pay him five rupees instead. She certainly has a valid point, but that's me. However, she is very meticulous and displays financial prudence and discipline and she provides the right balance I need in my life, a gifted finance manager. I call her the 'Home Minister', who manages the home finances, plans budgets, schedules annual vaccination and health budgets for Blackie and all of us including the insurance budgets, groceries, filing of documents, reminders on property bills etc.

The growing-up years of Aditya, our son, were a lifetime experience and Padmashri and me. We treasure the moments right from his infancy to teenage. We would play with him, carrying him all around, feed him and attend to all his requests and needs. His innocence, inquisitiveness, fearlessness, ever-smiling and playful approach reinvigorated and refreshed our childhood experiences. I must confess, as we grow up, we tend to smile less and less, become averse to taking risks and forget being playful, we tend to leave behind the child in us. As our son stepped into his teens, my wife and me stepped back and allowed him his space and freedom, while we continued to inculcate in him values, good thoughts, caring approach towards Mother Nature, respect for teachers and elders, honesty, integrity and respect for women. In fact, as a child, he never liked the idea of crackers during Diwali festival, as it injures people, causes trauma to dogs, birds and babies. To this day, we truly celebrate Diwali as a festival of lights, sans the noisy crackers and we are proud of Aditya's views. This has been a wonderful learning for both of us.

My recent journey of entrepreneurship opened doors to a host of financial challenges, but for my wife Padmashri, it wouldn't have been possible for me to overcome the challenges posed by this journey. With delays in the project, technology glitches, and the undesired lag in monetizing, the business opportunity had inflicted a tsunami of challenges, both emotionally and financially. This has by far been the most arduous journey of my professional life and she supported me immensely. During this phase, during one of my travels, I unfortunately contracted a deadly eye virus which almost damaged one of my eyes. But thanks to an expert ophthalmologist, my eye was saved, but required continuous attention. It had impacted my vision partially and it has taken me three months to overcome the same. My wife looked after me, while my eyes were watering, administering the drops as I groped with pain, swelling in both my eyes and partial vision for over two weeks, she looked after me like a mother. If I am back in shape and enjoying my vision, I owe it to Padmashri, my better half. She truly is my better half and I am proud and blessed to have her as part of my life. I wouldn't be able to cope with the above mentioned challenges and many more all through my life, without her.

All major decisions in our life are discussed between both of us, analysed by both of us, the pros and cons are evaluated and we arrive at the most optimum alternative. All our decisions are taken collectively, be it the admission of our child's education, choice of school, purchasing an asset or making an investment. Yes, we discuss, debate, evaluate, and weigh the options very critically. My wife and I have both been away from our parents since an early age, and hence both of us have learnt to take our decisions independently. In fact, during the days after our engagement, while we were staying in different cities, we would leverage long distance calls to talk to each other, discuss and arrive at a decision collectively. Now it has become a second nature and we would like our children too to become independent and take responsibility and accountability for their decisions and actions. My wife has played a significant role in making major decisions in our life and she has been a source of immense strength.

Living together, today, we are able to predict what each of us think and it has helped us. We know when each of us are happy or sad. And this has helped us care for one another. We care very much for each other. I take care of all her needs. Simple things like helping her in the kitchen, which I used to indulge in quite a lot before I embarked on my entrepreneurship, where, we would together spend time chatting while baking 'rotis', stirring a 'curry' or tasting a dish, are moments we have enjoyed together. Going together to buy vegetables, picking up groceries together is something we do even today, despite a punishing work schedule. While my wife takes care of everything right from ironing my clothes, packing breakfast, ensuring currency in my wallet, my personal grooming items, she literally manages most micro things to ensure that Aditya, Blackie and myself are comfortable. I cannot imagine life without her, she is my heartbeat and my lifeline.

Well, it would be noteworthy to mention here that we do not take each other for granted. However, we take each other into confidence, just like friends do. We give each other space for our ideas and thoughts and respect each other's opinions. We share our thoughts and express ourselves very frankly without any inhibitions and that has stood us in good stead. Being open and frank has helped us transform our life into an open book, allowing transparency and giving us freedom of speech, expression and living in a truly democratic way and translating it into a married life full of joy, peace and trust.

Right from our engagement, we have been extremely frank, honest, committed to each other and have trusted each other and our decisions and actions. We have been very open in our communication with each other, have been very patient with each other by listening to each other's views.

One understanding between us has been that beauty and money do not last forever but love, compassion and mutual respect are eternal and this very belief and our ability to overlook material things and living within our means and enjoy our relationship has helped us and will continue to do so. For a marriage to succeed, it is important to marry the 'soulmate' we can't live without.

While my wife and I both hold our parents in high esteem, we have maintained a respectful distance to ensure a warm and healthy relationship between us. My relationship with my parents-in-law has been very healthy. Especially with my father-in-law, Lt.Col (Dr) Y V Murali who has served the Indian Army as a dedicated soldier and has been a very warm and wonderful human being and my affable brother-in-law, Ashok Murali, who is a software engineer. I have now known them for over two decades and have enjoyed our relationship thoroughly.

My wife's relationship with my parents has been very cordial despite the fact that she never spent time living with them as my work kept me travelling to various locations across the country. Well, if we had an opportunity to stay with my parents, Padmashri would have been the most enviable daughter-in-law to my parents, as she is caring, sensitive and has the attitude of servitude. Let me narrate an initiative and suggestion made by her, which truly demonstrates her caring attitude. My mother was not keeping well. I had just spoken to my father over the phone and he mentioned with concern, that there wasn't any significant improvement in her health, despite being administered the best of medicines. After concluding the call with my father, I shared with Padmashri, the concern voiced by my father and the current state of my mother's health. Hardly, had I concluded my sentence that she made a suggestion to me, 'Srini, I think you should ask your mother to immediately travel to Bangalore, we can take care of her. She has been unwell for nearly a week, I believe she needs our care and attention.' I immediately called my father and they were here in two days. Thanks to my wife, my mother was treated well by our family doctor, Dr. Shiva Kumar and she was back in the pink of health within a fortnight. This demonstrated to me, how a life partner can play a very decisive role in managing relationships.

It is scientifically reported that fifty five per cent of communication comes through facial expressions, thirty eight per cent of communication gets accomplished by tone of voice and the rest seven per cent of communication relies on verbal exchange. My wife and I have experienced this and understand each other through our facial expressions, a deep-rooted understanding for each other has played a significant role in our marital success.

Our Pillars of Marital Success: Commitment, Frankness, Honesty and Trust

Marriage is like a well-oiled machine. We need not work on the marriage, the marriage needs to work for us, on its own. Does the fish work on the water it swims in? Not at all. It is the water which provides the ecosystem for the fish to live its life to the fullest. Likewise, marriage is a noble institution created by society, which not only works on its own, but allows the husband and wife to live, love and enjoy the moments of life and serve society in the most righteous manner for our next generation to honour and respect the institution of marriage.

We do not need to work on our marriage, instead husband and wife should respect, help, support, advise, praise and ensure that they live happily. The key to enjoying marriage is to forget that one is a husband and the other is a wife, instead they should be friends and partners who are frank, fun-loving, adventurous and supportive.

The mantra for a successful married life as experienced by us is

COMET(B) -5F

Co – Compassion, Caring attitude
M – Mutual respect
E – Effective communication
T – Trust

Compassion – Compassion has helped cobble our relationship and build a deep bond at a psychological level. This required either of us to change focus from 'I' to 'we' and from 'mine' to 'ours'. It is collective wealth in every sense of the word. We both think from each other's point of view. We acknowledge and appreciate each other. We exercise marital prudence in not only analysing each other's feelings (hurt, pain, anger or any form of emotion) and most of all give space for the other through the mantra 'Let Go' – Let go ego and negative emotions. We both have replaced ego with empathy.

Mutual respect – We treat each other like friends – with care and respect and not live as husband and wife. We always had a positive opinion about each other, of course while we have accepted weaknesses at either end respectfully.

Effective communication – Choosing the right occasion to remain silent, praise, being constructively critical, being open, frank, factual and adjusting, have helped maintain a very healthy relationship. Listening is as important. If a husband is reading the paper and wife is speaking, it is important to keep the paper aside and pay attention to what she has to say; continuing to read and listen would surely annoy her. Small events such as this are prone to irk and hence being prudent would help.

Trust – We have trusted each other right from the word go. The foundation of our relationship has been trust. We have never had an occasion for questioning one another on this aspect and I am blessed to have a wife who trusts me and vice versa. This has been a key element of our relationship and happiness.

Sense of belonging and ownership – Marriage itself has created a sense of belonging in us. We belong to each other and whatever we have belongs to us. We take ownership and accountability for all our actions. One common trait between us is that we do not believe in pointing fingers and devaluation. This has induced the sense of ownership and ability to intuitively take actions which are mutually beneficial leading to a sense of euphoria and ecstasy.

5F – Fun-loving, Forgive, Forgo, Forget, Forbear

Forgive: We both, and especially my wife, have always forgiven each other for any differences and it has done wonders for our marriage. We never gave each other an occasion to retaliate, perhaps we owe it to maturity bestowed upon us by our parents.

Forgo: We would forgo an event that may have been unpleasant by taking it in our stride rather than make a mountain of a mole hill. Nullify the ego all the more as far as the spouse is concerned.

It helps strengthen the relationship. So do not hang on to the unpleasant past.

Forget: We would forget past events and live in the current moment. This ability to forget things has helped us get rid of unnecessary baggage and has helped us enjoy living together. When we forgive, we are in no way changing the past, but surely changing the future for good.

Forbearance: My wife and I have practised forbearance and it is one of our mantras for success. Forbearance is defined as the exercise of patience or also as forgiving in advance. Patience helps one remain calm and stay in command of oneself. This leads to well-thought-out actions eliminating misunderstanding and conflicts and building a strong relationship between husband and wife. Like a calm sea allows a ship to sail safely and a rough sea can capsize that very ship, the ship of marriage is no different.

An often asked question in the context of a marriage is 'Do you think in your marriage one of you is the one who always adjusts? Or is it give and take?'

Just like the sun and the moon, the day being bright due to sunshine and the night being bright and peaceful thanks to moonlight, my wife and I adjust and play our respective roles without interference. Just to give you an example, she is the master of the kitchen, she has learnt the art of cooking by herself. My mother-in-law, Mrs. Indira died of cancer a few months before our engagement. She learnt cooking through recipe books and by experimentation. Today, we can ask for any dish and she ensures we have a lip-smacking meal on the table. Hence, I have ensured cent per cent non-interference in her cooking. The same applies to all activities in her life, I do not interfere, likewise, she too reciprocates the same and we accommodate each other and respect our strengths and weaknesses. At no point in our life have we ever crossed the 'Lakshmana-Rekha', the boundaries, to point fingers at each other over our weaknesses. We have accepted each other the way we are, thus helping us to live our life meaningfully and happily.

I remember someone once making a mention to me, 'The first fifty years of marriage are the hardest', and with nineteen years of married life behind me, I can hardly agree. However, looking back, and reflecting on my two decades of married life, if I have to make a few suggestions for a happy married life, then here they are:

Be kind and caring

As goes the saying, love is caring for each other even if you are angry. It is important to sow kindness and care into your marriage Just like a seed which is sown and nurtured with the key ingredients, a happy marriage needs a healthy mix of kindness and care. Random acts of kindness and care include appreciation, compliments, helping the wife in the kitchen, husband making coffee or tea early morning and sweetly surprising the wife, taking the wife out for dinner to give her a break from cooking.

Don't mix money, material and marriage

Marriage is between two individuals, it's not a marriage of two banks or two cars or two apartments. Money is required to live a happy life. Let money not become a stumbling block in marriage. One single reason why money or material things influence marriage is because of the devil named 'Comparison'. So and so is earning well, he has travelled abroad, he has bought a new car, he has even taken his family abroad … or the husband would retort, your father has gifted your brother an apartment, you don't seem to be on the horizon and so on. A marriage can live without these comparisons. Such a mindset will lead to an unhealthy argument, create a gloomy atmosphere and widen the marital gap. After all money, car and vacation are non living things, while husband and wife are living beings. Is it worth trading non living things for living beings? Let not money and material things weaken the sound foundation of marriage. It is worth remembering that money can buy a bed but not sleep, money can buy a car but not respect. Hence, let not money and material things come in the way of a happy married life. Material things are not permanent, your life is. Respect and enjoy it. And life is too short to be wasted.

Stick with each other through thick and thin

'Tough times never last but tough people do', is a popular quote and title of a book written by Robert H Schuller and it aptly applies to a happy marriage too. Tough times are like a passing cloud, they shall soon be history. It is therefore very important that both husband and wife support each other through the good and not-so-good times. The not-so-good times could be anything ranging from a business loss, job loss, injury, health problem and domestic issues. It is important to be together and face the situation rather than point fingers at each other. It is important to refrain from remarks such as, 'I told you, you never heeded my advice, all of us ought to face the problem. Had you not ventured into the business, we wouldn't have suffered this loss.' Such remarks should be avoided. Instead the spouse should dig in, be empathetic and support the other during the tough times thus paving the way for a strong emotional bond between the two and ensure a happy marriage. A word of encouragement during failure is worth more than an hour of praise for success.

Be liberal with praise

Do not hesitate to praise the wife if she has cooked a tasty dish or dressed well. As husbands, it is important to remember that a wife makes a house a home, a home to which a husband and wife return back after they are done with school and office respectively. If she serves a hot cup of tea, it's important to tell her that the tea is tasty. She would be happy to receive your gesture. It's a natural human tendency to point out silly and small mistakes, however most of the good done by the wife misses praise. Such errors in marriage can slowly widen the gap in a relationship and are detrimental for a marriage. So praise when she deserves it most.

Refrain from being abusive

However critical or difficult the situation may be, never abuse a lady either physically or verbally. No reason can justify this, more so when the relationship is that of a husband and wife. Any differences should be discussed privately away from children and parents, if necessary they should step opt for a private date or go on a long drive and sort out the misunderstandings. It is important to treat the wife with care. She is the individual who has left her place of birth and parents to resettle with the husband and hence she deserves to be treated with utmost respect and care. This is a very important aspect of a happy married life.

Commitment, Trust, Honesty and Frankness

Commitment is essential be it a teacher, a pilot, a father or a spouse. Both husband and wife should deploy equal amount of effort and time to nurturing the noble man-woman relationship. It should be a commitment, come what may. Both the lows and the highs of life should be faced with commitment. Life is a roller-coaster ride, challenges, hurdles and adversities can be overcome if and only if, both are willing to work through them by supporting each other. Divorce is not a solution, staying together and supporting each other, is. A relationship can survive any adversity if the husband and wife are really committed to each other.

Frankness helps maintaining open communication between husband and wife and brings each other closer and eliminates any misunderstandings and helps foster trust. Treat each other like friends as far as communication is concerned. Open channels of communication bring both the husband and wife closer and eliminates barriers.

Honesty is extremely important while we speak, write, and communicate. Honesty and frankness could make one vulnerable, however, it is important to be honest and frank anyway. Hiding facts, information can lead to distrust and the spouse could react in an unpredictable manner. Honesty fosters trust and more than anything else, it reduces the possibility of misunderstanding and helps avoid distress. Honesty and truthfulness go hand-in-hand. Husband and wife should be truthful to each other and hence eliminate the scope of deception which not only causes pain, but also derails the marriage. Be truthful, be factual, however difficult it may be. Even if the husband or wife have a difficult truth to share, they must do so, at least they stand an opportunity to re-work the marriage. Pushing it under the carpet will only lead to distrust.

Leave behind your past. The past is dead

To believe in something, and not to live it, is dishonest, said Mahatma Gandhi. It is therefore important to believe that once you are married, you ought to live it and be honest. Conduct a funeral of the past. The past is dead. Erase your past when it comes to all 'exes', ex-boyfriend, ex-girlfriend, father's riches, memories of being driven around in chauffeur driven cars while staying with parents and so on. Once married, the couple should delink themselves from the past, the past is dead. Indulging in extra-marital relationships with 'exes' or new affairs, will only harm your marriage. A wife should refrain from comparing a husband's financial status with that of her father, she should instead help and support her husband grow in his profession or business and extend all her support, because it is sense of belonging that counts and matters. Likewise the husband should not pester his wife for dowry, money from her father but should build an emotional and financial security for the family and be a role model for the children to emulate. Life sans comparisons, extra-marital affairs, cheating the spouse, references to the past, should be left behind to ensure a successful and happy married life.

Be content

I wish I had ten hands! Did this thought ever cross your mind, perhaps never. You are contented with what God had gifted. Would you like four eyes on your face? Would you ask for more, by comparing with others who have just two eyes? The answer would be an absolute 'No'. Likewise, in marriage it is very important, do not allow thoughts such as, 'What would it be like if my spouse was different or I were married to someone else?' The more you compare the more shall be the discontentment.

A spouse is not a car, motorcycle or a smartphone that can be compared, he or she is a human being. Accept them as they are and be contented. It is important to respect them for their strengths and as a life partner, help them overcome their weaknesses. A car, TV or a mobile will not cry if you are sick, nor will they help you when you are emotionally down, but a spouse can stand by you, administer medicine, escort you to a doctor, and support you morally. Hence, respect the soul within than the material things and be contented. The Law of Attraction states that you do not get what you ask for but get what you are or what you deserve and hence it is very important to stay contented and respect the law of nature. Husbands complaining about their wives should remember that there are men who are widowed and yet not married the second time and bringing up their children, so be happy, you have a wonderful wife. Please remember, there was a man who cried because he had no shoes until he met a man who had no feet. Hence we should learn to be contented. Comparison causes stress and breeds discontent. We should learn to appreciate and enjoy what is around us rather than yield to external pressures. This would help one enjoy marital bliss.

Lastly, I am absolutely lucky to have Padmashri as my life partner and as a soulmate. I lived like an absolute bachelor until she stepped into my life. I would come back to the four walls to sleep after a tiring day at work. After our marriage, as she stepped into my life, I was no more returning back to a house with four walls, but walking into a tidy home, to a smiling welcome, which was a 360-degree transformation in my life. She has brought fun, love and care into my life and we are proud parents of Aditya, who is now a teenager. In fact, I can't ask for more. She has been with me through thick and thin and has been extremely supportive. I am extremely thankful to God Almighty for having blessed me with such a wonderful life partner. She is truly my 'Ardhangini', my better half. This apart, she is a devoted mother, daughter and a daughter-in-law. She has been a pillar of strength for me and my son. To sum up, we are two souls and one heart in a bond for life and beyond.

Though she holds a degree in sociology and is an alumnus of IIM, Bangalore, she sacrificed her promising career, dedicated herself to our son, his demands for toys and special choice of home-cooked food and allowed me to focus completely on my work. She is both a wonderful mother and a wonderful wife. Words cannot express my feelings and gratitude, she is beyond words. She is the best gift of my life.

ABOUT THE AUTHOR

A former director at Symbiosis, whose name figures with Thomas Friedman and Dale Carnegie, Virender Kapoor, is the founder director and chief mentor of MILE-Management Institute of Leadership and Excellence Pune. A telecom engineer, he is a postgraduate in Computer Science from IIT Bombay and holds a masters degree in International Relations from the University of Pune. He is also a member of the HR committee of CII.

A wonderful Boss, PQ-passion Quotient–How it matters more than IQ and *Leadership the Gandhi way and Innovating the Einstein way* are his recent books in the self help space.

To know more about him-

www.virenderkapoor.com
www.mile.net.in
virenderkapoor21@yahoo.com
Face book Virender Kapoor
Twitter @virenderkapoor